A History of Ashtead

There is a history in all men's lives..

Shakespeare, Henry IV, Part 2, Act III, Scene 1

St Giles' Church, Ashtead. Photograph by M.T. Jenkyn A.R.P.S.

A HISTORY OF ASHTEAD

edited by
J. C. Stuttard

LEATHERHEAD AND DISTRICT
LOCAL HISTORY SOCIETY

1995

ISBN 0 9506009 2 X
Cover design by Linda Heath
Front Cover photograph by Gwen Hoad
Ashtead Pond 1995 facing north-east
Back Cover photograph from LDLHS Collection
Ashead Pond c 1913 facing south-west
Printed by J.W. Arrowsmith Ltd., Bristol

FOREWORD

This book has been produced by the Leatherhead and District Local History Society in response to many requests from local residents. The Society published *Ashtead, A Village Transformed* in 1977, which very quickly sold out. A second impression was produced in 1979, but this has also been out of print for many years. Instead of issuing a new edition, it was decided to produce a new book, with more emphasis on the 19th and 20th centuries. It is hoped that this book will complement rather than supplant the previous history.

Particular thanks are due to Jack Stuttard who, in addition to editing this book, has compiled the index and researched and written several chapters. The two other principal researchers and writers were Howard Davies and Alan Gillies, who were also members of a small group appointed to assist the Editor in producing the book. I should like to thank them and all those who have been involved in any way in the preparation of this book. Of necessity, much material has had to be omitted, but all of it will be stored in the Society's archives for use in future years.

Last, but by no means least, our thanks are due to Esso for their kind assistance in providing us with a most generous grant towards the cost of producing this book.

Linda Heath
Chairman, 1995

PREFACE

This new History of Ashtead concentrates on the 19th and 20th centuries, showing how Ashtead has grown from small beginnings in 1800 to become almost town-like in size in the 1990s, yet retaining some of the traces of its village origins. The early chapters relate how Ashtead people lived under the Romans, during the Anglo-Saxon period, in the medieval age and in early modern times. There follows a detailed description of life during the 19th and 20th centuries, with special chapters on Ashtead's churches, population, schools, the arts and sport and leisure activities. The final chapter describes the main buildings of architectural and historical interest.

Thanks are due to Linda Heath, the Society's Chairman, for co-ordinating the production of the book and writing the Foreword. The book has been written by an enthusiastic band of contributors, specialists in their field, and the unstinted time they gave to the work is much appreciated. Howard Davies and Alan Gillies, in particular, have contributed much to the book, as have Richard Butler, Roddy Clube, Mary Cree, Ernest Crossland, John Derry, John Hampton, Joan Harding, John Hopper, Cherry Pepler and Jack Willis. Monica McAllister wrote the section on St. Michael's Catholic Church. Brian Cooper and John Wadey provided valuable accounts of Ashtead's post offices and fire services while the late Michael Gale, Andrée Hicks and Molly Morgan wrote on scouts, guides and the Boys' Brigade. The fine drawings by Mary Cree, Betty Eldridge, George Lewis and Gillian Wilson add much to the attraction of the book. Acknowledgement must be made also to the many people who so generously provided photographs, and to Kathleen Davies and Janet Goldsmith for selecting them. Lewis and Edwina Vardey kindly advised on publishing matters.

No book of this kind could be produced without the help and advice of many individuals, libraries and learned societies. John

Blair's comments on the medieval chapter and Alan Jackson's on the 20th century chapters were appreciated. The writing of the Arts chapter depended on many willing helpers, including Derrick and Betty Battle, Hugh Bayley, the late George Bixley, H. Fane-Bailey, Joy Hallam, Ken Hardy, Mrs B. Higgs, Joan Hunt, Michael and Alison May, Christopher Morgan, Frank Plastow and Margaret Wingfield. Others who helped on this chapter are mentioned in the text. The Domestic Buildings Research Group (Surrey) contributed generously to the chapter on Ashtead's buildings; others who advised on these included Barry Coxe, Paul Eales, Meta Haywood, John Lewis, John Vickers and Daphne Wollaston. The Worsfold family provided information on the Ashtead Free Church from the late Jack and John Worsfold's collections. The Rev. C.C. Hughes, Rector, kindly gave permission for the use of church records. Useful information was given by Joan Messenger and Tom Devitt. Thanks are due to the Rev. Ernest Buckley for assistance with the production of the Wyburd map; also to D.J. Hyson for other cartographical assistance. Acknowledgement should be made to past and present Headteachers and staffs of Ashtead schools for their assistance, as well as to officials and members of the clubs and societies consulted. Dorothy Ashurst assisted in typing the church and 19th century chapters.

For access to published and unpublished sources, we are grateful to the British Library (Reading Room and Map Library), the Public Record Office, the London Borough of Lambeth Archives Department (Minet Library), the Surrey Record Office, the Guildford Muniment Room, the Surrey Local Studies Library and the Surrey Archaeological Society. Information from published Census reports is reproduced with permission of the Controller of Her Majesty's Stationery Office, C. Crown Copyright.

The Society's Library and Archives provided invaluable material, including that from late members of the Society, Geoffrey Gollin, Robert Lever and Lawrie Smith.

J.C. Stuttard
1995

CONTENTS

LIST OF MAPS AND ILLUSTRATIONS

Frontispiece: St. Giles' Church, Ashtead

MAPS

ILLUSTRATIONS

ABBREVIATIONS

BL	British Library
DNB	Dictionary of National Biography
LA	Leatherhead Advertiser
MVDC	Mole Valley District Council
PCC	Parochial Church Council
PRO	Public Record Office
Procs. LDLHS	Proceedings Leatherhead & District Local History Society
SAC	Surrey Archaeological Collections
SAS	Surrey Archaeological Society
SRO	Surrey Record Office
V & A	Victoria & Albert Museum

Chapter 1

THE PHYSICAL SETTING

Ashtead lies about 15 miles south-west of London and is one of the many parishes between Guildford and Croydon found close to the spring-line of the North Downs where the chalk dips northwards under the London Clay. Epsom and Leatherhead are its near neighbours to the east and west with Chessington and Headley touching its north and south borders. The highest point in the parish, 425 ft, is just north of Headley Court and the lowest is in the Rye valley near Links Road, 150 ft, rising again across Ashtead Common to reach 275 ft near the Chessington boundary. The Saxon name for the village was 'Stede' meaning site or homestead and it is spelt this way in Domesday Book. There were many variations of the spelling in medieval times and it is not clear when the present spelling became accepted but it it is now generally agreed that 'Ashtead' means the homestead among the ash trees[1].

Geology and Soils
In its northern parts, Ashtead consists primarily of clays and sands forming part of the structural downfold of the London Basin, and in the south chalk soils predominate with a quantity of flints[2]. London Clay underlies much of Lower Ashtead and Ashtead Common. Apart from a thin basement section of pebbles it is a heavy, bluish-grey clay which weathers at the surface to brown or yellow. This colour change is due to oxidation of the iron minerals within the clay. The general thickness is about 400 ft. The London Clay produces very heavy soils more suited to woodland than to crop-growing. In the Roman period and at various times since then it has been worked for brick-making. Some of the older houses in Barnett Wood

Lane have Ashtead brick in their walls. A brick pit, now filled with water, is to be seen just by the railway near Green Lane.

Apart from the London Clay, north Ashtead also has some gravel soils, often referred to as 'Taele' gravels, lying over low ground in the form of fans from around *Murreys Court* to just north of Barnett Wood Lane, and through the Woodfield area widening out at Ashtead Station. These gravels are believed to have been formed at the end of the Ice Age from material washed down through shallow, coombe-like depressions during the summer thaws. In addition to these gravel outcrops much of the London Clay area is covered with odd pieces of flint which probably arrived at the same time as the gravel fans.

South of the London Clay is a thin narrow belt of sands and clay made up of two differing beds. The first of these are the Thanet beds, barely 200 yards wide and only 10 to 15 ft thick, running from south-west to north-east. Where their base rests on the chalk there is a narrow band of unworn flints often coated with a greenish film (this is known as the Bullhead bed). Otherwise, the Thanet beds are formed of brown to greenish grey sand, and except during road construction work they are nowhere exposed. They adjoin another outcrop known as the Reading beds, 70 ft thick, and covering a wider area than the Thanets; they pass right through the centre of Ashtead, the shopping area of The Street being located on them. They are reddish clays mottled with streaks of green along with bands of sand. Little can be seen of them at the surface but they have often been revealed during building work.

The south of Ashtead is made up mainly of chalk, pure white in colour and containing much flint arranged as nodules in courses or as tabular layers. The chalk used to be exposed in small quarries for the supply of lime (marl) for farmers and it is still possible to see it at The Warren, but this quarry site is now occupied by Ashtead Hospital. The largest chalk pit was probably about half a mile north-east of St Giles Church, which in the 1930s had a height face of about 65 ft and numerous fossils were collected from this. It was known as Pleasure Pit or Bishop's Pit.

Drainage and Water Supplies

Springs

The chalk in the south of Ashtead and on the Downs holds large quantities of water in its fissures and joints and this water is forced up between the impervious cover of the London Clay and the chalk, escaping as springs along the line where the chalk reaches the surface. Heavy exploitation of this water since Victorian times has led to a fall in the water table. This is generally low between Epsom and Leatherhead so strong springs are absent in the Ashtead area, but the water level rises east of Epsom hence the spring at Ewell. Some seepages occur around Ashtead and these can more or less dry up during long periods of dry weather.

The Rye or Rye Brook

The Rye or Rye Brook is Ashtead's only watercourse of note. It starts behind Park Farm House near the Epsom boundary flowing in a northerly direction until forced by the topography to turn south-westwards north of Overdale. It is most likely that the Rye is now much shallower and narrower than formerly. Its own stretch of alluvium forms a narrow belt from where the stream flows under the A. 24 road to its junction with the River Mole just north of River Lane, Fetcham. It has a number of minor rills which act as tributaries of which only one appears on the 1:25,000 map. This originates in Ashtead Park and after going under the A. 24 it disappears into a culvert to reappear at the south-eastern end of Overdale. It then continues on a straightened course to join the Rye at a point to the north-east of Broadhurst. There are other minor streams, now mere drainage ditches: one leaves a culvert west of the Ashtead Recreation Ground; another is to be seen along Woodfield Lane.

Wells and Boreholes

There are several wells on Ashtead Common, sometimes referred to as springs. These are said to have the same medicinal properties as the famous Epsom wells.[3] Whilst the medicinal nature of these waters cannot be disputed one must treat with some reserve the view that they are due to Epsom Salts (magnesium sulphate). An analysis commissioned by the Epsom and Ewell Borough Council in 1989 indicated a surprisingly low content of magnesium sulphate. Since all these wells are on London Clay, the dominant chemical dissolved in the water is likely to be calcium sulphate, known as gypsum in its mineral form.

Wells provided Ashtead houses with water before a mains supply was introduced at the end of last century. Most of these wells were probably shallow and are now infilled. A map of 1871 marks wells in Rectory Lane, Skinners Lane and Woodfield Lane, but there must have been many others which have gone unrecorded.

There used to be a borehole, that is a very deep well, at Ermyn Way on the Ashtead/Leatherhead border, put down for the Rayon Manufacturing Company. It reached a depth of 1,141 ft and though it produced a maximum test flow of 1,126 gallons per hour the supply proved inadequate. The Company which began operations in 1928 was forced to give up the venture in 1932. Another borehole in Ashtead, recorded in the district geology review, was equally unsuccessful.

Ponds

The pond which everyone knows is that close to the road between Woodfield Lane and the *Woodman* sometimes called the Woodfield Pond. Maps early this century showed that the pond was then larger than it is now. Manorial rolls called it Oxmoor Pond and they also mentioned Outwell Pond at Street Farm. There is a small pond at the eastern edge of Newton Wood and others at the extreme western and eastern ends of Ashtead Woods Road. Since drainage is poor in the flat parts of Woodfield temporary pools sometimes form here after long periods of rain.

There are two ponds in Ashtead Park, the southern Island Pond, now without its island, dating from the very early 18th century and another north of this constructed by Pantia Ralli after he took over the estate in 1889. He built an ornamental wooden boat-house at its southern end.

Close to the Epsom boundary near the entrance to the R.A.C. Club at *Woodcote Park* are two ponds, one marked Fish Pond on recent maps and another called Willmore Pond on 17th century maps but now known as Baron's Pond. This may have drained at one time to the Hogsmill River near Ewell but any flow today is concealed in drains and culverts[4].

Water Supplies

Ashtead houses received piped water for the first time in the late 1880s, provided by the Leatherhead & District Water Company from a 200 ft borehole in Leatherhead. The pipes were very close to the surface in the early years, but after 1895 they were lowered

to a minimum of 3 ft, the standard level today. Water is now supplied by the East Surrey Water Company using boreholes at Leatherhead and Fetcham springs. The company's supplies also come from
other boreholes at Kenley, Smitham and Purley. The water is soft-
ened at the Leatherhead works producing large quantities of pre-
cipitated chalk. Hardness levels in present supplies have to conform
to European standards.

Woodlands

There are about 640 acres of woodland in Ashtead, mainly on the
Common in the north of the parish (see below)[5]. This is about a
quarter of the total parish area, high for a place so near London.
Adjoining the Common on the east is Newton Wood, which has
always been separate from the Common and is roughly the same
area as shown on the 1638 map of Ashtead (see p. 33).

The only woodland in the south of the parish is Addlestead
Wood, close to Thirty Acres Barn and the Headley Road. In the
17th century it was nearly twice its present size.

Weather extremes: Storms and Droughts

Weather contrasts have been a feature of the years since the war,
though severe cold, heavy rains, strong winds and long, dry spells
have been common enough at other times. There was a big freeze
in the winter of 1947 as well as in that of 1962/63. Some of the
worst flooding of recent years took place in September 1968.
Equally well remembered will be the great drought of 1976, when
every day, for over two months from mid-June onwards, was cloud-
less and blistering with its heat; the fields became brown and everyone was exhorted to use running water most sparingly. More
dramatic was the fearsome storm of October 1987 which left in its
wake many uprooted trees, wrecked cars and damaged houses.
There was often a long silence, then in the distance could be heard
a roar, becoming louder and deafening as the wind passed overhead.
Another gale in January 1990 was similarly destructive; it topped
two of the finest cedars in the drive to St Giles' Church and caused
much damage elsewhere. The 1990 summer was hot and dry, followed by a particularly cold winter. Rainfall figures were below
average between 1988 and 1992 but water levels have recovered
since then[6]. There were long spells of heavy rain in late 1994 and
early 1995.

ASHTEAD COMMON

Ashtead Common covers 519 acres and its boundaries have hardly changed since the earliest surveys. It lies on shallow sands overlying London Clay which becomes very muddy underfoot after rain, though the soil bakes hard in long, dry periods. The chief features of the Common are the Rye Brook and an undulating ridge of high ground parallel to it. From the village the land rises gradually to the ridge and then more steeply down the other side.

The Common is covered with deciduous woodland, scrub and some grassland. The main trees are oak, birch and willow, with a thick undergrowth of bracken. Many of the oaks have twisted and gnarled branches, some several hundred years old. Shrubs, bushes and 'meadow' grass dominate the parts near the Rye Brook and Woodfield. The Common has a rich variety of flowers and plants, as well as large numbers of birds. Roe deer can sometimes be seen.

Periodic fires have done much damage to the ancient oaks and to many of the other trees over a wide area.

Early History

Old documents refer to the area as the 'Waste' of the Manor and little is known about its management or its vegetation until the 18th century at the earliest. However, we do know that the area was used extensively for grazing of livestock and for the production of timber, probably for house building and other uses. Most of the older oak trees show signs of having been pollarded, a convenient method of cutting timber of a useful size while preserving the health of the trees for the future.

The Common in the 19th century

In the early 19th century, the Wyburd Survey (1802) and the early Ordnance Survey maps show that the thickly wooded area coincided chiefly with the higher ground, most of the lower lying land in the Rye valley being a mixture of scrub, grass and heathland with some clusters of large trees. Unlike Epsom Common, there seem to have been few building encroachments, although Duke's Hall and some cottages on the northern fringes of Woodfield might have been exceptions.

When the railway reached the district in the middle of the 19th century it brought coal for fuel and imported timber for house building. The practice of pollarding probably ceased at about that

Fig. 1. Woodland on Ashtead Common, c. 1908. Probably the Broad Ride. LDLHS Collection

Fig. 2. Bridge over the Rye Brook, from Broadhurst to Ashtead Woods. George Astridge and his son, Percy taking leaf mould, collected from under the oak trees, to the Virginia Nurseries in Skinners Lane, c. 1930. LDLHS Collection

time, though some pollards remain to this day.

Doubtless, there were many tracks and pathways across the Common but the principal ones were those from the village across Woodfield and the Rye to the Ashtead Gap, Rushett Farm and Chessington; from Woodlands Road, Epsom to the Epsom Gap; and from Farm Lane along the side of Newton Wood to Woodcock Corner and thence to Chessington or Horton. The two access roads through privately-owned land near the Kingston Road have always been known as the Ashtead Gap (or Cross) and the Epsom Gap, indicating the destinations of the traffic entering at those points.

In 1866 the Ordnance Survey produced its large-scale maps (1:2500) which contained much greater detail of open country than had been possible hitherto. On these, the general vegetation was much as Wyburd had shown some 65 years earlier but the positions of many individual trees were plotted and trackways were shown in meticulous detail. In the Woodfield area there was a ford across the Rye as well as two footbridges over it.

After over 200 years of ownership by the Howard family the Common was sold in 1885 to Thomas Lucas and then again in 1889 to Pantia Ralli. By the turn of the century any pressure there might have been to cultivate the Common died away but grazing continued and the Common was a rich source of domestic fuel.

When war broke out in 1914 the Common was used extensively for troop encampments and training.

The Common between the wars (1918–39)

With the death of Pantia Ralli in 1924 the Common was bought by A.R. Cotton who was soon to be involved with the dramatic excavation of the Roman tilery which brought a host of visitors to the site (see p. 15). The Common still had a rural setting. Cattle waded in and drank from the Woodfield Pond and grazed on its verges; bracken on the higher ground of the Common was cut in late summer and used by farmers as winter bedding for livestock; leaf mould was collected for sale to local nurseries and some standing trees were felled and the best wood hauled away.

A.R. Cotton granted shooting rights on the Common to a local sportsman, and his gamekeepers from Newton Wood maintained a strip of open land known as the Broad Ride, for shooting parties. By standing at one side the guns could get a good view of the pheasants and partridges as they were flushed out from the other side.

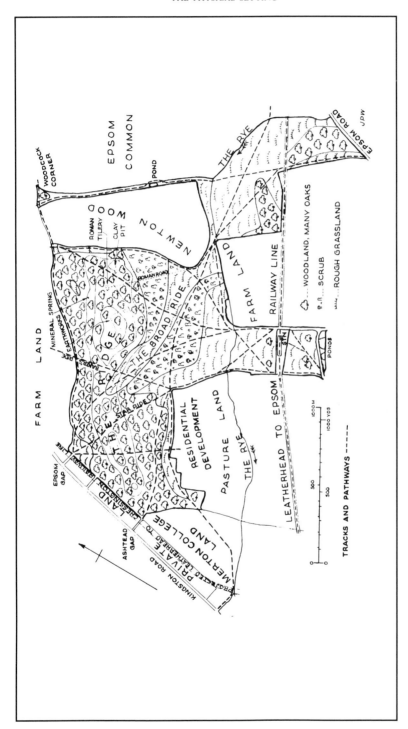

Ashtead Common in the early 20th century

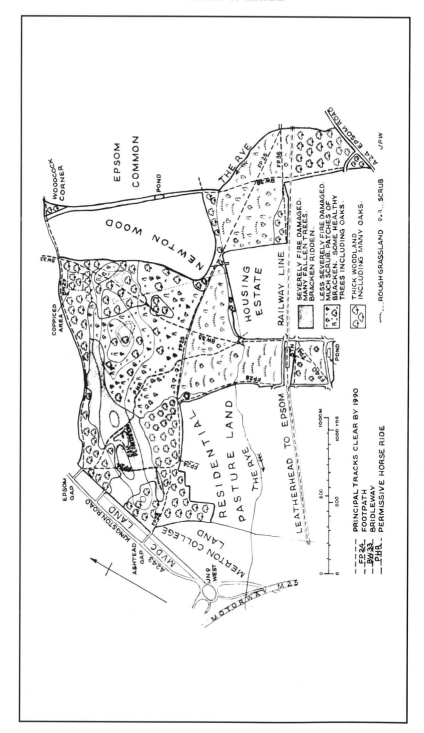

Ashtead Common in the late 20th century (to 1990)

Because of its closeness to Ashtead Station the Common had become a recreational area for Londoners. Parties of schoolchildren descended from the trains in their hundreds and the refreshment establishments as well as the funfair at *Windy Corner* by the footbridge did a roaring trade. At this point the refreshment place doubled as a bakery and it is thought that much of the flour for baking came from Rushett Farm via a track across the Common known as the Baker's Row Ride.

The Common in Wartime

During the last war, the Common was again used by soldiers, including the local Home Guard (see p. 139). Much of the lower land was ploughed for food production and many of the finest oaks were felled for war materials, while the *Windy Corner* restaurant was turned into a canteen for the troops. The restaurant continued for a few years after the war, but the use of the Common for widespread recreation never really returned.

The Post-War Years

A.R. Cotton continued to be responsible for the Common until 1962 when he sold it to Lord Barnby. About this time the Common had suffered a lot from storms and fires. Trees were being blown down in gales, branches were falling off and bracken spreading. Fires in the 1950s and 1960s destroyed great stretches of woodland and more bracken moved into the devastated area. Further fires during the drought of the mid-seventies, which coincided with the epidemic of Dutch elm disease, left the Common in a piteous state.

During the post-war years the area became registered common land, a Site of Special Scientific Interest and part of the London Green Belt; many of its network of footpaths and bridleways became regularised, each being given a right-of-way number. Lord Barnby established two permissive horse rides and a free riding area near the Rye. After a tussle with local opinion and with the government he was also able to get a set of bye-laws approved. After his death in 1982 his estate passed to a trust for the lifetime of Lady Barnby. In 1983 a statutory conservation group, the Lower Mole Countryside Management Project, was set up at Kingston and within a few years it became active in the management of the Common. Despite another bad fire and some discouragement from representatives of the trust, a quite dramatic transformation was achieved and within a few years the Common would have been restored to a healthy state. Unfortunately Lady Barnby's sudden death in 1988 meant that the Common was again up for sale.

After a short but heated debate locally, the Mole Valley District Council decided to purchase the Common but almost immediately transferred it into the ownership of the Corporation of the City of London, except for Woodfield south of the railway which it retained. Within a few months, negotiations had been completed and after some hundreds of years of local control and ownership Ashtead Common passed to the Corporation of the City of London in the spring of 1991. The new owners have been active in looking after the Common and have based their work for the first few years on the management plan researched and written by the Lower Mole Countryside Project before completion of the sale.[7]

Notes

1. J.E.B. Gover et. al, *The Place Names of Surrey* (1934) p. 11
2. For a detailed map of Ashtead's geology see the Geological Survey map (Sheet 286), 1:50,000.
3. *Victoria County History, Surrey* (1911), Vol. 3, p. 272
4. J.R. Clube, 'Ashtead's Missing River & Willmore Pond' *Procs LDLHS*, 5(5), 1992, pp. 146–8
5. R.A. Lever, 'The Woods and Copses of Ashtead' *Procs LDLHS*, 5(3) 1990, pp. 69–72
6. M. Davison & I. Currie, *The Surrey Weather Book* (1993)
7. 'Ashtead Common Plan' *Lower Mole Countryside Management Project*, 1991.

Chapter 2

PREHISTORIC AND ROMAN ASHTEAD

In southern England, over a period of at least two millenia prior to the Claudian invasion of AD 43, man progressed to a relatively settled agricultural economy. The evidence for this is widely dispersed, but it seems likely that the stresses created by an expanding – and sometimes decreasing – population led to tribal warfare. The political and land-use boundaries set up by an interplay of forces formed a pattern from which our present boundaries are but a distant reflection. As yet there is little to identify Ashtead in this Celtic background. 'Findspots' of material from the neolithic and bronze age are recorded, and, to support the concept of settled agriculture, two farm sites of the pre-Roman Iron Age have been found in the vicinity. One, at Hawks Hill, Leatherhead, comprised grain storage pits with pottery and animal bones. This site was excavated in the early 1960s and showed that at least by the end of the Iron Age stock could be over-wintered and grain stored[1]. A similar site in Park Lane, Ashtead, was less fortunate in its treatment: discovered in the 1920s, some fifteen pits were identified, one certainly and the others presumably the same as those on Hawks Hill[2-6]. The third site at the Old Quarry was said to comprise 'grain store pits', pottery, querns and loom weights[7, 8]. Limited excavations in 1974 did not identify the pits reported in 1933, but two were found possibly of 17th–18th century date[9]. So-called 'Celtic fields' appear on Leatherhead and Mickleham Downs: their date is uncertain, but it seems clear that they expanded from the late Bronze Age into the Roman period to cover much of the chalk downland in southern England.

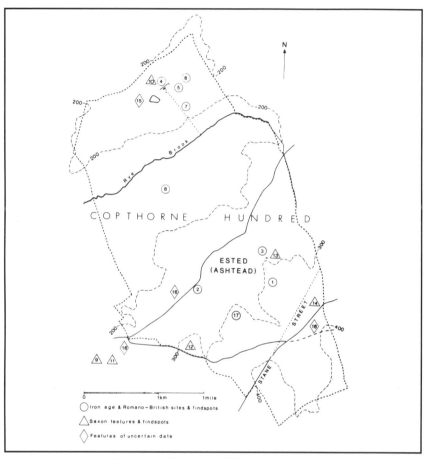

Iron Age, Roman and Saxon Ashtead
Based on OS 6" maps 1871–74: additional information, JNH & EC: drawn JNH.

Iron Age and Roman
1. Iron age and Romano-British 'farm' 1st c. BC to 3rd c. AD. 2. Iron Age pits, loom weights and quern stone fragments. 3. Roman building. 4. Roman villa and bath house. 5. Roman clay pits. 6. Roman pottery found (OS 6" map). 7. Roman road connecting the tile works with Stane Street. 8. Roman coins found (OS 6" map) 17. Roman coins found (Lowther, 1958)

Saxon
9. Leatherhead Church: original church built and endowed by King Alfred. 10. Saxon knife and pottery found on site of Roman Villa. 11. Late Saxon bronze pin found near Leatherhead Hospital. 12. Anglo-Saxon cemetery, Ermyn Way. 13. Ashtead Church with Roman tiles incorporated in south and former north walls. 14. Saxon burials south of Ashtead Park and near Stane Street. 15. Earthwork, Ashtead Common. 16. Trackways. (cf. deviant way to NE and post-Roman usage of Stane Street).

Stane Street and the Roman Occupation of Ashtead

The Roman road (Stane Street) from Chichester to London crosses the south-eastern part of the parish. It may reflect an early phase in the Romanization of Britain, dating from perhaps the AD 50s and was probably related to military needs, The road was known in medieval times variously as Stanstete (1279) and Pybyl-strete (1358).[10] The route survives as Pebble Lane, crossing the parish northward from Tyrells Wood to Thirty Acre Barn, where the bridleway Shepherds' Walk diverges to the north-east. The alignment of the Roman road then continues that of Pebble Lane across the fields to the Woodruffe Stables, attested by excavation[11] and crop marks recorded on air photographs. We can only speculate on the impact the Roman roads had on Celtic society; Stane Street passed near to the Iron Age farm in Park Lane. The grain storage pits, already referred to, produced Roman building material as well as pottery, and nearby was found a coin of Carausius (c. 290 A.D.). This evidence, coupled with that cited above, suggests that this farm began in the Iron Age and continued at least until the 3rd century – a life of perhaps four hundred years or more. Another Roman building has been identified near St Giles' Church, but it was destroyed by a later earthwork. Here, robber trenches suggested a building some 38ft by 10ft; only one corner was identified and the true nature of this structure remains enigmatic.

Roman Villa and Tileworks on Ashtead Common

The major Roman industrial complex on the Common is important and perhaps unique in southern Britain because the clay pits appear to have survived. The complex comprises a corridor villa and bath house probably surrounded by a 'precinct' wall with most of the clay pits to the east. The whole may represent a late 1st century investment in brick and tile making which lasted until the 2nd century. The site, in the centre of a ridge of heavy London Clay, rises to about 250ft above sea level and 100ft above the Rye Brook. Much of the area was in recent times covered with pollarded oaks, alas now sadly diminished. The choice of this area clearly relates to the presence of suitable clay and of timber for fuel.

The villa and bath-house were excavated between 1925 and 1929, and re-assessed in 1959[12, 13]. The 'Corridor' Villa is of a type well-known in the Roman Empire, but this is unusual in that there are two rows of rooms instead of the more usual single row. It is clear that the building had some architectural pretensions: the plan implies a near central portico approached by a road or drive, suggesting that the south-east facing facade was the focus of interest. This concept is supported by a series of half and quarter round tiles found in the corridor and *in situ* at the south-west corner of the building, indicating engaged half columns along the south-east face of the building. Furthermore, fragments of a carved sandstone block decorated with scrolls and cornucopia were found, strongly suggesting some type of dedication tablet. Although only brick floors were found within the villa, a small bath annexe contained several thousand small tesserae of various colours, clearly the remains of a mosaic, and this, when considered with the small finds, may imply some degree of wealth and taste.

The bath building, the first part of the site to be excavated by Lowther, incorporates a circular heated room and is a type often to be associated with Roman forts. Fair (1927) describes the circular building – 15ft to 20ft in diameter – as identified with the *sudatorium* or *laconicum* of Vitruvius and Pliny, a small, very hot chamber having its heat regulated by a shutter in the roof. Normally it is found that these *sudatoria* are entered directly from the cold room (*apodyterium, frigidarium*), in some cases from the open air; and they are heated by independent furnaces[14]. A late 1st to early 2nd century date is suggested for this type.

A survey by the writer in 1961–65 revealed the nature of the extensive clay pits and the areas of firing. An operation in 1991 to clear Flag Pond showed Roman debris on an old working surface, and it now seems probable that this is indeed a Roman clay pit. The largest pit, roughly triangular in plan with sides about 87 yds long, is about 6ft deep at its deepest point. Two 'kilns' (A and B) and possibly another (C) were identified on the periphery of the pit. (Fig. 3) It seems that the technique of firing at these sites was that of 'clamps' in which green tiles were stacked together with combustibles and the whole covered with clay or turf with air inlets round the base and smoke exits at the top; the rate of combustion was controlled by the amount of air allowed in through the base inlets. It is worth remembering that these techniques were still in use until the comparatively recent advent of mass production. Local brick production of this kind, where geology allowed, could be said to have been the norm until the late 19th century.

An important product was relief patterned flue tiles (Fig 4. These

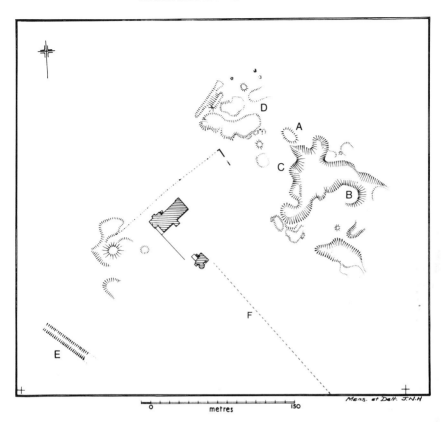

Fig. 3. Plan of Roman brick and tile works, Ashtead Common.
A, B, C, Site of 'kilns' and possible 'kiln' on the edge of the Roman clay pit. D.
Flag pond: now thought to be a Roman clay pit. E. Undated earthwork, probably
medieval. F. Road probably connecting with Stane Street.

box flue tiles, virtually rectangular clay pipes, were built vertically
into walls to carry the hot gases from the hypocaust below the floor
and were extremely useful for other building functions. The most
interesting feature of these box tiles is the patterns impressed or
incised on their wide faces. These patterns provided a key for plaster and were completely hidden from view. A wide distribution of
tiles similarly marked has been identified[15] but it not certain how
many came from Ashtead.

In an enterprise of this nature, transport was clearly vital to its
success. A road, almost certainly connecting the complex with Stane
Street, was identified by Lowther crossing the Common; and recent
aerial observation by the writer has suggested a likely junction
point.

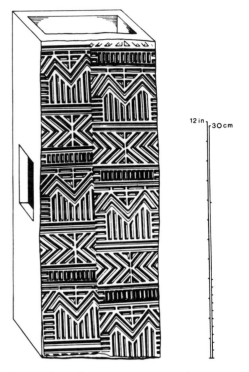

12 in   30 cm

Fig. 4. Roman box flue tile based on fragments recovered from the tile kiln at A. (Fig. 3.). The pattern has been impressed probably with a wooden roller which has been used twice across the face of the tile: note the mismatch of the design.

Whilst it is known that some settlements established in the Iron Age survived well into the Roman period and perhaps beyond, it is unclear how many of the present boundaries can be related to the Romanization of Britain. Blair (1991) has suggested that some of the modern boundaries between the Common and the village may well be based on a Roman land division of 2,300 ft squares[16.] Given the longevity of some of the boundary patterns in southern England this now seems not at all unlikely. Questions of this kind pose a challenge for the current programme of research into the landscapes of Surrey and underline the evolving nature of our knowledge.

Notes

1. F.A. Hastings, 'Excavations of an Iron Age farmstead at Hawks Hill, Leatherhead' *SAC.*, 62, 1965, pp. 1–43

2. A.W.G. Lowther, 'Cartographic Survey: Roman Period' *Procs LDLHS*, 2(2), 1958, pp. 41–2

3. A.W.G. Lowther, 'The Iron Age and Roman occupation site at Park Lane, Ashtead' *Procs LDLHS*,

2(6), 1962, pp. 164–8

4. A.W.G. Lowther, 'Iron Age pottery from sites at Ewell and Ashtead' *SAC*, 50, 1949, pp. 139–41

5. A.W.G. Lowther, 'The Roman site near the parish church of St Giles at Ashtead' *SAC*, 42, 1934, pp. 77–84

6. A.W.G. Lowther, 'The Romano-British site at Ashtead' *SAC.*, 38, 1930, pp. 197–202

7. A.W.G. Lowther, 'Bronze-Iron Age and Roman finds at Ashtead' *SAC*, 41, 1933, pp. 93–8

8. A.W.G. Lowther, 'Cartographic Survey...Bronze and Iron Ages' *Procs. LDLHS*, 2(1), 1957, p. 5

9. J.F. Barfoot, 'Excavations at the Old Quarry...1974' *SAC*, 76, 1985, pp. 76. 81–7

10. J.E.B. Gover et. al. *The Place Names of Surrey* (1934), p. 11

11. J. Fox, 'Stane St.' *SAC.*, 51, 1950, pp. 147–51

12. A.W.G. Lowther, 'Excavations at Ashtead, Surrey' *SAC.*, 37, 1927, pp. 2, 144–63; ibid, 38, 1, 1929, pp. 1–17; ibid, 38, 2, 1930, pp. 132–48

13. A.W.G. Lowther, 'The date of the Roman buildings and brickworks on Ashtead Common' *Procs LDLHS*, 2(2), 1959, pp 73–5

14. M.C. Fair 'Circular Bath Buildings in connection with Cohort Forts *Journ. Roman Studies*, 17, pp 220–24

15. A.W.G. Lowther, 'A study of the patterns on Roman flue-tiles and their distribution' *SAS* Research Paper 1

16. John Blair, *Early Medieval Surrey* (1991), pp. 29–36

Chapter 3

ANGLO-SAXON ASHTEAD

For most of the 600 years after the Romans left the country in AD 410 until the Norman Conquest in the mid-11th century very little is known about whether the Ashtead region continued to be settled by a farming community. Its position on a spring-line close to forests useful for timber had attracted a Romano/British settlement and these attractions were, of course, still there when the Romans left, but the constant wars and disturbances brought about by the Saxon and other invasions may wholly have disrupted and destroyed the rural scene here, at least in the 5th and early 6th centuries. It is believed that Saxons settled first in the northern parts of Surrey and only moved to points further south late in the 6th century[1]. Some may have come to Ashtead then and also in the next century, evidence from pagan burial sites supporting this. In the late Saxon period, during King Edgar's reign (959–75), Surrey, like other counties, was divided for administrative purposes into 'Hundreds' and at village level into 'Tithings' or groups of ten households. Ashtead (or 'Stede' as the Saxons called it) formed part of Copthorne Hundred but whether the village had 'Tithings' is not known[2].

It is doubtful whether there was ever more than a small hamlet on the present site in these Saxon centuries. Perhaps there were never more than 40 or 50 people at the most, living in timber or wattle and daub hovels, probably near the present Rectory Lane from which a rough lane would lead into the forest[3].

The only firm evidence for the presence of Saxons in Ashtead comes from burials adjacent to Ermyn Way (the Esso office site) and beside Stane Street near Ashtead Park; also an iron knife was found with a piece of pottery during the excavation of the Roman Villa on Ashtead Common. Nothing has been found to show where they lived, though the incorporation of Roman tiles in the south wall of St Giles' Church suggests that after they became Christians they occupied an area in its vicinity.

Saxon Burials at Ermyn Way

The archaeological potential of the Ermyn Way site was realised when A.W.G. Lowther found in 1927 a large pit in which were a number of dismembered skeletons which he and Professor Keith, the eminent pathologist, thought could be of Anglo-Saxons. In 1974 when a service trench was dug near the site of the Goblin Works a spearhead was found which gave further strength to the view that the skeletons were Anglo-Saxon.

Preliminary work in 1984 for the Esso building which was to replace the Goblin factory produced human bones. The company readily agreed to a detailed examination of an area which had not been disturbed by the foundations of the earlier factory. Three short periods of excavation produced evidence of more than 40 burials. Some graves contained artefacts (knives, buckles, bronze pins, a comb and a necklace of beads) showing that the bodies had been buried in the pagan tradition and their style dated them to the latter part of the 7th century, that is about the time when Christianity reached Surrey. These graves were well cut into the chalk sub-soil at about 3 below the surface at the time. This group of 18 or 20 bodies had their heads to the west and were well spaced out indicating that the location of earlier burials was known when later graves were dug.

Not all of the skeletons were sufficiently well preserved for the pathologists to be able to determine the age, sex and height. Only in the cases of adults is it possible to give the sex. Of the 18 where identification was possible there were eight men, four women and five children plus one adult of unknown sex. The children had died between the ages of four and five years. Most of the adults had been under the age of 45; their heights were approximately similar to ours.

Another group of burials had been in what can be described as no more than hollow scrapes in the ground at a shallower depth, and the bodies appeared to have been thrown in with little ceremony. Several had been decapitated and some had their hands in positions indicating that they had been tied together. The inference

Fig. 5. Saxon skeleton found during excavation of Esso Company site, 1989 (Courtesy, E.A. Crossland).

is that they had been hanged and so are judged to have been criminals. Of the 12 bodies in this category one was a woman, another under the age of 15; the rest were adult males. One severed head had been placed between the victim's legs.

With all the burials, apart from wearing down due to the grit in stone-ground flour, the condition of the teeth was good. There were some signs of arthritis in a few; one was clearly lame but none showed signs of battle wounds.

One of the children had been buried with what must have been a valuable necklace since it contained beads of amber glass and pottery with spacers of pieces of sea shell from a panther cowrie. A complete panther cowrie shell was found in another grave which also contained a small, two-sided bone comb. As panther cowries are only found in the Red Sea this is evidence of trade over a wide area in the 7th century; A large post-hole close to the burials could have been the site of a gallows tree[4].

Notes

1. Rob Poulton, *Saxon Secrets in Surrey* (1990) p. 7
2. John Blair, 'The Anglo-Saxon Period' in *Oxford Illustrated History of Britain* (1984) p. 88
3. A.W.G. Lowther, 'Ashtead and its History: Saxons, Danes & Norman' *Procs LDLHS*, 1(5), 1951, p. 24
4. Rob Poulton, 'Early Saxon Cemetery at the former Goblin Works, Ashtead' *SAC* 79 (1989) pp. 67–97

Chapter 4

THE MIDDLE AGES

According to Domesday Book (1086), Ashtead before the Norman Conquest was one of the many estates of Earl (later King) Harold, leased to a man called Thurgis.[1] After Harold's death at the Battle of Hastings his properties were divided among the Conqueror's close relatives and the Norman knights who had fought by his side. Ashtead was given to William's half-brother, Odo Bishop of Bayeux, though he allowed his Canons to hold it. This change to Norman ownership probably made little immediate difference to the day-to-day life of the villagers, but they doubtless resented the tax impositions and the personal services expected of them by each successive overlord.

The lords who ruled Ashtead were seldom resident and the manor would usually be left in the charge of a steward or bailiff. There is a tradition that the Warennes, Earls of Surrey, owned Ashtead for many years after 1088. There is also evidence that Laurence de Rouen held Ashtead from the Chamberlain of Tancarville in Normandy and that it passed to his descendants the de Maras. In the second half of the 13th century it was in the hands of the de Montforts who were related to the de Maras. Later lords of the manor were the Frevills and the Astons who held it into Tudor times.[2]

There was another manor in the village called Little Ashtead or Prior's Farm, owned by Merton Priory.[3] It lay in the west of the parish, comprising about 200 acres of farmland. There was a detached piece of 36 acres further south, though this may have been owned by Reigate Priory which is known to have had some property in Ashtead[4].

Over a long period there was an active land market in Ashtead, with some landowners not living here but leasing their land to tenants. In 1290, John Florentin of Guildford 'released' ten acres of arable land to Peter de Montfort, lord of the manor, with two acres of wood. Edith de Pariz, sister and heir of a cellarer in London, in 1304 granted her tenement and lands in Ashtead to Roger le Graunt, barber, of London. A few years later, de Montfort offered William Poundy, a shepherd, eight acres to hold for his life, at the rent of a rose. The Legh family of Addington and Headley held much land in Ashtead and there are many records of their property sales here; for example, there were two sales in 1317, five in 1321, ten more later in the century and eight in the 15th century.[5]

The Farming Community

After the Norman Conquest, Ashtead continued to be as in Anglo-Saxon times a small farming village. When the Domesday Survey was taken there were 53 families, made up of 33 villeins, 11 bordars and 9 serfs, all subject to the lord of the manor. If children were taken into account the total population was likely to have been between 150 and 200, all but a few living in primitive timber or wattle-and-daub houses with only a single storey. The water supply most likely came from natural springs and from a small lake or ponds. The village was probably linear in layout, with rows of dwellings, called tenements, facing each other and an unpaved road between them with some rough lanes leading towards the fields.[6]

Subsistence farming was the rule, at least in the early years after the Conquest, every working man seeking to produce what his family needed to feed themselves. The manor had its own 'demesne' land with some fields enclosed by hedges or fences, 'closes' being referred to in an Inquisitio Post Mortem of 1296, which also states that the lord had 320 acres of arable land, 60 acres of pasture and 18 acres of meadow, including also some woodland.[7] The manorial rules required the villeins to work for the lord two or three days a week. Ploughing, harvesting and carrying away the demesne produce were some of the tasks they had to do, under the supervision of the bailiff. As time went on, a few of the villeins may have exchanged their services for money payments.

The villeins who lived in the village farmed strips of land in several large open fields. Wheat, barley, oats and peas were grown. Care was taken that part of the land remained in fallow one year to maintain fertility. Marl and natural manure were used to improve the soil, the 'marl pit' of Ashtead being mentioned in a 1320 document.[8] The Domesday Survey reported that there were 14 ploughs but their number probably increased over the years. The ploughs were usually owned by more than one villager, the oxen working in teams. Horses were not used for ploughing until much later. Many of the villeins may have held a horse or two and perhaps a cow, some pigs and a few hens in their 'croft', adjoining where they lived; they may also have had bees to provide honey for sweetening and making mead.

Fixed cropping patterns do not seem to have been imposed by the Ashtead manorial court, as they were in the open-field parishes of the Midlands, though some loose system of crop control might presumably have been followed.[9] The pasturing of sheep, cattle and pigs was, by contrast, kept under strict management, stock only being allowed on arable and meadow lands after the harvest (usually completed by early August), folding and tethering taking place to ensure that this was done. The meadows were allocated in plots or strips by the bailiff to those who held arable land.

Livestock using the wastes and woodland were also controlled, a court case in 1433 referring to the lord's common as 'oppressed and burdened' by Richard Waley's 400 sheep being beyond the allowed number of 200.[10] It is clear that sheep-rearing for meat and wool was an important farming activity. Because of fodder shortage most livestock had to be killed in the winter and salted to preserve the meat for food purposes. The Ashtead woodlands were highly valued for their timber, used for making the many farming needs like poles, rakes, fences, baskets and shepherd's crooks. Payments called 'pannage' were made for feeding pigs in the woods.

Warrens for rabbits were common at this time, rabbits providing a source of food; their fur had its uses too. In the late 14th century, Sir Baldwin Frevill mentioned his rabbit warren in a lease to Adam Hyde.[11] The rights for the warren, thought to have been in or near Newton Wood, were closely protected, complaints sometimes being made in court against the 'digging out' of rabbits by ferrets and for stealing game birds like partridges and pheasant from there.[12]

An inventory of 1376 described Ashtead manor farm as having 24 oxen, as well as bulls, bullocks and cows, many hundreds of sheep and lambs, some pigs and hens and several horses. Its granary was stacked with wheat, barley, oats, peas and malt. There were six ploughs, a cheese press, and a farm wagon. This was clearly a large, mixed farm which must have brought in many villagers to fulfil its everyday tasks.[13]

The manor court had wide-ranging powers, protecting the lord's lands from illegal trespass and reproving tenants who were laggards in their work. It imposed what was called a heriot, the forfeit of a 'best beast' on the change of a tenancy, and exactions were due also on marriage. The court further required all cottages, fences, roads and footpaths to be kept in proper repair.

Although living off the land was the lot of most villagers, some would sally forth occasionally to nearby markets, perhaps carrying in simple carts some goods to sell. Some may have ventured further afield. The Gough map, drawn about 1350, showed that there was a network of roads leading to London from the south and from other directions.[14] The roads would be unpaved and muddy after rain, but they provided a reasonable measure of mobility for country folk.

The generally quiet tempo of village life here and elsewhere was broken in 1348/49 by the Black Death which in a few months killed about a third of the population in town and country.[15] Ashtead's farming community must certainly have been devastated, with few persons alive or well enough to gather the harvest. The high death rate and labour shortages led to farming difficulties throughout the country. These were one of the main causes of the Peasants' Revolt in 1381, though the spark for this was ignited by the new Poll Tax, hated by everyone. There is no record of rioting in Ashtead at this time, but some villagers might have found their way to join the London mobs, since Surrey men were known to have been there.[16]

In the 15th century there were no major upheavals as in the previous century, though in 1450 disturbances broke out in Banstead and possibly in villages even nearer, associated with Jack Cade's rebellion. The dynastic Wars of the Roses in the mid-century scarcely affected rural areas like Ashtead, well away from the fighting. The court rolls continued to list the many misdemeanors of the villagers and one, late in the century, complained about several 'natives' (villeins) having fled the manor without permission, a practice which was becoming more and more frequent. This was an indication of the breakdown of the old manorial system with many villeins finding pastures new or commuting their services for money payments and becoming 'free' tenants or copyholders. Villeinage, however, remained in some form in Ashtead down to the reign of Henry VIII.[17]

Craftsmen, Potters and Tile-makers

Most of Ashtead's household goods and farm equipment were probably made by local carpenters, wheelwrights and blacksmiths. Pottery-making was another village activity, traces of which have been found in Newton Wood Road. Several hundred fragments of vessels have been discovered, dating from about 1300, including parts of cooking-pots, dishes and jugs.[18]

Tile-making was an active industry here in the 14th century, and the works were believed to have been close to Ottways Lane or to Newton Wood Road. As many as 10,500 roof tiles were supplied in 1372/73 for the building of Banstead manor house. They were carted there in ten loads.[19] In 1376, Ashtead manor's inventory referred to 5,000 tiles being held in store and eight years later more tiles were being supplied 'for the lord's kitchen' The tile works closed down in 1400.[20]

Saltpetre was also produced in the village, probably by the burning of bracken.

Military Escapades

Ashtead men are known to have fought in the Barons' War of the mid-13th century, when Simon de Montfort and others challenged Henry III's opposition to their reforms.[21] In June 1263, Ashtead men demonstrated their sympathy with de Montfort's cause and their loyalty to Ashtead's lord of the manor, another de Montfort. They occupied Malden for three days, driving off farm animals and carrying away goods. Malden was an obvious target since it was owned by Walter de Merton, former Chancellor to the King, and eventually it became the location of his 'House of Scholars' later to be transferred to Oxford as Merton College. The Ashtead men also did rampage in Chessington and Cuddington. In June 1267, the raids were repeated though on a lesser scale, reflecting perhaps resentment following the King's victory over Simon de Montfort at Evesham the previous year.

So Ashtead men were not only tillers of the soil and payers of dues to their lord!

The Medieval Church

Early in the 12th century a charter of William Giffard, Bishop of Winchester, referred to the dedication of a church here, as a chapel subject to Leatherhead. It was built in about 1120 with an endowment from Laurence de Rouen.[22] The advowson, or the right to appoint priests, was held by Colchester Abbey until the mid-13th century when it passed to the lords of the manor. This early church, or chapel, probably had a nave and chancel only, incorporating some Roman tiles, and its shape is traceable even today. It was built close to the manor house, some distance from the village.

The Norman-built church probably became a church in its own right in the late 13th century after over 150 years as a chapel. The earliest Rector, Robert de Montfort, a relative of the then lord of the manor, was instituted about 1282. The early Rectors may have been non-resident since Vicars were also appointed between 1302 and 1482, no doubt to carry out all or most of the priestly duties. The Vicarage was endowed in 1331 with the tithes of lamb, wool, pigs, calves, geese, flax and hemp. It was about this time that Walter de Burleigh became one of the most distinguished of Ashtead Rectors: he had previously been tutor to the Black Prince and had written a treatise on Aristotle; after coming here in 1342 he obtained canonries in absentia at Chichester, Salisbury and York.[23]

Ashtead church retained its simple structure for many years, not being enlarged like Leatherhead and other Surrey churches, although a chantry chapel was established in 1261 by Mathew de Mara. The Priory of Newark (near Guildford) undertook to maintain it with three chaplains.[24]

The Vicar was a farmer as well as a priest, being responsible for the cultivation of about 30 acres of land granted to him at the church's foundation.[25] This was his glebe land, divided into strips and 'closes' and he depended on its produce for the part at least of the food he and his family required. He also had the tithes to support him. The parsonage where he lived adjoined the Little Ashtead estate in the west of the parish.

Notes

1. J. Morris (ed) *Domesday Book: Surrey* (1975)
2. *Victoria County History, Surrey* (1911), p. 248; Manning & Bray, *History of Surrey* (1809) II pp. 627–8
3. A. Heales, *Records of Merton Priory* (1878), App. LXVI
4. A.W.G. Lowther, 'Ashtead & its History, V' *Procs LDLHS*, 1(7), 1953, pp. 18–19
5. W.J. Blair, 'Medieval Deeds of the

Leatherhead   District'   *Procs LDLHS*, 4(6), 1982, pp. 153, 155; ibid, 4(8), 1984, pp. 207–10

6. John Blair, *Early Medieval Surrey* (1991), p. 58

7. Manning & Bray (1809) op cit, II p. 626

8. SRO 448/1

9. K.A. Bailey & I.G. Galbraith, 'Field Systems in Surrey' *SAC*, 74, 1973, p. 75; John Blair (1991) op. cit, p. 70

10. SRO 448/1

11. W.J. Blair, 'Medieval Deeds of the Leatherhead   District'   *Procs LDLHS*, 4(10), 1986, pp. 268–9

12. SRO 448/1

13. W.J. Blair (1986) op. cit. p. 269

14. R.A. Pelham, 'The Gough Map' *Geog. Journ* (1933) p. 34

15. P. Ziegler, *The Black Death* (1969) p. 230

16. E.B. Fryde, *The Great Revolt of 1381* (1981) pp. 14–15

17. SRO. 448/1

18. D.F. Renn, 'Some Unusual Pottery from the Ashtead Kiln' *Procs LDLHS*, 3(2), 1968, pp. 58–9

19. H.C.M. Lambert, *History of Banstead* (1912) p. 129

20. A.W.G. Lowther, 'Ashtead & Its History' *Procs LDLHS*, 1(6), 1952, p. 24

21. 'Fitznells Cartulary' *SRS* XXVI (1968) pp. 1xx, 1xxi, 1xxiv

22. John Blair (1991) op. cit. pp. 124–6

23. Society Records, 110

24. H.E. Malden, 'Ashtead and the de Mara Chantry' *SAC*, 7, 1906, pp. 27–32

25. D. Robinson, *Pastors, Parishes and People in Surrey* (1989) p. 4

Chapter 5

TUDOR AND STUART ASHTEAD

When Henry VII became the first Tudor king in 1485 the harvests throughout the country were among the best for a long time and they continued to be above average for the next ten years.[1] For Ashtead farmers, as for farmers everywhere, this long sequence of fine weather was a good augury for the new reign. No-one in Ashtead was to know that their future under the Tudors and Stuarts would lead to changes in the look of the village, with improved cottages to live in, as well as the creation of fine houses and parkland. There were to be changes also in the traditional pattern of church-going, brought about by the many religious reforms. Village life was disturbed in 1588 by the call for men to join the Surrey musters when an invasion was threatened by the Spanish Armada.[2] These were the years of Shakespeare and perhaps a few in the village managed to see at least one of his plays in London. During the Civil War in the 1640s there was no fighting or skirmishing at Ashtead, though Cavaliers and Roundheads were active sometimes in the neighbourhood. Ashtead, like the rest of Surrey, was on the Parliamentary side, but, after the war ended, many here were probably shocked by the King's execution in 1649, the abolition of the monarchy and the creation of a republic, all within a few weeks. The farmer, of course, had to worry about his crops and a series of good harvests in the 1650s helped him to forget the political storms.[3] After the Restoration, Samuel Pepys and John Evelyn paid several visits to Ashtead, recorded in their diaries. During these years, Ashtead became a favoured retreat for London merchants and leaders of fashion.

Ownership of Ashtead Manor

The ownership of Ashtead Manor changed hands many times in this period. The Aston family, owners for many years, disposed of the manor to the Crown in 1543, which in turn soon passed it to Henry Fitzalan, Earl of Arundel. After his death, it was held for a time by the Duke of Norfolk and then, in 1582, by Lord Henry Seymour. Queen Elizabeth passed the manor late in her reign to the D'Arcy family, but it was soon acquired again by the Howards. They held the manor for much of the 17th century, except for a brief spell in the Civil War when Lord Maltravers lost the property because of his Royalist sympathies; he had to pay a fine of £6,000 to repossess it. In 1680 the Duke of Norfolk sold the estate to Sir Robert Howard who in a short while transformed it into a gentleman's country seat.

Little Ashtead Manor

This manor in West Ashtead, owned by Merton Priory, was seized by the Crown following the Dissolution of the Monasteries in 1538. After this, it was held first by Ann, Duchess of Somerset, then by the Earl of Arundel and later, though briefly, by the Duke of Norfolk[4]. In 1578, it was granted to the Newdigate family and in the last year of Queen Elizabeth's reign George Cole became its owner. His lands here were shown on John Lawrence's map of 1638. Late in the 17th century, the Knightley and then the Wyke families were the owners of this land. The ownership passed to the Dackombe family during the next century.

Farms and Farming

There had been signs of a breakdown in Ashtead's old manorial system well before Henry Tudor became King (see p. 26). Many who lived and worked here were now copyholders instead of villeins, though this change of status carried with it some degree of thrall to the lord of the manor. The more active sought ways of becoming a freeholder. Thomas Otway's inventory of 1568 showed that mixed farming was still the rule, with cereals grown and livestock reared; bushels of malt were also mentioned, a clear pointer to the making of ale in the home.[5] Price rises for farm products encouraged farmers to extend their holdings; the manor court in July 1579 agreed that 'a day be given to tenants for ploughing part of the Downes never ploughed before'.[6] This practice continued into the next century.

KEY TO MAP OF ASHTEAD IN 1638   *demesne land   †Lady D'Arcy

1. Chaffers Mead*
2. Rennams*
3. Long Meadow*
4. Rennam Copps
5. Broadfield (La. Darcy)†
6. Sheephouse Field (La. Darcy)
7. Pawns field (La. Darcy)
8. Piggott Field (La. Darcy)
9. Cray (La. Darcy)
10. Broadhurst (La. Darcy)
11. Stoney Croft*
12. Great Teasly Field*
13. Little Teasly Field*
14. Long Field*
15. —(Mr. Peeps gent.)
16. Petters (La. Darcy)
17. Bramley Field (La. Darcy)
18. Harms Field (John Hether)
19. —(John Hether)
20. Cobs (John Hether)
21. Walters Mead*
22. Sheephouse Fields*
23. Jealous Mead (La. Darcy)
24. Nine Acres*
25. Jealous Mead (La. Darcy)
26. Philpot Mead*
27. Piggott Hay (John Hether)
28. Carter's Grove*
29. —*
30. Little Threshers*
31. Threshers*
32. Marld Meadow*
33. Grigs (Nicholas Dingley)
34. —(Simon King)
35. Lanthorns (Mr Mann)
36. Swallowes Hay (La. Darcy)
37. — (Wm. Hilder)
38. —(Michael Richbell)
39. —(Michael Richbell)
40. Rosefield (Wm. Hilder)
41. Lower Rosefield (Robert Hillar)
42. Grigs (Eliz. Mathew)
43. Lyars Field (Widdow Cooke)
44. —(Mr John Bragg)
45. Gossecers Mead*
46. Perry Croft (Mr John Peeps)
47. Perry Croft (Mr John Peeps)
48. Sapres*
49. Gasson*
50. Barbers Grove*
51. Blakes (La. Darcy)
52. Culver Hay*
53. Pen Grove*

54. Sayle Field*
55. Berry Piece*
56. The Ham*
57. Hanging Lands*
58. Ninwood Close*
59. Ninwood Copps*
60. The Breach*
61. Upper Ninwood Close*
62. King's Grove*
63. Down Close*
64. —(Sir Francis Stydolf)
65. —(Mr Cole)
66. Stagly (Edward Otway)
67. Tomletts (Edward Otway)
68. —(Richard King Senior)
69. Seamers (Robert Quennell)
70. —(Richard King Senior)
71. —(William Otway)
72. —(William Otway)
73. —(William Otway)
74. Dicks (William Otway)
75. —(William Otway)
76. —(William Otway)
77. The Gullet (William Otway)
78. Tomletts (William Otway)
79. Fraudings (Mr Cole)
80. Fraudings*
81. Fraudings*
82. Jack Adams' Meadow (Wm. Otway)
83. —(Eliz. Jordan)
84. —(Wm. Otway)
85. —(Eliz. Jordan)
86-94. The Marsh*
95. The Horse Close (Mr Cole)
96-98. —(Edward Otway)
99-103. —(John Hatcher)
104-105. —(Wm. Otway)
106. —(Edward Otway)
107-109. —(Wm. Otway)
110. Taleworth (Wm. Otway)
111. —(Thomas Knightley)
112. Long Field (Mr Cole)
113. —(Mr Cole)
114. —(James Styles)
115. Old Court (James Otway)
116. —(Thomas Mathew)
117. —(Mr Cole)
118. The Parsonage
119. Michells (Ed. Otway)
120. Frownsers (James Styles)
121. Glebe
122. —(Mr Cole)

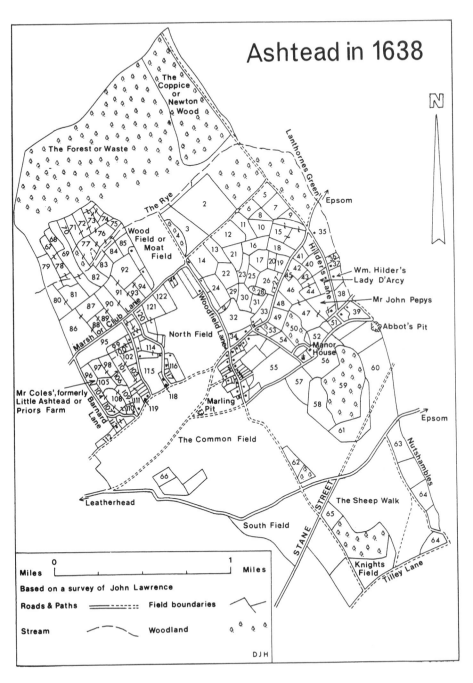

Ashtead in 1638

The Coppice or Newton Wood

The Forest or Waste

The Rye

Lanthornes Green

Epsom

Wood Field or Moat Field

Hilder's Lane

Wm. Hilder's
Lady D'Arcy

Mr John Pepys

Woodfield Lane

North Field

Abbot's Pit

Manor House

Marsh or Club Lane

Mr Coles', formerly Little Ashtead or Priors Farm

Barnard Lane

Marling Pit

The Common Field

Epsom

Leatherhead

Nutshambles

The Sheep Walk

South Field

STANE STREET

Knights Field

Tilley Lane

0   1
Miles |_____| Miles

Based on a survey of John Lawrence

Roads & Paths =======

Field boundaries

Stream

Woodland

DJH

John Lawrence's map of Ashtead, 1638 (redrawn)

For many Ashtead people the land and what they grew was their whole life and the Elizabethan poet, Nicholas Breton, delightfully expresses what it must have been like here in summer when 'The broad oke comforts the weary labourer, while under its shady boughs he sits singing to his bread and cheese...the medow grounds gape for rain, the corne in the ear begins to harden...the little lads make pipes of straw and they that cannot dance will yet be hopping; and a little later on in the year 'the medowes are left bare by the mouths of hungry cattle and the hogges are turned into the corne field...the winds begin to knock the apples heads together on the trees and the fallings are gathered to fill the pyes for the household'[7].

The enclosure of open land was still piecemeal only and some open fields lasted until the 19th century. The John Lawrence map of 1638 showed these enclosures as well as the open fields, with the names of their owners, also the areas of woodland and waste. The numerous small enclosures north and west of the Rye were most probably on land at one time forest or waste. What Lawrence called 'The Common Field' lay between 'North Field' and 'South Field', all three of which were probably open fields. A terrier or land survey in 1656[8] complemented the 1638 map and showed there to to have been 12 freeholders and 40 copyholders owning and working the land. At this time and later in the century some of the farmers were most likely to have experimented with the new farming methods much vaunted in the Stuart period. Fodder crops like clover were advocated by many agricultural writers of the day, as were sainfoin and lucerne. In 1697 at least one Ashtead farm had six acres of clover; another was growing sainfoin. Wide acceptance of these new crops was however probably delayed until the early years of the 18th century.

The inventories of Ashtead farmers in the late 17th century, showing what they owned in house and farm, revealed their prosperity and well-being. According to William Menheire's inventory of June 1671 he owned 110 acres of farm land (probably part of Little Ashtead Manor) and in his house, there were leather chairs in the hall, a damask table-cloth in the dining room, feather beds upstairs with 'eight pairs of fine sheets'; and in the yard, eight horses and carts.[9] The Page family, who lived in the timber-framed house now incorporated in *Ashtead House*, appeared just as affluent if not more so. Their inventory of December 1681 referred to 20 pewter dishes in their hall and six feather beds upstairs; a cheese press and two churns in the 'milk-house'; grains were stacked in the barn and there was a special wool loft which held 840 bundles of wool; some cattle and pigs were kept and as many as 220 sheep.[10] A husbandman, Thomas Snells, was said to have had five horses, a coach, two carts and a wagon, according to his inventory of June 1697.[11]

Population and Occupations

Early in the Tudor period, Ashtead had about 200 inhabitants, based upon the 1524 Lay Subsidy returns and upon an estimated number of wives, children and servants not included in these returns. The figure arrived at is not much more than at the time of the Domesday Survey, but it had certainly fluctuated much since then, losing perhaps a third during the Black Death of 1348/49 and regaining its former strength in the next century. It may well have declined in number after the 1524 returns were made, since in 1556–58 there was reported to be a high death rate all over England due to a serious influenza epidemic. The Archdeacon of Surrey's return of communicants in 1603[12] gave the figure of 120 for Ashtead, so taking into account children and perhaps a few others the total was not very different from the earlier estimate. There was, however, a marked increase by 1664 when the Hearth Tax returns showed that there were 68 houses (172 hearths), so with an average ratio of 4.5 persons per household the total would come to 306.[13] The Compton Census of 1676, on the other hand, recorded only 169 churchgoers, but children and others would increase this appreciably.[14] Whatever the truth, Ashtead's population appeared to have increased during the Stuart period.

Although farming was the main occupation of most Ashtead people, there were many other activities often associated directly or indirectly with farming, like carpenters, turners, blacksmiths and wheelwrights. Humphrey Whitlocke, a butcher, was also the village Constable. Small tradesmen included a brickmaker called Symes whose father was a weaver with three looms at his home. Many of the village houses had a thatched roof so it is not surprising to find a thatcher among Ashtead's working men. There were, it seems, no local brewers, though many homes would brew their own ale. There were references in 1655 and 1684 to a possible ale-house called the *Three Horse Shoes*, maybe on the site of the present *Leg of*

Mutton & Cauliflower but it seems to have disappeared by the end of the 17th century.[15]

Several Ashtead families sent out their sons to learn a trade as apprentices, usually for a period of seven years. Those going to Kingston are known from surviving lists, but they may have gone elsewhere as well: the sons were sent to cordwainers, butchers, blacksmiths and tailors and at the end of their training the apprentices, if deemed worthy (as all Ashtead ones were), received a parting gift of 'double apparel', that is, two suits for working days and holidays, also sometimes a money payment.[16]

Some Ashtead People

It is always difficult to recreate what life was like so many years ago, but something may be gleaned from a brief look at a few of those who lived in Ashtead at this period.[17] Many were fairly modest farmers like the Otways whose family had lived here since the early 1400s, becoming prosperous in the 17th century and living well at *Tileworth* (or *Lee House*); others like the Simms or Symes, a common name here, were farmers but some of this name were spoken of as gardeners and thatchers and one was Steward of the manor from 1673 to 1684. Some people retired to Ashtead, as John Browne and his wife did after Queen Elizabeth in 1591 granted them a house and land here in recognition of his service as 'Sergeant of the Woodyard'.

A revealing look at life in Ashtead is given in Samuel Pepys' Diary, recounting the happy days he had spent as a boy at his cousin John's house in the village which he called 'my old place of pleasure'. When he came here in 1663 his cousin had died and he stayed the night, rather uncomfortably, in 'Farmer Page's house' near to his late cousin's house then occupied by 'Mr Rouse, called the Queen's Tailor'. In the summer of 1667 Pepys walked on the Downs near Ashtead with his wife and cousin, Mrs Turner. They found an old shepherd with a horned crook to control his flock of sheep and a little boy reading the Bible to him, 'the most pleasant and innocent sight that ever I saw in my life.'[18]

One of the most fascinating of Ashtead characters at this time was Sir Cornewall Bradshaw, who lived in a house thought to be incorporated in the present *Ashtead House*, though his London interests meant that he must have been a frequent absentee.[19] Bradshaw was the City Chronologer from 1665 to 1668, the last to be appointed to this odd post. He was a successful City businessman, becoming Controller of Customs at Bristol and other ports, a lucrative pursuit. He was knighted by Charles II in 1682. After his death in 1698 his natural son, Caesar, let *Ashtead House* to a succession of tenants, including Admiral Sir James Wishart. Cornewall Bradshaw's inventory of his possessions referred to hunting horns, fishing equipment and a fowling piece; he also had a black sword and bayonet, an iron crossbow, three horses, two carts and an old 'travelling chariot'.[20]

No account of Ashtead people in this period would be complete without mentioning Sir Robert Howard who became the owner of Ashtead manor in 1680. He was born in 1626, son of the Earl of Berkshire, his mother being Elizabeth, daughter of William Cecil, Lord Burghley.[21] He had a distinguished career after leaving Magdalen College, Oxford, fighting for the Royalists in the Civil War and being knighted when only 18 years old for his gallantry at the Battle of Cropredy Bridge in 1644. He was imprisoned at Windsor Castle during the Commonwealth period but after the Restoration became M.P. for Stockbridge, Hampshire and created a K.C.B. He was soon given a Treasury appointment and from 1677 onwards he held the rewarding post of Auditor of the Exchequer.

Sir Robert Howard was as well known in literary and dramatic circles as at Court and in politics. His poems were admired by John Dryden, who married Robert's sister, Elizabeth. He became a successful playwright, the most acclaimed of his plays being *The Indian Queen* and *The Duke of Lerma*, the King and Queen attending one of its performances in 1668. During his years at Ashtead, Sir Robert had close relations with the composer, Henry Purcell, who composed the score for the operatic version of *The Indian Queen*. Purcell is known to have given music lessons to Sir Robert Howard's daughter, Katherine, at Ashtead.[22]

When Sir Robert Howard bought Ashtead Manor and its lands in 1680 he soon decided to build a more prestigious house to live in, consonant with his status. It took four years to build, Howard presumably living in London for much of this time. The old manor house had fallen into some disrepair, though John Evelyn had paid a visit to it when Lady Mordaunt was living there; the house, part of which had been used as a dairy, survived until the end of the next century. Evelyn was invited to the new house soon after it was completed, admiring the Verrio paintings on the staircase and the 'swete park upon the Downe'.[23] Celia Fiennes, who travelled round most of England at this time, described Howard's house as of brick with 'an abundance of pictures' and 'very good tapestry hangings' in all the rooms.[24] Sir Robert made much of the old demesne land round the house into a splendid Park. He entertained profusely at the new house, his guests including Charles II, James II and William III.

Sir Robert Howard was four times married, his last wife being Annabella Dives, a maid of honour at Court. He died in 1698. Howard was said by Evelyn to be not particularly amiable, but he was certainly a gentleman of fashion with wide gifts in politics and the arts (Fig. 6).

Church and Parish

For nearly half a century, the church enjoyed the peace established by Henry VII after the end of the Wars of the Roses in 1485. At some point in this period, work was carried out on the fabric of St Giles' Church, especially on the tower.[25]

Between 1535 and 1559, Ashtead experienced eight changes of Rector![26] Some of these had been through death, but others because of the upheavals following Henry VIII's break with the Pope over his divorce in 1534. Under his successor, Edward VI (1547–53), the ultra Protestant authorities ordered the removal of all Catholic ornamentation from St Giles, and the destruction of the remains of the chantry in the church, established in the 13th century by the de Maras.[27] On the death of Edward in 1553, a Catholic priest was appointed to the living by Queen Mary to restore the Catholic faith.

The Rev. Ralph Kirkham, Rector under Edward VI, returned after the accession of Queen Elizabeth in 1558 and remained Rector until 1586. He was made responsible for ensuring that the Protestant faith was seen to be restored: the Book of Common Prayer in English, the Holy Communion in place of the Mass, and the reading of homilies prepared by the state.

The state made use of the existing parish organisation, laying considerable responsibilities on the Vestry and the churchwardens. The Ashtead Vestry Minutes have disappeared; the early books are believed to have been lost in a fire at a churchwarden's house. No doubt the Parish Constable, Overseers of the Poor and Waywardens kept order, looked after the sick and poor and watched over the highways as in Leatherhead and elsewhere. Not every parishioner would have welcomed the interference of the church as the organ of the state, especially the fines for non-attendance at morning service on Sundays.

In the early years of James I's reign, parishioners in Ashtead and elsewhere had to get used to hearing the new Authorized Version of the Bible read to them at services. A copy was issued to every church in 1611. Further religious dictats and reforms came in the 1640s, starting with the Protestation Oath requiring all those over 18 in every parish to swear that they were 'against all Poperie'.[28] The abolition of episcopacy soon followed. The Rector of Ashtead clearly had reservations about the ways things were going, since Whitehall agents suspended him from his living in 1643 shortly before he died. He was succeeded by William King, a Parliamentary nominee, reported in the *House of Commons Journal* as being a 'godly and orthodox divine'; he would be expected to concur with the Book of Common Prayer being replaced by the Directory of Public Worship, the abolition of Christmas and other Feast days, also the forbidding of all sports and pastimes on Sundays. While these far-reaching changes were being imposed, the government sought to promote the 'classical' Presbyterian system with ministers and lay elders, but this was never achieved and even William King may have carried on the normal church routine he was used to. During the Interregnum, what most people disliked was the introduction of civil marriages, no church weddings being allowed after September 1653, and the continuance of the ban on festivals.

All these tiresome restrictions were swept away at the Restoration in 1660 when Charles II became King. Many priests felt that they could not in their hearts return to the old Church of England ways and those refusing to sign the Act of Uniformity in 1662 had to resign their living. William King was one of those ejected and he was replaced by Elkanah Downes who was Rector for 21 years, followed by William Duncombe.

After being ejected, William King is said to have stayed on in the district and to have concerned himself with 'conventicles' of 'Non-Conformists' at Ewell and Dorking. There were believed to be no 'conventicles' in Ashtead in the mid-1660s, but ten years later the Compton Census referred to 17 'Non-Conformists' in the parish and even more surprising that there were 12 'Papists', a large number since in the whole of Surrey their numbers were only 122 at this date[29]. These figures reveal for a small village a high proportion of non-Anglican worshippers. They would fear prosecution for their beliefs until William III's Toleration Act of 1689 and even that did not apply to Papists.

Fig. 6. Sir Robert Howard (1626–98) by Sir Godfrey Kneller. From copy in LDLHS Collection

Notes

1. W.G. Hoskins, 'Harvest Fluctuations, 1480–1619 'Agric. Hist. Rev, XII (1964), p. 39

2. 'Surrey Musters' SRS (1914), pp. 6, 150

3. W.G. Hoskins, 'Harvest Fluctuations, 1620–1759' Agric. Hist. Rev, XVI (1968), pp. 15, 31

4. Alan A. Jackson (ed) Ashtead: A Village Transformed (1977) pp 42–3.

5. PRO: HW/B-162; transcribed by Marion Herridge, 1984

6. SRO 203/1

7. N. Breton, The Twelve Months (1626), pp. 12, 18

8. SRO 203/1

9. PRO: Prob 4/1674; transcribed by Marion Herridge, 1991

10. PRO: Prob 5/2207; transcribed by Joan Holman, 1987

11. PRO: Prob 4/21551; transcribed by Marion Herridge, 1991

12. B.L.: Harleian Mss, 595

13. C.A.F. Meekings, 'Surrey Hearth Tax, 1664' SRS, (1940); Alan A. Jackson (ed), (1977) op. cit. pp 164–6

14. SRO 255/1: Compton Census

15. Alan A. Jackson (ed), (1977) op. cit. pp 53–5

16. Ann Daly, Kingston upon Thames, Register of Apprentices, 1568–1713 (1974)

17. R.A. Lever, 'Notes on Some Ashtead Personalities, 1543–1732' Procs LDLHS 4(10), 1980, pp 287–8

18. Pepys Diary, 25 July 1663; 14 July 1667

19. G.J. Gollin, 'Cornewall Bradshaw of Ashtead' Procs LDLHS, 5(3), 1990, p. 85

20. PRO: Prob 5/686; transcribed by Marion Herridge, 1991

21. DNB

22. F.G. Zimmerman, Life of Purcell (1983), pp. 228–9, 252–3

23. Evelyn Diary, 19 July 1687

24. C. Morris (ed), The Journeys of Celia Fiennes (1947) p. 339

25. Winchester Diocesan Registry, Fox's Register, II f. 31

26. For details of Rectors see Society Records (AX 350)

27. Alan A. Jackson (ed) (1977) op. cit. pp. 120–1

28. H. Carter (ed) 'The Surrey Protestation Returns' SAC, 59, 1962, pp. 35–68

29. SRO 255/1,2

Chapter 6

THE 18TH CENTURY

In 1701 the manor of Ashtead became the sole possession of Sir Robert Howard's daughter-in-law, Lady Diana, upon the untimely death of her husband, Thomas Howard. In the course of the next 30 years, she kept a firm hand on the management of the estate, her account books surviving. She married William Feilding as her second husband in 1707. Lady Diana had a sad life, witnessing the death of her three children, grandson and daughter-in-law. Outliving her second husband by 10 years, she died without heirs in 1731, aged 73. She was a lady of fashion; her portrait painted by Sir Godfrey Kneller survives (Fig. 7). She is commemorated by a fine monumental bust and coat of arms in St Giles' Church; the monument was moved from the chancel to the nave in 1891.

After Lady Diana's death, the Ashtead manor passed through the hands of several members of the Howard family, including successive Earls of Suffolk and Berkshire and Lady Andover. A private Act of Parliament was required in 1789 to enable Lady Andover's daughter, Frances, and her husband Richard Bagot, to purchase the manor. For six years it had been held by Sir Michael le Fleming and his wife, Diana, under a marriage settlement made by her deceased father, another Thomas Howard, who had bought it but not paid for it![1] Richard Bagot took the name of Howard on his marriage to Frances in 1783. A new mansion was built in Ashtead Park in 1790–92 on the site of the old one[2] (see Fig. 8).

Several notable people lived in the large houses to the north-east of the Park. Lord North used *Ashtead House* for some years in mid-century before he became Prime Minister. Capt Nathaniel Smith of

Fig. 7. Lady Diana Howard (later Feilding) by Sir Godfrey Kneller. From copy in LDLHS Collection

the East India Company and his widow, Hester (née Dance), leased the house for some 50 years before it was bought for his descendants in 1813. The family, whose name later changed to Denshire by marriage, has its own vault beneath the chancel of St Giles' Church and a memorial window. Another important family associated with this part of Ashtead were the Beckfords[3]. They lived in or owned at various times *Newstead House, Blake's Close* and *Ashtead House*. The Beckfords were an affluent family with wide city interests, one member twice becoming Lord Mayor of London. The last Beckford to live in Ashtead – at *Penders*, later *Ashtead Lodge* in Parker's Hill – was from the branch of the family with large estates in Jamaica. Late in the century, Thomas Tyers, a man-about-town and close friend of Dr Johnson, held a house in Ashtead where he died in 1787.

Ashtead's Population
The difficulty of obtaining any reliable estimate of Ashtead's population before the taking of the first Census in 1801 may be illustrated by the widely differing figures which were quoted in the Bishops' visitations of 1725 and 1788[4]. At the earlier of the two dates the Rector, Peter Hamelot, said that 'the number of souls may be about 200 including children', which seems surprisingly low, in view of the fact that the 1801 Census recorded a total of 552 persons. William Carter, Rector in 1788, appears to have attached far more importance to his return, stating that 'the exact number of the inhabitants is 510'. This seems to fit in with the parish registers of births and deaths which suggest that there was an increase in Ashtead's population after 1750.

Most Ashtead people in the 18th century were connected with the land, though a 1791 directory listed a tailor and a watchmaker, also some other trades not related to farming. One of the fashions of the day was to keep a black servant and there were references to this in the parish registers for 1704, 1768 and 1771.

New Farming Methods
Some Ashtead farmers had discovered in the late 17th century the advantages of growing turnips and grasses like clover and sainfoin, giving extra fodder for winter feeding and cutting down the amount of fallow time needed. William Thornton's inventory of Jan 1793 referred to his owning 9½ acres of turnips, while his two hogs,

weighing 18 stone and 20 stone respectively, revealed no shortage
of year-round food[5]! Thornton, a tenant of West Farm, was a typical 'mixed' farmer, his barns being stacked with sheep and lamb's
wool and bales of wheat, oats and barley; and in his dairy there
were two butter churns. He also grew the common fruits, including apples from which cider was made. Whether Thornton had
made use of the many improvements in farming equipment, like
Jethro Tull's seed-drill, seems doubtful though some of the tools
listed in the inventory may have been 'modern' ones.

Most Ashtead farmers grew wheat, barley and oats as their main
crops, in rotation with turnips; peas were also favoured, with some
rye, beans and a few potatoes. The fire at the Park Farm in 1731
burnt down the farmhouse and destroyed many tons of hay as well
as quantities of wheat, oats and horse fodder[6]. Although many of
the new farming methods had been accepted, the open fields
remained; their working continued to be supervised by the manorial court, with heriots paid when copyholds fell vacant. Leasehold-
ing was soon to be the most common landholding, as more and
more land was acquired by large estates.

Towards the end of the 18th century and early in the next century, there was an increasing national interest in agriculture which
fed its way into the counties. Several studies were made on farming
methods in Surrey and elsewhere with a view to their improvement.
Ashtead was not often specifically mentioned, but attention was
drawn to the increased productivity which would ensue if its open
fields were to be enclosed[7].

Roads and Road Transport

The pattern of roads and tracks in Ashtead existed long before the
Georgian period but only then were there serious and successful
attempts made to improve the road surfaces and maintain them in
a good state of repair. The Waywardens or Surveyors of the Highways appointed in Tudor and Stuart times were usually unable to
carry out adequately all the needed road repairs, but the Turnpike
Act of 1755 ensured by a toll system the better maintenance of the
main road from Leatherhead through Ashtead to Epsom.

The road system at this time was well shown on John Rocque's
map of 1770[8] and on the the first Ordnance Survey map printed in
1816. There were frequent stage coach services from Leatherhead
and Epsom to London, Guildford, Kingston, Dorking and towns on

the south coast. It is likely that Ashtead people who wished to visit these places would ride or walk to Leatherhead or Epsom. Most travelling was indeed still done on horseback or on foot. Horse riding continued to be a common means of transport for many right through this period and beyond. On race-days at Epsom and during the times when the Wells there were popular Ashtead men and women probably walked or rode to these places, and they would also frequently find their way to the markets and fairs in the neighbouring towns.

The Church in the Community
There were five Rectors of Ashtead during the 18th century. Peter Hamelot, a French Huguenot refugee, held the living for over 40 years from 1698/99 to 1742. His four successors, Robert Grahme (or Graham), Thomas Denton, Thomas Martindale and William Carter were all from the North Country. Denton was curate to Robert Grahme before succeeding him as Rector; he published poems in the style of Spenser and was associated with the Biographical Dictionary of 1761. Carter was Rector for nearly 40 years (1782–1821).

Fig. 8.   Ashtead Park House, 1790–92. LDLHS Collection

Since Queen Elizabeth's reign, care for the sick and poor, for the highways and for law and order had been in the hands of the Vestry. This was presided over by the Rector or curate and attended by the churchwardens, the appointed Overseers of the Poor, the local Constable and other parishioners. Some of the meetings were known to have been held at the *Leg of Mutton & Cauliflower'*, but most were probably at the church or the Rector's house. Details of their meetings have not survived, but it may be presumed that all cases of distress brought before them would be handled as best they could, the money for their help being found from a Poor Rate levied on the householders. It is known that an almshouse existed before 1668 and a large one for six poor widows was built from funds left by Lady Diana Feilding. This was one of several charities watched over by the church, including that of Mrs Sarah Bond in 1712, linked with Mr. Smith's earlier grants of cloth to the poor. In 1725 David White left an annuity for the education of eight poor children (see p. 179). Friendly Societies to help those in need became popular in the late 18th century and one at Ashtead is mentioned in 1772 as meeting at the *Berkshire Arms*[9]. Its members paid a small subscription which went towards any who fell on bad times. It was also a social club.

The church did more than be responsible for the village welfare, since it was very much the centre of village life, as of old. Its traditional feast days and its patron saint's day (1st. Sept) were yearly celebrated as were May Day, the Rogation-tide procession round the bounds of the parish and the day when the harvest had finally been gathered in.

Notes

1. G.J. Gollin & R.A. Lever, 'The Ownership of Ashtead Manor' *Procs LDLHS* 4, 4 (1980) pp. 110–12

2. Alan A. Jackson (ed) *Ashtead: A Village Transformed* (1977) p. 83

3. G.J. Gollin, 'The Beckford Family and Ashtead' *Procs LDLHS* 4, 5 (1981), pp. 134–40

4. W.R. Ward, 'Parson and Parish in Eighteenth century Surrey: Replies to Bishop's Visitations' *SRS*, XXXIV, 1994, pp. 4, 88. See also Alan A. Jackson (ed), (1977) op. cit. pp. 164–6

5. PRO: PROB 31/833/117; transcribed by Marion Herridge, 1992

6. Alan A. Jackson (ed) (1977) op. cit. pp. 142–3

7. W. James & J. Malcolm, *General View of the Agriculture of Surrey* (1794); J. Malcolm, *Compendium of Modern Husbandry: Surrey* (1805)

8. *SAC*: M 2/9/2

9. Quarter Session Records, *SRS*, 1931

Chapter 7

INTRODUCTION TO THE 19TH CENTURY

During a century when London and the industrial towns were growing fast, Ashtead remained a predominantly small rural area of farms and open spaces. Only in the last 25 years of the century, as the land changed hands and the new professional middle class began to move in, was the age-old order disturbed. The population of Ashtead grew, slowly at first from 552 in 1801 to 684 in 1851, but more rapidly to 906 in 1871, more than doubling to 1,881 inhabitants by 1901[1]. The chief occupation for most inhabitants was to make some sort of living from the land. Until the last decade or so the farms were Ashtead's life, encompassing the whole of the parish. After 1875 the farms began to decline as they did elsewhere because of the import of cheap American grain. For many years there was a scattering of cottages and a few large houses. The village centre was quite small. Half-a-mile from it stood the *Ashtead Park Mansion* and the parish church of St Giles, dating from the 12th century.

The Howards at the *Park Mansion* were the lords of the manor and owned virtually all the land in Ashtead by 1840. This branch of the family also had extensive estates at Castle Rising in Norfolk, Levens in Westmorland, Elford in Staffordshire and Charlton Park at Malmesbury, Wiltshire[2]. The owners spent a portion of their time at each estate. Richard Howard (formerly Richard Bagot) and his wife Frances Howard had become established in their new mansion in the Park by the beginning of the century. Their only surviving child, Mary, who had been brought up in Ashtead, married the Hon. Col Fulk Greville Upton in 1807, he taking the name of Howard. Mary inherited all the estates when both Frances and Richard died in 1818. She had no children. She outlived her husband who died in 1846 by 31 years. Col and Mrs Howard were both strong supporters of St Giles' Church, contributing generously to the restoration and extension of the church building. Mary was a benefactress here as elsewhere, founding the Church School in 1852 and providing funds for many good causes. On her death in 1877, the Ashtead estate passed to her father's family, the Bagots. Some land was sold piecemeal in 1879 to clear mortgages and debts. The remainder was subsequently sold to Thomas Lucas and others. Lucas sold the *Mansion* and the Park estate to Pantia Ralli, a banker, in 1889.

The first few years of the 19th century were particularly unsettling to life in Ashtead as elsewhere because of the serious threat of a French invasion during the Napoleonic Wars. The recruitment in 1803/4 of 80 Ashtead men to the Epsom Brigade of the Surrey Volunteer Infantry and Yeomanry, an early 'Home Guard' which was never called into action, was a temporary potential disturbance[3]. The pressure on farmers to increase production during the war was much more demanding. After peace was made in 1815, the next 100 years were largely a time of peace for local people, interrupted by the Crimean War in mid-century and other far-off wars. News travelled slowly for many years but by the end of the century, with the wider use of the telegraph and the invention of the telephone, events such as the Boer War in South Africa were quickly reported.

At the beginning of the century few could read or write. The early schools helped but an improvement began with the founding of the Church School in 1852. By the close of the century the Parish Magazine was being distributed to every home. The coming of the railway first to Epsom in 1847 and then to Ashtead in 1859 made travel much easier for all. The penny post of 1840 and later the telegraph made communication easier. The water mains laid in the 1880s, the arrival of the luxury of piped gas about the same time and the digging of sewers in 1900 were raising the standard of life. These developments, coming at the same time as the sale of the estate, attracted the developers and the new inhabitants that were to shape Edwardian Ashtead as the next century began.

Notes

1. Census table (p. 178).
2. 'Some records of the Ashtead Estate and its Howard Possessors' (1873), unpublished work attributed to the Rev. Francis Paget.
3. J.R. Clube, 'Leatherhead & District Home Guard in the Napoleonic Wars' *Procs LDLHS*, 5(4), 1991. pp. 103–6.

Chapter 8

A FARMING COMMUNITY, 1800–1875

At the beginning of the 19th century, when the Wyburd Survey was made, Richard Howard of Ashtead Park possessed much more land in Ashtead than any of his more recent predecessors, 1,624 out of 2,571 acres. Soon after 1802, he acquired more land fom small owners, including copyhold land in the North and South Fields. Although Aquila Dackombe, Joseph Syms and a few other landowners maintained independence, this concentration of property in one owner's hands continued to grow in the next 40 years and must have produced a dependency culture in the parish.

Farms and Farming in the early 19th century
The Wyburd Survey of 1802 showed nine farms in Ashtead[1]. Seven of these were owned by Richard Howard, farmed by tenants, another belonged to Aquila Dackombe and the remaining one was farmed by the Rector, the Rev. William Carter. The majority of Ashtead's population, 552 at the 1801 census, worked on the farms or in trades and crafts connected with them.

Five of the farms were large in comparison with the others. The largest was the Home Farm (or Ashtead Park Farm), 407 acres in extent, surrounding the *Mansion* and the Park and including Newton Wood. It was based on *Park Farm House* in Farm Lane, stretching from the Common to Pebble Lane (Stane St). Similarly, Street Farm, 350 acres, stretched from the middle of Woodfield Lane (then known as Common Lane) to the borders of Headley parish, its swathe of land widening out considerably to the south. The farmhouse was situated centrally on the north side of The Street. The same pattern in modified form was to be found in other farms. New

Fig. 9. Park Farm House. LDLHS Collection

Purchase Farm, so called because only recently purchased by Mr Howard, had extensive fields between Barnett Wood Lane and the Rye Brook and in Agates Lane. It had blocks of land also in both the North and South Fields, stretching continuously from the footpath later known as Northfields Passage to the old Green Lane at the south of the parish. Its farm buildings were on the future site of *Murrey's Court*. West Farm was smaller: the farm buildings at the top of Harriotts Lane lay between the fields on the east side of that lane and its more extensive blocks of land in the North and South Fields, also extending south to Green Lane.

The fifth of the larger farms, Whitehouse Farm of 193 acres, was owned by Aquila Dackombe, a non-resident, and farmed by Jefferys. The farm buildings were next door to those of West Farm. Its fields were scattered round the west side of the parish from north of the Rye Brook to Addlestead Woods on the Headley border, some land being isolated within Mr Howard's property. It was an example, then surviving, of the old system of strip farming, together with some hedged fields.

The outline of these farms on the Wyburd map shows that each

THE WYBURD SURVEY 1802
Ashtead Village

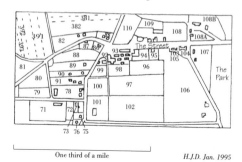

One third of a mile   *H.J.D. Jan. 1995*

Key to the Wyburd Survey: Ashtead Village 1802

	OWNER	TENANT(s)	PROPERTY
71	Joseph Syms	John Larpent Esq	House & garden [Howard House]
72	Charles Monro	In hand	Orchard
73	Joseph Syms	John Larpent Esq	House & garden
75	Mrs Baker	Mrs Bloss	House & garden
76	Luke Richardson	In hand	House & shop
78	Charles Monro	In hand	House & 2 cottages [Ashtead Lodge]
79	Richard Howard Esq	Charles Monro	Meadow
80	William Finch	In hand	Meadow
81	,, ,,	,,	,,
82	,, ,,	,,	House & meadow [The Limes]
85	Richard Puttock	Widow Bates	House & garden
86	Richard Howard Esq	Huck & Lunn	2 Tenements
87	,, ,,	Samuel South	Barn, stables etc.
88	,, ,,	,, ,,	Orchard
89	Sarah Waters	Richard Puttock	House, garden [Fowler's later]
90	Mrs Chitty	In hand	,, ,, [Applebough]
91	Francis Mellish	In hand	House, garden etc [Forge]
92	Richard Howard Esq	Samuel South	House & garden [The Cottage]
93	,, ,,	,, ,,	Public House [Leg of Mutton]
94	Joseph Syms	Pinnion	House, Blacksmith's shop etc
95	Richard Howard Esq	Richard Hatcher	House & garden
96	,, ,,	Samuel South	Orchard & meadow
97	,, ,,	,, ,,	Meadow
99	,, ,,	Thomas Davis	Garden
100	,, ,,	,, ,,	,,
101	William Hambley Esq	In hand	House, etc [Old Rectory later]
102	,, ,,	In hand	Meadow [Glebe later]
103	Parish	Poor people	Poor houses
104	Lady Diana Feilding		Hospital
105	Parish	Poor people	Poor houses
106	Richard Howard Esq	William Weston	Barn & meadow
107	Joseph Syms	Sundry tenants	Houses, gardens etc
108	Richard Howard Esq	William Weston	Meadow
108A	,, ,,	,, ,,	2 cottages, shop etc
108B	,, ,,	,, ,,	Public House (Berkshire Arms)
109	,, ,,	,, ,,	Street Farm house, barns etc
110	,, ,,	,, ,,	Meadow
381	Rev William Carter	In hand	Strip in North Field 1 acre
382	Richard Howard Esq	George Weston	,, ,, 2 acres
391	,, ,,	William Weston	,, ,, 2¾ ,,
392	,, ,,	,, ,,	,, ,, ½ acre
393	Mrs Pinnion	Thomas Pinnion	,, ,, ½ ,,

[In hand = no tenant except owner]

HJD
2/95

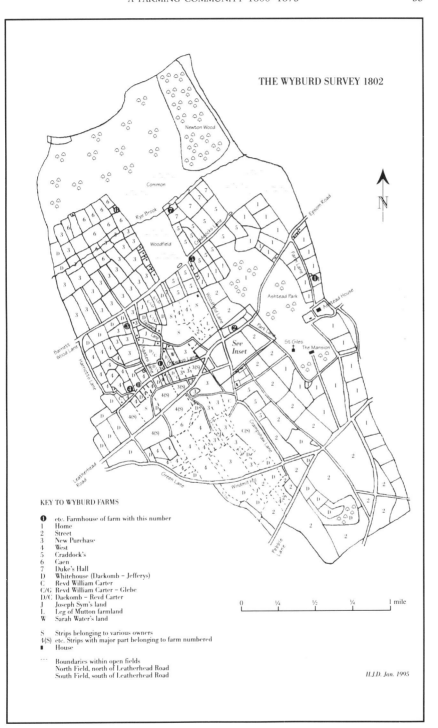

THE WYBURD SURVEY 1802

KEY TO WYBURD FARMS

❶ etc. Farmhouse of farm with this number
1   Home
2   Street
3   New Purchase
4   West
5   Craddock's
6   Caen
7   Duke's Hall
D   Whitehouse (Dackomb – Jefferys)
C   Revd William Carter
C/G Revd William Carter – Glebe
D/C Dackomb – Revd Carter
J   Joseph Sym's land
L   Leg of Mutton farmland
W   Sarah Water's land

S   Strips belonging to various owners
4(S) etc. Strips with major part belonging to farm numbered
▪   House

··· Boundaries within open fields
     North Field, north of Leatherhead Road
     South Field, south of Leatherhead Road

H.J.D. Jan. 1995

0   ¼   ½   ¾   1 mile

had a mixture of soils from north to south whether by custom or design, making full use of the dip slope (see p. 1). Much of the parish was hedged by 1802. The open, unhedged North and South Fields had been greatly reduced since the Lawrence survey of 1638. The North Field still stretched from Woodfield Lane to Grange Road, narrowing down in the west to the land between Ottways Lane and the Leatherhead Road. The South Field extended from the Leatherhead Road to Pebble Lane. By 1802 many of the former strips of land had been joined together to form blocks of land farmed by the large farmers, ripe for enclosing with new hedges. William King of West Farm had several blocks of six or more acres; John Lynn of New Purchase Farm had four with over six acres each, the largest being 13 acres. Jefferys farmed one block of 11 and another of nine acres for Dackombe. All these blocks were in the South Field.

The three farms in the north of the parish, Craddock's (later Woodfield Farm), Caen and Duke's Hall, were different, each having hedged fields in the clay region. Craddock's, however, also had 20 acres of the 'Church Field' east of Crampshaw Lane, and Caen a small portion in the South Field. Coffin at Duke's Hall astride the Rye Brook had hedged fields between it and Craddock's Farm.

The last of the nine farms mentioned in the Wyburd Survey was held by the Rector, the Rev. William Carter. He had 11 acres of glebe land along Barnett Wood Lane (Glebe Road was later built on part of it), and 17 acres of glebe strips scattered in the North and South Fields. He also farmed a block of 30 acres in the South Field, interspersed with some strips which belonged to other owners, to the west of Crampshaw Lane, and a variety of small strips elsewhere. The parsonage at the corner of Skinners Lane and Ottways Lane had farm buildings and a barn opposite, Mr Carter being the tenant of Dackombe for the surrounding fields. If the Rector received a tithe of all the corn produced in the parish as was his entitlement, he must have been a substantial and busy farmer. It is, therefore, surprising to find him in debt in 1816, having relinquished most of his land and dying penniless in 1821.

There were some smaller farms, including that farmed by the landlord of the *Leg of Mutton* inn. Several of his farm buildings were on the south side of The Street opposite Street Farm. He farmed land near the inn and on the west side of Woodfield Lane.

Crops and Farming Methods

By far the largest proportion of Ashtead's farming land, described by the Wyburd Survey, was arable, whether enclosed or not, most of the remainder being meadow or woodland. The areas of pasture were the Common and small enclosures close to the farm buildings. There were some pieces of common land beside the roads, for example, by Pebble Lane and the King William Avenue. If the meadows were intended for hay for winter feed, such cattle as there were would have been grazed on the Common or on the stubble in the fields.

At the crop census, called by the government in 1801[2], the returns for Ashtead were as follows:

Ashtead crop acreages, 1801

Wheat	397	Turnips	276
Barley	374	Peas	288
Oats	459	Beans	9
Rye	19	Potatoes	7

Total acreage: 1,828

The demand for crops was high during the Napoleonic Wars but fell sharply in 1814–16, bringing ruin in its train. The Rev. William Carter may have been a victim.

The large acreage of turnips in Ashtead in 1801 may indicate that Richard Howard was influenced by the new farming methods which had long been practised in Norfolk; he would be familiar with these through his ownership of the Castle Rising property in that county. This is supported by the actions of his successor at Ashtead Park, Col Howard, who in 1824 sought a farmer for Norfolk for one of the vacant Ashtead farms. His agent there could not provide a farmer, but recommended Norfolk's method of farming for the light chalky soils in the south of Ashtead: a rotation of turnips, barley, two or three years' 'layers', that is, leys or grasses grazed by sheep, and then wheat.[3] Sainfoin, of the pea family, and other plants had been in use as leys in Ashtead in the 1690s[4] and there was no indication of any fallow ground in 1802. The application of these methods old and new in Ashtead would account for the high level of corn production in the 1830s, compared with other parishes.

Where the people lived

There were three main groups of houses in the parish of Ashtead in 1802. The principal group was in and around Rectory Lane (then known as Headley Road) and in The Street, forming the village. The second group was in the Lanes to the west, the area known as Lower Ashtead. The third settlement was on the west side of the Common, known as the Woodfield. There were several large houses in addition to the substantial farm houses. Those in the centre were *Howard House*, *Ashtead Lodge* and *Hambley's*, later the *Old Rectory*. The large houses in Farm Lane had been reduced to two, *Ashtead House* and *Park Farm House*, the centre of the social scene having shifted to the new *Ashtead Park Mansion*. Most of the remaining houses in the parish were cottages.

Enclosure of the Open Fields, 1839

In Ashtead, the process of creating blocks of land within the fields had been taking place for some time. In 1838 Col Howard, Mr Legge the Rector, Daniel Dackombe, successor to Aquila, and one or two others met at the *Leg of Mutton* and carved up the remaining 'common fields'[5]. Col Howard took 293 acres, most of which he already owned, and Dackombe 62 acres. The Rector received the freehold of the (old) Rectory and surrounding fields in exchange for most of the former glebe land including the fields in Barnett Wood Lane. The tenant farmers found that the land allocated to them largely coincided with the areas they were already cultivating within the two main estates. Such strip cultivation as had survived by 1839 was abandoned. Across the former South Field a long thick hedge was to run from north to south, eventually marking the boundary of Howard and Hackblock (formerly Dackombe) land. More hedges were planted in the former North Field.

The Church Tithe

For as far back as could be remembered landowners had paid a tithe or tenth of all their produce to the church each year. In practice, this had become confined to the main produce, corn, which included wheat, barley and oats. The payment of a cash equivalent had been growing and was made compulsory in 1839 by an Act of Parliament of 1836. The value of the tithe was assessed on the average price of corn over the years 1829–35, producing in Ashtead parish a total cash equivalent of £553 per annum. The high value of the

Fig. 10.　Colonel Fulk Greville Howard by George Richmond, c. 1841. From copy in LDLHS Collection

Ashtead tithe, based on an average annual income of £55,300 from the sale of corn, points to the success of the Howard farming methods. The tithe in Leatherhead was a mere £244, representing £24,400. The tithe total was fixed for a century, remaining the same after the redistribution of the tithe in 1887. In 1840 Col Howard owned 1,698 acres and paid £458 tithe, Dackombe 211 acres, £63 and 31 others 84 acres, paying £32 between them[6]. The tithe charge was passed on by the landlords to their tenants in the rent. In good years the new system favoured the farmers but in bad years ate into the profits.

The Farms in 1840

By the early 1840s there had been changes only partly brought about by the enclosures. New Purchase Farm had absorbed Caen Farm, Michael Agate farming 374 acres stretching right across the parish. George King of West Farm was farming 63 acres of Dackombe's land and 11 of his own allotted in the Enclosure agreement, as well as 157 acres of Col Howard's land. Woodfield Farm, formerly Craddock's, had absorbed Duke's Hall Farm and had land on both sides of Crampshaw Lane. Thomas Smith of the *Leg of Mutton* had over 40 acres mainly in the former North Field. Maydwell at Street Farm had land stretching from the bottom of Woodfield Lane to the borders of Walton and Headley parishes in the south. Dackombe's Whitehouse Farm land, farmed by James Harriott, had been consolidated in a swathe round the south-west side of the parish with 25 acres at Windmill Hill. Each of the six farms that remained enjoyed an enhanced cross section of Ashtead's soil. It was recorded that the area of arable land in 1839 was 1,251 acres, meadow and pasture 614, Common 512 and woodland 144 acres.[7] The change in proportion from 1802 may indicate that there was an increase in livestock farming.

The Houses in 1840

The settlements continued to be centred on the village, in the 'Lanes' and in Woodfield. During the previous 40-year period about 14 houses had been built, including *Northlands* off the Northfields Passage, and three of the Lodges in the Park. The remainder were cottages, including two in Newton Wood.[8] Cottage after cottage each housed several families with large numbers of children of all ages, dependent adults and lodgers.[9] The houses were overcrowded and lacked water or proper sanitation. Privacy was at a premium, children sleeping several to a bed. There was nothing romantic about living in a 19th century cottage in rural Ashtead. Over 200 lived in the confines of the village centre and 74 in Woodfield and Newton Wood, not far off half the population in 1841.

Mid-Century Prosperity

The middle years of the century were a time of prosperity for farming with good prices being obtained for corn which was in demand from the growing population especially in the towns and cities.[10] Ashtead farmers no doubt shared in what has been called the 'Golden age of farming'. With four farms of 350 to 400 acres each, Park Farm, Street Farm, New Purchase Farm, and West Farm (which was then joined with Whitehouse Farm), Col Howard's farmers enjoyed a considerable income and were the principal employers of labour. Between 1851 and the late 1860s there was full employment in Ashtead, women and boys together with families settling from outside Ashtead being called upon.

One farmer gave up his tenancy at the top of the market. Maydwell of Street Farm from the early 1830s until the late 1860s had been more than an Ashtead farmer: he owned a large acreage at Newdigate and sold cattle, brought from all over the country and Ireland and fattened on his land, to the market at Smithfield and local markets. Livestock such as his in passage did not appear in official statistics. His assistant, John Hoyland, who lived in the cottage next door to the *Leg of Mutton*, carried on his business, though not the Street Farm, after Maydwell's retirement. Street Farm, 364 acres, had gone to John Smith by 1871, separate from Maydwell's Newdigate farm of 400 acres. Arguing in favour of the building of an Epsom and Leatherhead Railway before two Parliamentary Committees in 1856, Maydwell was looking for a means of transporting manure from London streets, a substance in short supply apparently in Ashtead! He had depended hitherto on oil cake brought to Kingston by barge and spread on the fields[11]. Maydwell kept a good house at Street Farm with distinguished visitors, but was often away on business. In spite of Maydwell's expectations it is unlikely that the railway, with its one little siding, made much difference to Ashtead farmers. The line to Guildford was not open until 1885 and there was never a direct route to Kingston.

Fig. 11.   Street Farm, Ashtead, 19th century (Courtesy, Worsfold family). The house on the right is on the site of the present Esso garage.

The Gathering Clouds

Problems began to arise in the 1870s. The price of wheat which had reached 63 shillings a quarter in 1869 compared with the normal 45s dropped drastically as a result of over-production and the arrival of American cereal imports from 1875.[12] Bad weather added to the farmers' problems. Tithe payments were fixed and had to be made together with rents whatever the income from sales. Col Howard's death in 1846 had deprived Ashtead of its guiding light, affairs being left in the hands of land agent, bailiff and solicitor.

In 1872 as the old Rector was dying at the *Mansion* and Mary Howard, attended by her faithful companion, Lady Harriet Paget, had her 87th birthday, the farming community was poised, unbeknown, on the threshold of the events that would change the face of Ashtead.

Notes

1. The description of the farms and settlement in 1802 is based on the Wyburd Survey of Ashtead in that year, undertaken for Richard Howard. The survey includes a full-scale map of Ashtead and a ter-

rier of owners and occupiers. The original is in the SRO, Kingston, 2703/4. The LDLHS holds 2 copies, AM8, and a copy of the terrier. The reproduction does not show the many separate strips in the North and South Fields.

2. PRO/MAF 68
3. SRO 203/31/11
4. Ashtead Court Rolls; in unpublished paper by R.A.Lever, Society Records
5. SRO LA7/2/8 Plan & Common Fields Award, 1838. Copy of Plan in Society Records
6. PRO IR 29/34/6: Terrier of Tithe Apportionment, 1838/9. A tran-
scription by G. J. Gollin, with his tracing of the map, is in Society Records
7. PRO IR 29/3416 Report of Tithe Commissioner, George Smallpiece.
8. Terrier of Tithe
9. Census return 1841. Transcript, G. J. Gollin, Society Records.
10 J.M.Stratton, *Agricultural Records* (1978).
11 Evidence to Select Committee, House of Commons, Epsom & Leatherhead Railway Bill 21 May 1856. House of Lords Library, Group E4.
12. J.M.Stratton (1978) op cit.

Chapter 9

THE LAND CHANGES HANDS, 1875–1900

The death of Mary Howard in 1877 coincided with a long and severe agricultural depression in Britain. The Howard estate broke up, farming declined and developers moved in, while the population doubled from 906 in 1871 to 1,881 people in 1901.

The sale of the Howard Estate in 1879
The enforced sale of the Howard estate after Mary Howard's death triggered the changes in land ownership in Ashtead. By mid-19th century the Howards had possessed most of Ashtead, about 2,450 acres out of some 2,670. Of the remainder, less than 200 belonged to the former Dackombe estate, owned by John Hackblock. He had tried and failed to sell much of this land in 1872. The whole former Howard estate of 4,000 acres, including 1,550 in Headley, was offered for sale in 1879 by the trustees of Major General E.R. Bagot, deceased, who had inherited it.[1] General Bagot had incurred two very large debts in 1855 and 1869 which had to be met from the proceeds of the sale, while much of the estate was found to have been mortgaged.[2] About 1,400 acres in Ashtead and 1,050 in Headley were sold, many lots going at 'knock down' prices. Because of the depression few wanted to buy farm land. Ashtead Park, the *Mansion* and its 684 acre Home farms together with several other lots were withdrawn from the sale when they failed to reach the reserve price.[3] Details of the sale will be found in the eight areas described below.

The agricultural depression
Farming conditions were very bad in the year of the Sale, which

was said to have seen the worst harvest of the century. The winter of 1880/1 was the hardest in living memory. The price of wheat dropped to 30 or 35 shillings per quarter because of the flood of U.S. imports, falling to 25 shillings in the mid-1890s.[4] Not surprisingly, the wheat yield from the remnant of the Ashtead farms in 1886 was a quarter of that 20 years earlier.[5] Farmers turned over their fields to livestock, supplying dairy products to local institutions and the London market, but the sale of fresh meat was also hit by the import of frozen meat from South America which began in the same period.

Ashtead was saved from the ruinous state of much of the English countryside by its proximity to London which made it attractive to property developers and, because of its convenient railway and picturesque wooded setting, to new upper middle class settlers. The worst sufferers were the agricultural labourers, many being forced onto such parish relief as was available (see p 92). Some doubtless found employment on the new building sites and on the building of the new drainage and sewers as general labourers, though navvies came from other parts. In 1891 there were very few Ashtead-born employees at the *Mansion* or as living-in domestic servants in the increasing number of large houses.

Most of the former Ashtead farms were broken up by 1887 and property had been distributed between eight major landowners and many smaller ones. Similar changes in many areas of Britain, especially in and near the expanding towns, had made the 1839 arrangements for cash tithe payments out of date; a new apportionment was needed and was ordered by Parliament. There is a finely drawn map showing the re-apportionment of the Ashtead tithe payments in 1887. This map and its accompanying list of owners, tenants, acreages and tithe sums opens another window into the Ashtead scene similar to that provided in 1802 by the Wyburd Survey.[6] The description which follows uses this information together with the particulars and maps accompanying the 1879 estate sale, the Census abstracts of 1871, 1881 and 1891, the revised Ordnance Survey maps (1:2,500) of 1895 and 1896 and several local Directories.[7] Each part of Ashtead developed in its own way and at its own pace. It can be conveniently considered in eight separate areas. We discover a society changing from a farming community centuries old and preparing to enter the world of the 20th century.

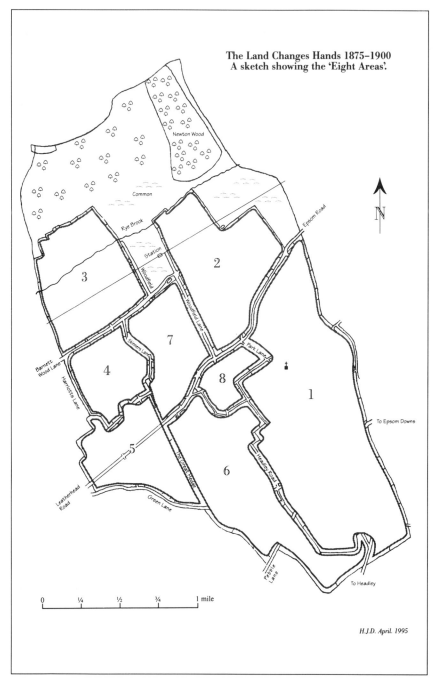

The Land Changes Hands 1875–1900
A sketch showing the 'Eight Areas'.

"Eight Areas" of Ashtead, 1875–1900

1. Ashtead Park

The "Palatial Mansion" standing in the midst of a 'majestically timbered deer park' of 200 acres dominated the eastern area. It was enveloped in each direction by unspoilt farmland, bordered on the east by the Epsom estates and on the south by Headley and the Downs. *Ashtead House* in Farm Lane was almost the only house within this area to be independent of the Park regime.

The Park had been divided into two parts for the 1879 Sale, the *Mansion* and Park itself together with a Farm Homestead known as Thirty Acre Barn, a total of 514 acres, and the Home Farm, 170 acres. The Farm Homestead consisted in the main of the former Street Farm land to the south and south-west of the Park as far as the border with Headley and included a piece in Walton on the Hill parish. In practice it was worked from the Home Farm, labourers living at the Thirty Acre Barn homestead. The Home Farm was based at the fine Georgian *Park Farm House*. The whole 684 acres which had been withdrawn from the sale in 1879 were sold to Thomas, later Sir Thomas, Lucas in 1880. He also bought the advowson, the right to choose a new Rector, with the church, rectory and glebe, all of which had also been withdrawn from the sale. Lucas acquired several other pieces of land including the school fields. In 1885 he bought the manorial rights, which included Ashtead Common, from the Bagot Trustees, and Newton Wood. His land thus stretched from the Headley border round the east of Ashtead to its north-western border. In 1889 Sir Thomas sold the whole property and all the rights to Pantia Ralli, a banker, for £101,000.[8] Much of this part of Ashtead was to remain unchanged and has given the place its characteristic ambience.

On the Epsom Road in this area, there were four properties subdivided into tenements, including the old workhouse (see p 91). An influx of population increased the residents in these from 13 in 1851 to 79 in 1861, the total declining again from 74 in 1871 to 23 in 1891. Of these, the numbers in the former workhouse, described as 'not paupers', increased from three in 1851 to 34 in 1871, falling right down to two in 1891 after Mr Lucas had bought the property, known as *Moorwood Place*, in 1883. Most were working class families originating in Ashtead.

Fig. 12.   Ashtead Park c. 1890. Drawing by George Lewis.

2. The North-East Area (excluding the Common and Newton Wood)

This area stretches from the Epsom Road to the Common, east of Woodfield Lane. Throughout the earlier 19th century it had been divided between the Home Farm of the Park, Street Farm and Woodfield Farm. Street Farm had been one of the major farms but it was probably deliberately divided into two parts for the 1879 Sale, the large area in the south which was less attractive to the speculators being separated from that north of The Street, a rump of 108 acres. The latter was sold for £11,000; it soon came into the hands of the Ashtead Land Company but was leased to Mr Lucas. Large houses were built on the east side of Woodfield Lane, commencing before 1887 at the north end with *Hockham Lodge* and *Claverton*, both since demolished. These were followed by *Crofton*, *Mawmead Shaw* and *One Oak*, round the site of the future Roman Catholic church. In 1890 the Land Company leased all the 108 acres, except the land on which these houses had been built, to Pantia Ralli as meadow or pasture, with the proviso that land could be called in when required for building.[9] This the company did, building the large houses in the future area of The Marld. *Lagham*, where the Marshalls, the influential family of the first quarter of 20th century Ashtead, were to live, was erected in Woodfield Lane.

By 1901 there were fourteen of these houses, together with *Street Farm House* and four more building sites. They were all leased and were offered for sale in that year, figures mentioned ranging from £970 to £2,700 according to size and modernity.[10] Plans had been made to build villas over the whole 108 acres, roads having already been drawn on the map. This did not happen, the area remaining rural until occupied by the Council estate and Hillside Road in years to come. *Fountain Cottages* and two cottages on the north side of The Street were also included in the 1901 sale. In 1883 two smaller houses had appeared at the top of Woodfield Lane. (For *Forest Lodge* see pp 232-3).

Pantia Ralli leased a former Street Farm plot in Woodfield Lane from the Ashtead Land Company for a cricket ground, making no charge to the Club. The tree-lined field was retained by the Club throughout the next century.

At the northern end of this area stood Woodfield Farm, with fields on both sides of Craddocks Lane, a private road to a pond beside the railway later to be re-routed as Craddocks Avenue. The farm had been divided by the railway in 1858, its two parts being connected by a subway known locally as 'the cattle creep'. Sold for £6,100 in 1879, it was being farmed by James Weller in 1901. It was advertised in that year's sale as an excellent investment for building, with plans for a recreation ground, refreshment rooms and shops for excursionists north of the railway to the east of the station. The remaining part of the farm was offered for sale separately, a recently built cow shed and mixing-house erected by Weller to be regarded as his own property. Weller later appeared as the owner of all this Woodfield Farm area which lay undeveloped until the 1930s.

Next to the farm stood a terrace of six cottages and two others, all eight owned jointly by David Taylor and James Chitty, the carman and coal merchant who lived in one of them. There were also two above what was later Meadow Road.

The attraction of Woodfield Lane and much of area two lay in its proximity to the railway station.

3. The North-West Area

An area bounded by Barnett Wood Lane, the Woodfield, the Common and the Leatherhead boundary, this had formed the northern part of New Purchase Farm, one of the largest of the Howard farms. The main farmstead was outside this area in Agates Lane but the former Caen Farm buildings were in use near the northern boundary. New Purchase land had been divided by the railway in 1858 but was connected by a 'field crossing', known as Agate's.

This northern part of the farm was offered as a whole for purchase in the 1879 Sale, together with land in Agates Lane and on the south side of Barnett Wood Lane, but was withdrawn when the reserve price was not reached. The farmer, John Agate, to whom the land had been leased since the late 1850s, died in 1880. The whole area was bought up by developers, the chief of whom was Joseph Soames who had 61 acres in 1887 north of the railway line and on both sides of the Rye Brook. In that same year, the year of the Tithe Apportionment, the representatives of the late William Fitzhenry, who had lived at *Oakfield Lodge*, administered 37 acres between the railway and Barnett Wood Lane, including the land on which the Caen Wood Road estate would be built and the future Floral Pool then used as a quarry for brickmaking. Richard Heald owned and was living in *Sunnyside*, one of the first large houses in Barnett Wood Lane. Others who had purchased fields included Walter Cassells who built a large house in the far north-west corner, 28 acres; Henry Turnill of the *Laurels*, Agates Lane; William Goodwin who owned the *Caen*, the first house in the future Links Road and Payne Jennings, 16 acres in Barnett Wood Lane (see Area 7). The Suburban Land and Cottage Company which had built the Glebe Road houses (see Area 7), had ten acres on both sides of Links Road, and the Land and House Company Ltd, eight acres at the east end of Links Road. The Housing and Improvement Association had eight acres nearer the western end of that road.

Development was very slow indeed north of the railway, in spite of the fact that the future Links Road and Ashtead Woods Road had been marked out by 1894. There were endless arguments and disputes over access with the railway and the manorial landowners of the road across the Woodfield. The developers failed to obtain a road-crossing at Agate's crossing from Barnett Wood Lane; the railway replaced the crossing at Woodfield by a footbridge, under an obscure Act, and the roadway from the east of the station was deemed private land.[11] On the south side of the railway building began, large houses along Barnett Wood Lane and small terraced and semi-detached houses in Caen Wood Road. The railway had formed a barrier to the growth of Ashtead to its north and land continued to be worked as farmland for nearly a century.

While speculation in land went on, the cottagers along the western fringe of the Woodfield or Common continued to eke out an existence, the men mostly labourers, with one or two having specific jobs such as those of the three railway employees. In 1891 there were 108 people living as tenants of various landlords in 19 houses or cottages. Well-to-do families with servants lived in *Woodfield House* and *Oakfield Lodge*. By 1895 Curwood had built a refreshment room and complex south of the railway, the *Rosary*, a temperance establishment mainly for excursionists, the cottages being termed 'Curwood's'. *Felton's Bakery* was run in the 1890s by Mellish on the north side of the railway beside *Woodfield House* and was also a centre for refreshment and amusement.

4. Lower Ashtead

This area is bounded by Barnett Wood Lane on the north, Skinners Lane on the east, Ottways Lane on the south and Harriotts Lane and the Leatherhead boundary on the west. (This is the correct meaning of Lower Ashtead, historically.) Excluding the New Purchase Farm buildings on either side of Agates Lane and *Merry Hall*, most of this area had belonged to West Farm, owned by Col. Howard, and Whitehouse Farm, owned by the Dackombes earlier in the century.

By 1851 Bowman, the bailiff, was working both farms from *West Farm House*. *Whitehouse Farm House* had been occupied by farm labourers for some years before it was rebuilt in 1851 and let to private tenants who were not farmers. James Harriott, who in 1839 had worked Whitehouse Farm, was working the combined farm of 400 acres in 1861 from *West Farm House*. In 1863 John Hackblock, who had bought the Dackombe estate including Whitehouse Farm ten years earlier, exchanged land in Lower Ashtead with Mary Howard for a similar sized area which she owned south of the Leatherhead Road suitable for shooting (see Area 5). Peter Harriott took over both farms from his father before 1871, with land stretching to the southern border of the parish. In 1887 Peter Harriott owned six cottages at the south end of Agates Lane but lived at *West Farm House.*

When the Howard estate came up for sale in 1879 the West Farm land which belonged to it in Lower Ashtead (86 acres) was sold as a separate lot to J Sudbury, a solicitor from Hereford. Sudbury, who became the owner of *Wonersh Park* in Surrey, sold off some of the land to others, including George Masterman, a race-horse trainer. Masterman had bought *Merry Hall* in 1882 and by 1887 he owned most of the area between Skinners Lane and Agates Lane. Master-

Fig. 13.   West Farm House, a recent photograph. LDLHS Collection

man's land was sold off in parcels in 1898 after his death, initiating the fragmentation of land that would characterise the next century in Ashtead. The bulk of West Farm land remained undeveloped until the building of the 1920s and 1930s.

The New Purchase Farm buildings on the west side of Agates Lane were bought by Col Gleig in 1880, after they had been withdrawn from the 1879 Sale on failing to reach the reserve price. Gleig moved in and changed the name to *Murreys Court*. He also bought the adjoining fields, Great and Little Murreys, and added two along Barnett Wood Lane which he bought from Sudbury, leasing them to Peter Harriott for farming. Large houses were to appear in the latter two fields before long. The farm buildings and large field on the other side of Agates Lane through to Skinners Lane had been bought by Masterman. Thus, New Purchase Farm, created by Richard Howard and Col F G Howard, had ceased to exist by 1881.

5. The Copthorne Estate of John Hackblock

This estate was situated in the west of Ashtead, bounded by Ottways Lane, by a line drawn southwards from the south end of Skinners Lane to the Leatherhead Road and a long boundary hedge to Green Lane in the south, and from thence along the boundary with Leatherhead parish back to the Leatherhead Road. It then followed the boundary back to Harriotts Lane and thence to Ottways Lane. This was part of the former Dackombe Estate, about 211 acres, bought by John Hackblock, a merchant from London, in 1853. Hackblock, who never resided in Ashtead, also bought adjoining land in Leatherhead parish. He was a founding director of the Leatherhead and Epsom Railway (see Chapter 11).

Hackblock was a prosperous businessman with little interest in farming who sought to entertain his friends with sporting activities. For this purpose he acquired land south of the Leatherhead Road from Mary Howard in exchange for an equal area in Lower Ashtead (see Area 4). This included Little Stagley and Great Stagley but he failed to obtain a licence for an hotel, *Wayside*, for his visitors, on the Leatherhead Road opposite and had to pull it down.

The first of the new, large middle-class houses were built on or near these areas. The first was *Parsons Mead*, built by Captain (later Colonel) Gleig, who bought the plot from Hackblock in 1859 (see Area 7). This was followed in the 1860s by the *Marions*, renamed *Gateforth House*, then a private school and later Downsend School, on the Leatherhead Road; *The Grange*, later St. Andrew's School; and *Grange House* on the west side of Grange Road. *Uplands* was built in the 1870s on the Leatherhead Road and sold to the father of Frederick Hue Williams, the latter being a member of the Stock Exchange, and churchwarden for 40 years from 1881. Also on the Leatherhead Road was *The Cot*, what was left of the *Wayside Hotel*, and, behind it with a private road to Ottways Lane, the curiously-named large house called *The Hut* which Gleig, now Colonel, owned and to which he moved in 1876.

To these were added several more, one in 1882, *Hillfield*, a large house in extensive grounds with a drive to the Leatherhead Road, now traversed by the M25. It stood on the south side of the Linden Pit Path, hard by the Leatherhead boundary. *Lynwood* had been built by 1887, owned by Hue Williams and occupied by General Payn, just inside the Ashtead boundary and in the path of the future M25 near the Knoll roundabout. The *Long House* also appeared by 1894, the future *Milner House* beside the future Esso offices. All were on land belonging to Hackblock and Dackombe before him, several remaining the property of his family and his Trustees.

The new residents of these large houses played a significant part in church and society in Ashtead. They were professional and business men who had begun to take the place formerly monopolised by the aristocracy before the effects of the 1879 sale of the Howard estate had been felt.

In 1891 Samuel Andrews, farm bailiff for the Copthorne estate, was living at the *Whitehouse Farm House* (later *Dormers* see p 231). After the sale of West Farm in 1879, the parts of the former Whitehouse Farm which belonged to the Hackblock Trustees became once again an independent farm, known locally as Andrew's Farm. The farm had land on both sides of the Leatherhead Road, including the site of the future Goblin Works, where the Esso offices would be built 100 years later. Sudbury who had bought much of West Farm (see Area 4) was also the tenant for 56 acres of Copthorne land in the Stagleys. This may have been used for sporting as it had been in previous years, being the piece exchanged with Mary Howard.

6. The South Area
This area is bounded by the Leatherhead Road, the edge of the village from Parker's Hill to Crampshaw Lane through to Thirty Acre Barn, Addlestead Wood, the Headley and Leatherhead parish

boundaries to Green Lane and thence by the great dividing hedge to the Leatherhead Road.

The whole of the area was offered for sale in 1879 in three lots. The largest, Lot 41, 150 acres, included all the land north of Green Lane, including the three north to south swathes of land agreed in 1839, belonging respectively to West Farm (27 acres), New Purchase Farm (96 acres) and Woodfield Farm (27 acres). Advertised as ripe for building, the whole was bought by Roger Cunliffe of Tyrrells Wood for £10,900. John Agate's lease of New Purchase Farm expired at Michaelmas 1879 and the farm with its 96 acre field then ceased to exist. Lot 40, 59 acres, being arable land on Windmill Hill between Green Lane and Pebble Lane, including New Purchase Farm (11 acres) and West Farm (27 acres) land, was sold to Sheldrake. A third portion was offered as part of Lot 45 (Headley Court Farm): the hop-garden field (23 acres) and the Forty Acres (44 acres), also sold to Sheldrake.[12]

By 1887 Cunliffe had possession of all the land bought by Sheldrake. He was leasing part of this and the former New Purchase farm land in the south to G.W. James. Peter Harriott of West Farm retained the lease of 54 acres (Parr's Bridge and part Windmill Hill) from Cunliffe, and William Webb of Woodfield Farm the lease of 27 acres along Crampshaw Lane. Part of the area of the future Warren Estate appears to have been used by the Ashtead Golf Club. It was to be some years before Cunliffe's investment was to pay him dividends! The southerly part, like the Hackblock land to its west, the Stagleys area, remained rural, some for the whole of the 20th century.

7. The 'North Field' Area.

This area includes all the land between Woodfield Lane and Skinners Lane, bordered on the north by the Woodfield and Barnett Wood Lane and on the south by the Leatherhead Road. This is a central block, formerly a large part of the Ashtead common field, the North Field. The principal owners who emerged after the sale of the estate in 1879 were Payne Jennings and Frederick Peake, both of whom played a major part in Ashtead in the last decades of the 19th century and the beginning of the 20th century.

Payne Jennings, photographer and publisher (see p 206), whose relatives had lived at *Meadow Bank* in Skinners Lane, newly-built on former West Farm land in 1881, bought a large portion (43 acres) of the former *Leg of Mutton* land north of the Leatherhead Road. This land had been withdrawn from the Sale in 1879 when the reserve price was not reached. Jennings' land included the west side of Woodfield Lane, a good investment. Between 1887 and 1891 seven large houses were built on this stretch and between 1891 and 1894 seven more. Behind the houses was a large area, which he also owned, called Greville Park, honouring the memory of Col Fulk Greville Howard, former Lord of the Manor. A footpath ran through the park to the station, lined with tall poplars. It was not until the 1920s and 1930s that houses were built on this land.

In 1895 the names of Payne Jennings and James Cadett were linked with the Greville Works, which, together with their large, newly-erected house, *Monte Rosa*, stood at the southern end of the footpath to the station across Greville Park and adjoining the Northfields Passage. The factory which was built in 1889 originally belonged to Mawson and Swan. A second factory had been built by 1895, the Crampshaw Works, on land behind West Hill (Leatherhead Road); in 1897 this had been taken over by Cadett and Neall Ltd. Cadett also built the Victoria Works on the north side of the Leatherhead Road. Jennings built himself *Gayton House* nearby. These factories brought employment to a number of Ashtead men and women.

Jennings also bought 16 acres of former New Purchase land on the north side of Barnett Wood Lane (Area 2 above) most of which was later to become the Council Estate of Read and Taylor Roads but with villas fronting the Lane.

Most of the remainder of the *Leg of Mutton* land north of the Leatherhead Road, 21 acres, was purchased after the 1879 sale by Frederick Peake, a London solicitor who had moved into *Parsons Mead* as a tenant in 1876. Peake bought that house from Col Gleig in 1880, adding it to Gravel Piece, 17 acres, a large area of former New Purchase land between Ottways Lane and the Leatherhead Road which he had bought in 1879. Peake was a stalwart churchman, being a churchwarden from 1878 to 1892. Within the compass of the *Parsons Mead* land lay a 'Churchwarden's Field' and a field of glebe land belonging to his namesake, the Rev. E. C. Peake, the Rector in 1886. On Ottways Lane nearly opposite *Parsons Mead*, the almshouses known as *The Haven* were built in the 1880s on the site of the former parsonage, land bought by Peake in the 1879 sale. At the other end of Peake's land, in Barnett Wood Lane, the Iron Church was built for the parish in 1882.

Peake's land stretched from the Leatherhead Road to Barnett Wood Lane, a swathe adjoining Payne Jennings' land and covering both sides of the southern end of Skinners Lane and the whole of both sides of the future Oakfield Road, top and bottom. Large Edwardian houses would be built on this road which, in the 1880s and '90s, was marked only by footpaths through the fields.

Within 'Area 7', on the south side of Barnett Wood Lane, a little to the west, a field forming part of New Purchase Farm which had earlier in the century been glebe land was the site for the erection of semi-detached cottages for labourers, Glebe Road ('Glibes' Road at first). Developers were Joseph Soames, William Goodwin and the Suburban Land and Cottage Company (also at work in Area 3). There were 24 cottages in 12 pairs by 1887, two occupied by brick-makers who worked at the brickworks in the adjoining field. The Ashtead Gospel Mission was built on Barnett Wood Lane in the latter field by 1895 (see p 171). The first shop in Barnett Wood Lane stood at the north-west corner of Glebe Road by 1887, occupied by a fishmonger in 1891.

There were several ponds between the *Woodman* and Woodfield Lane. Beside the pub there was a field belonging to Goodwin which was later to be the Recreation Ground. Beside the largest pond, which was to remain for the next century, six semi-detached cottages had been built by 1894, and six semi-detached villas facing Woodfield Lane. These were all on former Woodfield Farm land.

There were several properties which did not figure in the 1879 sale. One was *Northlands*, with fields and a cottage (later to be the area of The Paddocks and, later still, Paddocks Way), 13 acres on both sides of Northfields Passage owned by Dorcas, inheritor of the Syms land. The second was *Timber Lodge*, a house built earlier in the century at the junction of Ottways Lane and Leatherhead Road. It was owned in 1887 by Llewelyn Harris, a stockbroker, who also bought a plot nearby on which *Timber Hill* was built later. The remainder were cottages, mainly in Ottways Lane, inhabited by families of labourers, but one the bakery, which had stood near the south end of Skinners Lane throughout the century, was owned by a freeholder tradesman.

8. Village Centre

If an 18th century inhabitant who had died early in the 19th had returned seventy years later, he or she would have been able to recognise most of the village centre. Fashions had changed but the buildings were much the same in 1879 as they had been in 1802 (see inset to Wyburd map on p 52).

Fifteen years later, however, in 1894, the village had taken on a new appearance. Buildings had been demolished and new ones built along the south side of The Street. Many of these were to remain for a hundred years, hiding later behind new shop fronts but revealed in the upper storeys and at roof level in many cases. The north side of The Street on the other hand remained virtually unchanged before 1900, with fenced fields, *Street Farm House*, cottages and sheds. Rectory Lane, formerly Headley Road, had surrendered its position as the chief road in the village community to The Street by 1895, more than a century after the latter had become the Epsom to Dorking turnpike road.

There were three groups of inhabitants in the village centre throughout the century. Proximity to the *Mansion* in Ashtead Park meant that most village people were aware of their proper status in society. No doubt caps were doffed or forelocks pulled to the gentry, the first group, the Parkers of *Ashtead Lodge*, the Rectors, the Chesters at *Ashtead Cottage* (*Howard House*), as well as to Mary Howard, her notable visitors and her successors. The customary deference was tinged with some reservation as the new rich moved into other parts of Ashtead at the end of the century.

The middle group in the village was composed of the craftsmen and, to a lesser extent, the tradesmen. There had been a blacksmith in The Street near the *Leg of Mutton* for many years but his smithy had disappeared by 1891. The wheelwright's in Rectory Lane grew in importance in the last quarter of the century. George Wyatt, the wheelwright, owned the house and forge in Rectory Lane in 1887 and employed several craftsmen, wheelwrights, blacksmiths and apprentices. In the same year, a little way up the road, Anne Harman owned the bakehouse opposite the (Old) Rectory. She took in boarders, including a novelist and her friend and, in 1881, the young curate, the Rev. E. C. Peake. By 1891 John Fowler, the builder, had bought the cottage in Rectory Lane which was to be named after him.

By the mid-19th century postal services had been established in

Fig. 14. Garden staff, Ashtead Park c. 1900. The picture includes William Lisney and his son George, Edward Chitty, his wife Harriet (tea lady) and their son Arthur, James Batty and George Munday. The Chitty, Lisney and Batty families lived in the three Park lodges at various times. (Courtesy, Mrs Dorothy Chitty).

the village. Robson's Commercial Directory of 1838 recorded that Thomas Smith, landlord of the *Leg of Mutton*, was 'Receiver of the posts for Ashtead', but the first post office was not authorised until 1845. This was staffed by a Receiver and a foot messenger with William Newport as the first Postmaster. He soon retired, and was succeeded by James Penny who was also the schoolmaster. He had come from Levens, Westmorland where the Howards owned the estate. Penny is believed to have run the counter from *Parkside Cottage* at the far end of The Street, but by 1862 the post office had moved to the *Leg of Mutton*, where it remained for nearly 20 years. In 1881 William Hogsden became Postmaster, in the shop which he and his wife ran at 78 The Street. John Webb was their courier. After William died in 1890, his wife and daughter took over the post office for a few years. By 1895 Alfred Borer had become Postmaster. Ashtead was then despatching mails four times a day (once on Sundays) and making deliveries three times a day (no Sunday delivery).

Fig. 15. Fowler's Cottage, Rectory Lane. Photograph by J. C. Stuttard

In the new building which had recently taken the place of an old *Leg of Mutton* property, there was in 1891 a grocer, a corn dealer, a greengrocer/dairyman and a factory superintendent. Farther up The Street there was another grocer, a builder, and a butcher whose young assistant was Harry (Pip) Page of the later 'Page & Clatworthy' and father of Alick Page who carried on the business until the early 1990s. There were still very few shops before 1900. Unusual residents in The Street in 1891 were an Assistant Director of Navy Contracts with a B.A. degree and a shop which may have been run by his wife, an Epsom jockey and his family and the proprietress of a coffee house which she ran in conjunction with the church. Many in this middle group were able to own their own houses and to live in reasonable conditions.

The third group, which formed the majority of residents in the village centre, consisted of labourers (some more skilled than others), former working people living in rented accommodation, houses divided into tenements, sometimes whole extended families occupying no more than four rooms. Among these there were gardeners, dressmakers, domestic servants and other manual workers.

At the bottom of Park Lane, *Parkside Cottage* in the Epsom Road was occupied by James Cadett in 1891 with a family of independent means next door, while two of the five houses round the corner were occupied by schoolteachers. The population of the village centre had increased from 200 in 1841 to about 276 in 1871, with only a very small number of extra houses, but it stabilised at that number while new houses were being built, thus reducing overcrowding by the end of the century.

Notes

1. The Ashtead Park Estate, Sale Catalogue, *SAS* M14/AST/5(1–10); BL, MAPS 137 b3(10) and elsewhere.

2. Conveyance of Estate, 1880, Trustees of General E.R. Bagot to Thomas Lucas Esq. By courtesy of the Headmaster, City of London Freemen's School.

3. *Surrey Standard* 1 July 1879. Original copy by courtesy of M. Worsfold. The cutting contains details of offers accepted at the 1879 sale.

4. J.M. Stratton, *Agricultural Records* (1978)

5. PRO: MAF 68/Surrey. Table in Alan A. Jackson (ed) *Ashtead: A Village Transformed*, (1977) p. 157.

6. SRO: PSH/ATD/GIL/13.11. The terrier is in PRO: IR29/34/6. (A handwritten transcript by G.J. Gollin is in the Society Records)

7. The information for the remainder of this chapter is to be found in the above map and terrier, the Sale catalogues of 1872 (Copthorne Estate) and 1879 (Howard Estate, Bagot Trustees); the Ordnance Survey maps of Surrey (1:2,500) 2nd Ed., 1895 OS sheet 18.12 and 1896 OS sheet 18.16, copies in Society Records AM 417 & 418; the Census returns for 1851 to 1891, PRO H0107/1592, RG9/419, 10/798, 11/761, and 12/546 and Directories.

8. Conveyances of Estate, 1880 and 1889, by courtesy of the Headmaster, City of London Freemen's School.

9. Indenture 23 December 1890 between The Ashtead Land Company and Pantia Ralli.

10. The Ashtead Estate, Sale particulars, plan etc 1901, by courtesy of T. Devitt.

11. *Ashtead Parish Magazines*, e.g. Vol 25 (1910), p 295, 296. Also Minutes of the South Western and Brighton Railway Companies Joint Committee, PRO RAIL 197:2&3.

12. *Surrey Standard* op cit. A copy of the 1879 Sale catalogue, loaned by T. Devitt, has the name of Cunliffe pencilled in as the buyer but this may have been added later.

Chapter 10

ROADS AND ROAD SERVICES

Road Pattern

A comprehensive picture of the road pattern in and around Ashtead at the beginning of the 19th century may be gained from the wealth of cartographic material surviving from previous centuries. The fine maps by Rocque and others, dating from the 17th and 18th centuries, show that roads whose modern counterparts include, for instance, Agates Lane, Farm Lane (formerly Hilders Lane) and Barnett Wood Lane (formerly Marsh Lane) were established routes two or three centuries ago. The roads depicted by Rocque, in particular, correspond to main roads in Surrey today.[1] Wyburd's map of 1802 and the first edition of the Ordnance Survey one inch map, dating from 1816, confirm the picture given by the earlier maps.[2]

The turnpike from Leatherhead to Epsom, through Ashtead, constructed during the 1750s, was the last major road development locally, until the present century.[3] This and the other turnpikes in the district, however, did not prove to be of the lasting significance which was anticipated when they were built. Within about a century they had been eclipsed, for a time at least, by the coming of the railways – a fate which could not have been foreseen a hundred years before.

In the early 19th century significant changes were made in the layout of the roads through Ashtead Park, for amenity reasons to remove such roads from close proximity to the new manor house built in 1791–92.[4] These changes included, in particular, diversion of the public road passing initially between the new manor house and St Giles' Church, to its present position north of the latter in Rookery Hill.

The history of Woodfield Lane is of particular interest. Its original track, shown on Lawrence's map of 1638 and now a service road, lay to the west of the main carriageway. It has been described as part of an ancient way which crossed the Downs from Ashtead Woods to Headley, and in 1816 it was portrayed by the Ordnance Survey as part of a route between Ashtead and Chessington. Historically, Woodfield Lane was known as 'Common Lane', and this name was used on a map which showed the Ashtead properties of the Beckford family in 1750. The nearby hamlet of Woodfield was shown as consisting of a line of cottages running north towards the Rye Brook, which Woodfield Lane would have linked to Ashtead village. Common Lane was once a track, but it had become a road by the closing decades of the 19th century, when it was known as 'Station Road', which suggests that it may have been constructed following the opening of the railway in 1859.

Road Services

Early 19th Century
The first reference to the route taken between Leatherhead and London and which afforded proof of a service through Ashtead, related to the post in 1793, which left Leatherhead at 10.00 p.m. each evening and travelled by way of Epsom and Croydon. There was a daily coach through Leatherhead to Brighthelmstone (Brighton). Coaches from Leatherhead ran also to Dorking, Guildford and Horsham at this period.[5] Around the year 1800, a coach from Dorking to London, which passed through Ashtead, made the journey one day and returned the next. In later years, the journey time was reduced to three hours, including the time taken to change the horses.[6] By contrast, in the 1870s and early 1880s, a four-horse coach arrived at Dorking from London at 2.00 p.m. and started the return journey 90 minutes later, presumably with fresh horses![7]

The Box Hill coach, the *Rocket*, commenced in April 1803, and travelled to London by way of Leatherhead, Ewell, Kingston and Barnes. This was the era of named coaches when, for instance, in 1815 *The Times* and *The Star*, passed through Ashtead, their journeys to London from Guildford and from Horsham taking four and four-and-a-half hours respectively.[8]

In the 1820s William Broad of Dorking drove a coach with a team of four grey horses through Ashtead to London. It has been suggested that he was the prototype for Tony Weller, the father of Sam, in the *Pickwick Papers*.[9] In 1823 eight coach services linked Leatherhead with London, including one to the City by way of Epsom, Ewell and North Cheam.[10] Three years later, 106 coach departures, including a reduced number on Sundays, were listed each week from ten hostelries in the City, Southwark and Charing Cross.[11] Various regular van and wagon services ran from Leatherhead to Bishopsgate, the City, Holborn and Southwark. Probably, the majority of these would have served Ashtead.

By 1836 12 coaches were passing through Leatherhead and serving Brighton, Guildford and Worthing.[12] Three years later regular coaches left Epsom for London, and services ran from Epsom to link with the London and Southampton Railway, probably at the original Surbiton Station (then known as Kingston Station), which opened in May 1838 at the Ewell Road bridge, and was moved to its present site in 1845.[13] Coaches were passing through Epsom and Ashtead daily at this period, from places such as Brighton, Guildford, Horsham and Worthing on their way to London.

Directories for 1845 listed a large number of carrier services to London operating from Epsom.[14] Such services probably drew their custom from a wide surrounding area, including Ashtead. Carriers listed as passing through Epsom from Dorking, Guildford, Horsham and Leatherhead, would have served Ashtead.

In Hand with the Railway

Although no precise date was given, a picture might be drawn of the coach services to London, which passed through Ashtead and Epsom just before the opening of the railway to Epsom on 10 May 1847. The first coach of the day started from Epsom at 8.00 a.m. Coaches from Dorking, Horsham and Guildford passed through the town during the next couple of hours. Further coaches included those from Worthing and Bognor, which reached Epsom at mid-afternoon on alternate days. The final London-bound coach of the day passed through Epsom at 4.30 p.m., from Dorking. Coaches from London reached Epsom on the return journeys between 11.00 a.m. and 6.30 p m., the final coach terminated in the town – so anyone from Ashtead who left it until the last coach would have had to walk! Coaches passing through Ashtead probably stopped at one of the hostelries in the centre of the village, or at the *Haunch of Venison*, near the present site of *Forest Lodge* (see p 232).[15]

Long-distance road transport was eclipsed by the expanding railway services, the first indications becoming apparent in the district by the mid-19th century. The London, Brighton & South Coast Railway station, off what is now the Upper High Street in Epsom, provided a service to London Bridge by way of Croydon. The railhead attracted daily road services from as far afield as Ockley. The timings indicated that separate services ran from Dorking and from Leatherhead. The attraction exerted by Epsom Station was illustrated further by the fact that the coach continued to run from Dorking, two years after the South-Eastern Railway had opened Boxhill & Leatherhead Road Station (now Deepdene) in 1849. The latter would appear to have been far more convenient than Epsom Station for travellers from Dorking, but the route to London via Redhill was circuitous! The service to Epsom would have passed through Ashtead, and would have enhanced its residential attraction.

By 1851 there were fewer long-distance coach services passing through the district than in earlier years. There were daily services from Dorking and Leatherhead to London. The former was routed via Mickleham and Epsom, and must have passed through Ashtead. The only other long-distance coach services known to be running at this date were one which ran thrice weekly from Brighton to London via Leatherhead, and one which ran daily from Guildford to London, via Leatherhead and Epsom.[16]

The number of carts, vans and wagons running between Leatherhead and London had fallen to three services weekly by 1851, apart from services passing through Leatherhead from further afield; e.g., from Dorking and from Effingham. This represented a substantial fall below the earlier level and suggested that the data may have been incomplete; particularly as the railway was not to reach Leatherhead for a further eight years.

With the opening of the railway to Leatherhead in 1859, the pattern of road services through Ashtead was to change. Leatherhead rather than Epsom was the rail-head with flys and coaches from the Swan Inn meeting all the trains. A daily coach ran from Horsley, Effingham and Bookham to link with the 9.20 a.m. train from Leatherhead to London, and to meet the train due from London at 5.14 p.m. It seems unlikely that there would have been corresponding services from Ashtead into Epsom Station, but more likely that Ashtead people would have missed-out – they had their own station – having benefitted hitherto from services from further afield, which passed through the village.

A number of carriers continued to operate from and through Leatherhead, despite the presence of the railway and it would be of interest to know whether they operated in co-operation or in competition with the agents appointed by each of the two railway companies to handle the onward delivery of goods.[17]

Revival in road use

Interest in roads was revived in the late Victorian period with the increasing popularity of cycling and the arrival of the motor car. There was also a brief revival of the stage coach, in a small way, partly for pleasure, and also, for a few years after 1887, to carry some of the mail.

Notes

1. K. Cooper, 'John Rocque's map of Surrey- a disregarded historical reference' *Bull. Soc. Univ. Cartographers*, 6(1), 1971, pp. 1–7
2. Alan A. Jackson (ed) *Ashtead: A Village Transformed* (1977) p. 197; R.A. Lever, 'Ashtead in Maps from 1753 to 1816' *Procs LDLHS*, 4(10) 1986, pp. 280–3
3. G. Joan Fuller, 'The development of roads in the Surrey-Sussex Weald and coastlands between 1700 and 1900' *Trans Inst. of British Geographers*, 1953, pp. 37–49
4. Alan A. Jackson (ed) (1977) op. cit. pp. 83–4
5. *Universal British Directory*, 1793. The terms 'omnibus' and 'coach' were used in the sources without differentiation. The term 'coach' has been used throughout the present study.
6. Charles Rose, *Recollections of old Dorking* (1878) p. 72
7. William Dinnage, *Recollections of old Dorking* (1963) pp. 53–3
8. A.H. Lock, *Surrey in 1815* (1974) pp. 10–11
9. Charles Rose (1878) op. cit pp. 73–6
10. Pigot's *Commercial Directory*, 1823
11. *Post Office London Directory*, 1826
12. A. Bates, *Directory of stage coach services, 1836*
13. Pigot's *Royal National and Commercial Directory and Topography* (1839) pp. 613, 629
14. *Post Office Directory of the Six Home Counties* (1845) pp. 494, 531
15. Gordon Home, *Epsom- its History and Surroundings* (1901) pp. 29, 31 The details given on the coaches correspond fairly closely with those for Leatherhead taken from A. Bates (1836) op. cit.
16. *Post Office Directory of the Six Home Counties* (1851) pp. 617, 734, 644
17. *Post Office Directory of Surrey* (1862), p. 1395

Chapter 11

THE COMING OF
THE RAILWAY

The railway was opened through Ashtead on 2 February 1859. Several plans had been made for lines through the Mole Valley gap in the North Downs which would have passed through Ashtead from Epsom Common to Leatherhead. One of the most significant of these was the proposed main line from Battersea, Nine Elms, to Brighton which was rejected in 1836 in favour of a direct line from London Bridge to Brighton via Croydon and Red Hill. Another was a direct line on the 'atmospheric' principle from London Bridge to Portsmouth via Croydon and the Mole Valley, proposed in 1844. A line from London Bridge via Croydon terminating at Epsom was built in 1847 and was taken over by the London Brighton and South Coast Railway (LB&SCR, or 'Brighton Company').

In 1856 a group of mainly local businessmen sought and obtained an Act of Parliament authorising 'The Epsom and Leatherhead Railway Company' (E&LR). A line was to be built from Epsom to a station on the east side of the turnpike road to Kingston about half a mile east of Leatherhead. A station would be included at Ashtead although this was nearly dropped as an economy measure[1]. Two of the Directors had Ashtead connections: Daniel Maydwell, tenant farmer of Street Farm, and John Hackblock, non-resident owner of the former Dackombe estate. Most of the land required in Ashtead was owned by Mary Howard. One of the first acts of the E&LR was to make an Agreement with Mary Howard for the purchase of farm and common land[2]. Maydwell and Michael Agate were the only recorded representatives from Ashtead at the ceremony of the 'turning of the first sod' which did not take place until 2 June 1857 in a field near the junction of Barnett Wood Lane and the turnpike road to Kingston at Leatherhead, the site of the proposed terminus station. A procession of notables was accompanied by constables, navvies on horse and foot, children and teachers and a military band[3].

The construction of the line by the well-known and experienced Thomas Brassey took place very slowly. The single track followed the route already surveyed by the Portsmouth Railway Company for a railway from Croydon to Portsmouth. The route followed the easiest gradient which coincided with Mary Howard's alleged desire to place it as far away as possible from the Park. The line was three-quarters of a mile from the village. Delays were blamed on the weather, shortage of labour, men who deserted them at harvest time, and lack of materials. The Company blamed lack of funds. Mary Howard was blamed for holding up the work at one point when she demanded a subway under the railway on Woodfield Farm, later known locally as the 'cattle creep', in place of a bridge agreed for her private use from the end of Craddocks Lane to the Common[4]. The first sign of the coming railway was the erection of fences. Clay was shifted by horses from the cutting being made on Epsom Common to build the embankment on the Ashtead side of the border. Ashtead Station consisted of one short, low platform and a rudimentary building, both on the 'Down', that is, the south side of the line, the work being completed in the autumn.

The first trains began to run on 1 February 1859, worked by the London and South Western Railway (L&SWR)[5]. For the first two months, all passengers for London had to transfer by road at Epsom to the Brighton Company's Epsom Town station. On 4 April 1859, a junction was made at Epsom between the E&LR and the newly-completed Wimbledon and Epsom line built by a second independent company, the 'Wimbledon & Dorking', also worked by the South Western. Trains then began to run from Leatherhead via a new Epsom Station to 'Waterloo Bridge station', seven each weekday in each direction.

An unusual Joint Railway
On 8 August 1859 LB&SCR (Brighton Company) trains began to run from London Bridge to Leatherhead but continued to use that Company's Epsom Town Station. An Act of Parliament of August 1860 authorised the two companies, South Western and Brighton, to purchase the line from the E&LR and to take it into their joint

ownership. The line was managed by a joint committee presided over alternatively by the two chairmen. Each company ran its own trains but station staff at Ashtead and Leatherhead were appointed jointly[6].

At first none of the six Brighton Company trains in each direction stopped at Ashtead but in 1860 three did. The two best South Western trains to Waterloo in the morning did not stop, but later one of these 'Gentlemen's trains' did, by request. For years the best train of the day was the 5.25pm from Waterloo which reached Ashtead in 33 minutes.

The electric telegraph from Waterloo came to Ashtead station in 1861. A single wire was slung on poles erected on the 'Down' side of the track. A second wire was added in 1873.

In 1866/67 the track from Epsom to Leatherhead was doubled to take the increased traffic which would arise from the opening of the Brighton Company line from Leatherhead to Dorking, Horsham and Brighton, via Steyning and Shoreham. The Kingston Road station was closed and two stations built at Leatherhead nearer the town, one for each company. Ashtead then became the only jointly owned station on the line, with a new short platform on the 'Up' side added to that on the 'Down' side but apparently no further building. In 1874, a house was built for the jointly employed stationmaster on the 'Up' side platform beside the crossing. This was at that time described as a private occupation crossing giving access to the Common. The road from the bottom of Common Lane (later Woodfield Lane) to the station had been made up by the South Western in 1859 with ballast provided by Mary Howard from the Common at 6d per load. The avenue of trees was planted much later. Porters were jointly employed to control the two crossings at Ashtead, the other being a Highways Board road to the houses on the north portion of the Woodfield. The porters were also responsible for signal lamps in the early days. A cottage was later built for a gatekeeper at what became known as 'Lady Howard's Crossing', an apparent misnomer.

Ashtead was not regarded as an important station before 1885. Neither the majority of Brighton Company trains nor the best morning train to Waterloo called at the little station. There was a siding for goods, one train per day stopping for a few minutes in each direction when required. In 1872, the advertisement for the sale of Hackblock's Copthorne estate in Ashtead which described it as 'about 18 miles from London and served by stations at Ashtead and Leatherhead on two lines of railway .. to five London termini' drew no response[7]. Lt Col Ponsonby Bagot complained in 1878 that there were no facilities at Ashtead for loading private horse carriages on to the trains; he had to go to Epsom. In 1879 he also requested a loading dock for horses, cattle and sheep without success, indicating the limited use of Ashtead's yard for agricultural purposes.

Improvements at the end of the century

New sidings were constructed on both sides of the main line in 1883 and 1885 to hold excursion trains bringing children and families from London for a day out on Ashtead Common. The platforms were lengthened and raised and in 1885 new station buildings were erected which were to last until 1969[8]. The waiting room with a fire on the 'Up' platform and a canopy took the place of a temporary shelter. Although land had been acquired in the Woodfield in 1883, the yard was not developed until 1903. New interlocked double gates were installed on the easterly level crossing with wicket gates for passengers in 1886. The signal box stood on the 'Up' platform. A central footbridge was built in 1897.

The stationmaster from 1873 until 1905 was Mr Sims. He and his family lived in the house beside the Up platform. As Agent appointed by the Joint Committee, he was responsible for the sale of each Company's tickets. He was paid weekly until 1898 when he was put on the salaried staff. He was assisted by his daughter, his son also being in the employ of the railway. When he retired he was presented with £106 and a framed address by the villagers in the station waiting room[9]. In retirement he ran the newsagent's in Barnett Wood Lane, his wife having previously carried on the business from the station.

A few L&SW trains were extended to and from Guildford in 1885 when the line via Bookham and Horsley was opened (Effingham Junction Station and Depot were built later) but otherwise travellers experienced little change. There were few early morning trains to London, the first being the LB&SC 7.19 slow to London Bridge and the next the L&SW 7.57 which took 43 minutes to Waterloo. The earliest to Victoria was at 11.32, an LB&SC slow from Brighton. Both the 'Gentlemen's morning trains were timetabled to call at Ashtead by this time. An hourly service from Waterloo ran in the evening between 4.30 and 7.38, the best train,

Fig. 16. LB&SCR Stroudley Class A1 0-6-OT built in 1875. Known as 'Terriers', locomotives of this class painted in deep yellow livery worked suburban trains between Dorking and London Bridge and Victoria calling at Ashtead for many years. (Courtesy, National Railway Museum, York).

Fig. 17. Ashtead Station as it was from 1885, photographed in 1909. The stationmaster's house is on the 'Up' platform. (Courtesy, Surrey Local Studies Library)

the 5.30 taking 36 minutes. It was necessary to leave the City early to come back on a train from London Bridge that stopped at Ashtead. When the Waterloo and City line opened in 1898 the L&SW route to Waterloo became the best way to the City.

While the L&SW developed its suburban service from Leatherhead in the next years, with all trains calling at Ashtead, the LB&SC used the route mainly for through trains to Horsham and the coast. Some 15 fast or semi-fast LB&SC trains passed through Ashtead in each direction, few inhabitants, other than cottagers, living near enough to be disturbed by the clatter of wheels and sounds of steam. One LB&SC train which called at 9.0 a.m. enabled a day to be spent in Brighton, arriving back at Ashtead soon after 10 p.m..

Notes

1. 19&20 Vic c xcii, House of Lords Records Library and associated papers.
2. E&LR Terrier, PRO RAIL 414:525.
3. *Surrey Standard*, 6 June 1857, LDLHS, LX612.
4. Minutes of .. the E&LR, PRO RAIL 197:1.
5. H.J. Davies, 'The Epsom and Leatherhead Railway, 1856–59' *Procs LDLHS*, 5(6), 1993, pp 170–2
6. Minutes of the South Western & Brighton Company Joint Committee PRO 197:2
7. *The Times* 6 July 1872 in G. J. Gollin, *Bygone Ashtead* (1987).
8. PRO RAIL 414/199
9. *Ashtead Parish Magazine* 21,242.

Chapter 12

CARE FOR THE COMMUNITY TO 1900

Poverty

At the beginning of the 19th century there was a workhouse and a group of almshouses in the parish. The workhouse, on the south side of the Epsom Road not far from the parish boundary, was provided under the Statute of 1723 and paid for out of the Poor Rate. The Almshouse, sometimes known as 'The Widows' House', was founded by Lady Diana Feilding, Lady of the Manor, about 1730, and was supported out of her bequest and voluntary giving; it was at the east end of The Street at the corner of Park Lane. The workhouse had itself begun life in the late 17th century as an 'almshouse', voluntarily provided until 1723. The new Almshouse provided six widows with two rooms each. Entry to and oversight of the workhouse was the responsibility of the Parish Overseers of the Poor who also collected the Poor Rate from property owners. The Almshouse was administered by the Rector and the trustees of Lady Diana's bequest.

The parishes of Ashtead, Epsom and Ewell, Cheam and Leatherhead were combined into one Union by the Act of 1834 for Poor Law purposes. The Ashtead workhouse was closed and the inmates sent to the workhouse in Epsom (sited near the Epsom General Hospital). The Almshouse was not affected. The new workhouse was controlled by the Guardians of the Poor appointed by the Act, one of whom came from Ashtead, usually the Rector, with the assistance of the Overseers and Assistant Overseers who did the day-to-day work and were appointed by the Vestries. A poor rate was set annually by the Vestry Meeting and levied on all householders, tenants paying through their rents. The rate in 1888 was 1/7d in the pound and was collected by the Assistant Overseer, then Mr Swindells, a retired Church School teacher who was also Collector of Taxes in the 1880s.

In 1852 Mary Howard had the Almshouse enlarged to accommodate eight widows and added to the endowment. She met the cost of reinstating the whole building in 1873 and on her death four years later she left £500 to be invested and income applied to augmentation of the widows' allowance. In 1872 the Rector, Mr Legge, left £250 in his will in aid of 'The Widows' Houses'. Two plaques record the benefactions which were still being administered in the 1990s.

The Parish Burial Registers record burials 'from the poorhouse', 'from the workhouse', and 'a widow from the Charity House'. In 1813, Elizabeth Saker, 'widow from the Charity House' was mentioned, and in 1818 Elizabeth Terrey from the 'Ashtead Charity House'. Ages varied: John Collingham, labourer, 1813, and William Kiffen, 1824, both aged 87, from the workhouse; William Page, eight months, 1813, and John Arthur, five weeks, 1825, both from the workhouse. Between 1840 and 1849 sixteen funerals took place in Ashtead from the Epsom Union Workhouse, six over forty-five years old, four teenagers and, saddest of all, three children in one family, aged eight, six and fourteen, within six weeks, in the winter of 1848–49. The Rev. Barrington Taylor, Mr Legge's bachelor curate for 46 years, was chaplain to the Epsom Union Workhouse from 1840 to 1866.

The former Ashtead workhouse, which became known as the old workhouse, continued to be inhabited by poor families. In 1851 and 1861 James and Eliza Reid and Joseph Page lived there, in 1861 with the addition of three children; in 1881 William Skilton and his wife and nine children had moved there.[1] The old workhouse was pulled down in 1901.

Poor relief was not confined to the inmates of institutions. In 1851 Elizabeth Fleetwood, 97, Almswoman, and Elizabeth Newport, 71, living in cottages, were in receipt of 'Parish Relief'. In 1878–9, £17 16s.0d was distributed to 77 families[2] and aged people in the parish from a charity established in 1712 by an Ashtead inhabitant, Sarah Bond, 'for poor people not receiving Parochial relief': the beneficiaries were selected annually by the Lord of the Manor and Rector as executors of the bequest. In the same period, £5 0s.9d was paid to 22 families requiring assistance through sick-

Fig. 18.   Mary Howard (1785–1877) from a painting c. 1870 by Weigall, formerly at Ashtead Park, now at Levens Hall, Cumbria. (Courtesy, Hal Bagot).

Fig. 19.   Almshouses, The Street. Drawing by Mary Cree.

ness or old age out of a fund provided by Denton, a former Rector, and added to by Mr Legge in his will. The fund became an authorised Charity in 1892 and the payments were made by the Rector at Epiphany. Under Legge's will of 1872 eight old men of 65 and over each received a sovereign annually on 21 December.

Ashtead was one of several parishes, including Leatherhead, which benefited from the will of Henry Smith in 1627, a respectable Cheapside trader. In 1878/9, tickets were given to 108 families and aged people, to be presented at specified stores: 49 for groceries at Mrs Sanders', 26 for bread at Mr Taylor's, 19 for drapery at Messrs Williams & Co, and eight and six at Mrs Harman's and Mr Felton's respectively, also for bread, a total of £31 8s.0d, drawn from Smith's charity.

From a legacy left by Mary Howard, 99 pairs of blankets were provided for the poor at a cost of £50 in 1878/9. Seventy-one members made monthly payments into a Clothing Club from which £102 15s.6d, including subscriptions from the gentry, was paid to Messrs Williams & Co the draper. The club managers in 1898 reminded the members that they would not pay for trimmings or furs, ribbons or laces, or artificial flowers, the club being intended for blankets and winter clothing. Coal was bought for 105 families and old people, one bushel each per week for eight weeks, paid for by subscription from the better off. Soup was sold at one penny per quart. Unemployed farm labourers and their families qualified for soup distribution when times were hard.

A Sick and Poor Fund was administered by the church. By 1878, the practice had been established of giving the offertories on the first Sunday of the month and on Christmas Day to this fund, amount-in 1878/9 to £36. The money was distributed to the poor and widows for groceries, meat, wines and spirits, and coal.

The church struggled to meet the demands of mendicants who appeared regularly at the doors of the parish. A Parish Coffee Room had been established in the 1880s with a manager. A scheme was adopted in 1886 for the sale to parishioners of meal tickets at 4d and 6d each for giving to beggars. On presentation of a ticket at the Coffee Room (also called the Coffee Tavern) the beggar would be given a meal. The scheme was successful at first but the lease could not be renewed. In 1889 the manager, Mr Brown, opened another room in one of the Street Farm cottages and continued the scheme, providing "temperance refreshment". His venture did not succeed: in spite of a 'Grand Concert' to raise funds and other special events hosted by Rector and churchwardens, with supper, songs and tobacco for the choir and others, it disappeared by 1892.

Charitable giving was very important to the poor in Victorian Ashtead, with little or no provision by the State. It must have involved the giving of much care and time by the better-off families as well as by the Rector and the parish officers. The year 1878–9 is typical of the last quarter of the century, although sums dispensed grew less as the income from investments, especially Consols, declined in the 1890s and later[3].

Health

Although the health of the population in Britain had improved during the 19th century, sickness was still a major problem and one not confined to the poor. For example, two rectors of that period struggled with ill-health during their time in Ashtead. Adamson (1875–85) suffered 'a melancholy decline in health', leading to an early death in office in his forties: Lucas, for all his sporting prowess, was forced on several occasions, particularly in the winters of 1899 and 1900, to travel to Egypt because of ill-health and increasing deafness.

The average age of death in 1887 in Ashtead was 51, comparing favourably with the country as a whole. In 1888 the Epsom Union Rural Sanitary Authority reported deaths in Ashtead below the average of 27.4 per thousand in the district and births above the average of 13.3 per thousand. In spite of much potential poverty and primitive sanitation, Ashtead was not an unhealthy place in which to live by the standards of the time.

For the ordinary people, especially the poor, a trained parish nurse, Nurse Martin, was appointed for the first time in 1888 and one penny a day was charged for her services. Subscriptions were invited from the well-to-do towards a nursing fund of £80 per annum, plus the costs of the initial outlay on medicines, and appliances. In 1889 the nurse had bought a water-cushion and in 1890 a concert was held to raise funds for a water-mattress. There was a measles epidemic which closed the school in October 1890 but a year later the parish lost its nurse because of insufficient subscriptions. Mrs Giberne, of the Cottage in the Park, enrolling member of the new Mothers' Union (MU), rallied support for another nurse but this time the 'cottagers' were asked to pay a subscription of 2/-

a year to become members in order to benefit. Mrs Bunyan, who was appointed and lived at 2 *Woodfield Cottages* (in 1994, renovated and standing at the bottom of Woodfield Lane), made an average of 56 visits per week. There was a serious outbreak of influenza leading to some child-deaths in 1893. By the end of the year the arrival of the first resident doctor in Ashtead and his establishment of medical clubs for the poor made the services of a resident nurse unnecessary.

The Rector called a meeting to consider Ashtead's affiliation to the Dorking Nursing Association. This was agreed and the scheme was started in January 1894. Subscribers to the nursing fund would receive the services of a nurse when needed at a pro rata cost per week from 2 shillings for the labourers to 10 shillings for the gentry. The nurse would live-in, for example, during childbirth and would receive free board and lodging when possible for her work. The scheme was primarily for the poor, but nurses were also available for 'the upper and middle classes'. The funds supporting this were soon over-stretched, so in 1897 the gentry were excluded.

Although Ashtead had always had its untrained midwives, it was made a separate 'Poor Law medical district' in 1887, Dr. William Smythe being appointed as Medical Officer of Health. Smythe was a well-known figure in the village in the 1890s, living in *Street Farm House*, and his appointment was seen as a boon to the poor who were dependent on the 'Parish Doctor'.

First-aid classes were started in 1898 and the first ten certificates were gained after 'Ambulance Lectures'.

Public Services
The Leatherhead & District Water Company supplied Ashtead with piped water in the 1880s. Until then it had depended on wells and springs. Gas was provided for street lighting and the home at about the same time. There were frequent discussions at the Ashtead Parish Council on how many gas lamps there should be and for how long they should be lighted. A Lighting Committee was formed in 1897 to negotiate with the Epsom & Ewell Gas Company about these matters[4]. Electricity was not introduced widely until after 1900, though some of the large private houses had their own generators before this.

In the last years of the 19th century the drainage and methods of sewage disposal in Ashtead were radically improved. The Epsom

Sanitary body in 1891 had sought stiff new by-laws regulating cess pools and drainage in Ashtead, as pressure increased through new building in an area without sewers. Special meetings of the Vestry had to be called to consider this but the problem was too great for the old parish organisation. In 1897 the new Epsom District Council which included Ashtead proposed a drainage plan for Ashtead, at an estimated cost of £6,000, but when the work was placed on contract with Bell of Tottenham two years later this had risen to £7,863. Delays were caused by compulsory purchase problems and by dependence on the connection with Leatherhead's sewer outfall under a different local council. As the work at last began in November 1899 Ashtead inhabitants were warned in the *Parish Magazine* that the roads would be unpleasant. Children were told not to loiter because of danger from 'bad smells and fever germs' as cess-pits and sewage-soaked soil were disturbed. Ashtead celebrated 1900, the last year of the 19th century, by moving from the earth closet to the water privy! As 150 navvies moved-in the Council warned of traffic delays. W.H.Holt of the Navvy Mission Society was employed to minister to the navvies in the district. A list of subscribers to the fund supporting Mr Holt included the following note: 'A Working Woman in sympathy . . offers her mite, 6d'. Open-air services were held in Glebe Road. The Rector of Ashtead urged continuing support when the navvies went on to construct the outfall works at Leatherhead.

Law and Order

The Vestry employed a beadle who was paid 10s.6d. per quarter and Mr Millichap, described as 'constable' in 1851, who collected the church rate and was paid £2 2s.0d per annum. In 1871, Millichap was called the beadle; both roles were probably filled by the same man. The enforcement of law and order was shared. In the early 1820s Col Howard's game-keeper arrested two poachers with the help of the blacksmith and two others, brought them before the JP in his own home, and held them in custody at the *Leg of Mutton* until the fine was paid or, if not paid, taken to the Brixton 'treadmill'[5]. In 1857, prisoners were transported via Kingston by magistrates from Epsom and Dorking to the Wandsworth Common House of Correction. George Cubitt of *Denbies*, Surrey Magistrate, advocated a railway from Epsom to the Waterloo line for the purpose[6]. Visitation fees for Quarter Sessions, twice yearly at Epsom and Kingston, were paid by the churchwardens, including £1 for expenses.

Parish Councils established

Under the 1894 Local Government Act a Parish Council was established for Ashtead. A Parish Meeting was to be held annually, to elect a councillor for the Epsom District Council and nine for the Parish Council. The first statutory election was held on 4 December 1894, some animosity being experienced (political, personal and sectarian) from a faction of parishioners. There were 23 nominations for the Parish Council so an adjournment for a deed poll on 18 December followed. George Sayer, of the *Brewery Inn* and a former Overseer, topped the poll easily and the other successful candidates were also well-known figures. Battle, licencee of the *Leg of Mutton* who had appeared at a Vestry Meeting in 1889 as a defender of the working class (much to the displeasure of churchwarden Hue Williams), failed to get elected. The Rector, Lucas, was elected as District Councillor and was subsequently elected for a second term which he concluded in 1900. The new council arrangements finally separated ecclesiastical and parochial affairs, the Vestry retaining only the former – the church building and church moneys.

In June 1900 the following item appeared in the *Parish Magazine*: 'A touching tale to end the Century.....

John Hawkins of the 'Old Workhouse' on the Epsom Road, has asked us to express his thanks to all those who kindly subscribed towards getting him a new Donkey, which was purchased last month from a well-known Boxhill Donkey Dealer for the sum of 55/-. John Hawkins is over 80 years of age and very lame in both legs, but he will now be enabled by means of his new Donkey to get outside his own grounds in order to sell the produce of his garden. He is "at home" most days and both he and his garden are well worth a visit to those who can spare the time to look in'.

On 28 July 1900 John Hawkins was buried, aged 82.

Notes

1. Census reports, 1851 and later
2. Ashtead Parochial Report, 1878/9: SRO, PSH/ATD/15/4.6(2
3. Figures for Charities, 1873/87; SRO, PSH/ATD/GIL/15/4@2–4; see also *Parish Magazines,* 1886–1900
4. Parish Council Minutes, 1897
5. Howard Papers, SRO, 203; D. Robinson, *Surrey History,* 1V, No. 5, 1993, p. 279
6. Evidence to House of Commons on W&D Railway Bill, 4 June 1857. House of Lords Library

Chapter 13

SOCIAL LIFE IN THE
19th CENTURY

THE FIRST 75 YEARS

For three-quarters of a century the life of Ashtead was dominated by the Howards at the *Mansion* in Ashtead Park. Absent though the owners were for long periods on their other estates, their periodic arrival in Ashtead heralded a bustle of activity amongst the thirty or more resident servants and a quickening of the pulse in the village. The *Mansion* was frequently peopled with refined guests who received a hearty welcome and generous hospitality. The perfect gardens, tended by a dozen gardeners, produced an exquisite array of fruit, not least the choicest grapes from the well-known vineries[1]. Col Howard engaged in a round of hunting and shooting on his many estates, which in Ashtead included Newton Wood, Addlestead Wood and 'the 100 acres of shooting'[2]. These acres included the fields and woods south of the Leatherhead Road which his widow, Mary, who herself is reputed to have ridden with the hunt, exchanged with John Hackblock after her husband's death in 1846. In her latter years Mary Howard is found in the company of one or more 'Ladies' including her constant companion, Lady Harriet Paget.

The handful of gentle folk and prosperous tenant farmers had substantial households and also entertained guests. Margaret Silvester, a Professor of Music, was a guest at Street Farm in 1861. At *Merry Hall* in the same year Rebecca King, widow, lived with no less than five unmarried daughters between the ages of 20 and 27, two sons, 19 and 16, and a younger daughter, as well as her 44 year old brother and one servant! Meanwhile the Rector, Mr Legge, kept a bachelor household[3].

Of the social life of the common people during the first 75 years of the century nothing specific is known from the Ashtead records. Working hours were long with little time for leisure. There were no bank holidays, May Day being the main celebration of the year.

INNS AND PUBLIC HOUSES
THROUGHOUT THE CENTURY

At the beginning of the century, all three 18th century Ashtead inns had been acquired by Richard Howard: the *Berkshire Arms*, the *Haunch of Venison* and the *Leg of Mutton & Cauliflower*[4]. They catered not only for local needs but in particular for traffic passing through Ashtead coming to and from London. The *Berkshire Arms*, standing back at the north-east end of The Street and run by the Westons then at Street Farm next door, disappeared in the late 1820s, although the grocer's shop in front of it continued to trade. The *Haunch of Venison*, later the site of *Forest Lodge* (see p 232), was frequented by the carriers with heavy wagons travelling from the coast to the growing London metropolis with, for example, French merchandise and fresh fish from the port of Shoreham. It was also a local tradesmen's and farmers' club, a sort of unregistered Friendly Society which also organised an annual May day festival in the village. The opening of the railway from the Sussex coast to London via Redhill in the early 1840s killed off much of the lucrative trade from the carriers. The local railway did the same for the passenger coach traffic in the early 1860s (see p 83). Terms were agreed for the transfer of the licence and business to the *Leg of Mutton*, the *Haunch* becoming a private residence.

The *Leg of Mutton & Cauliflower*, or the 'Leg' as it was commonly called, in the village centre, was a farm as well as an inn, having $13\frac{1}{2}$ acres in 1802, some behind the house and the rest in the North Field[5]. The yard and farm buildings were extensive (see inset to Wyburd map, p 52) but the accommodation was very limited at the end of the 18th century, with no bedrooms for guests[6]. The inn was used for meetings of the court baron, the coroner's court and for the landowners' allotment of enclosed fields in 1838. Felons were kept temporarily in its custody[7]. In mid-century, with the demise of the other inns, the *Leg* became the principal posting house.

By 1879 the *Leg of Mutton* had become the most important Public House, with Skilton, as the licensed victualler. The farm had

Fig. 20.   Leg of Mutton & Cauliflower Inn, 1860. LDLHS Collection

increased to 74 acres, extending over much of the former North
Field west of Woodfield Lane, as well as land at the centre of the
village. Skilton, in 1860, advertised that he not only supplied families with new-laid eggs, milk and butter but also the Royal Benevolent College at Epsom since it had opened in 1855. The inn in
1879 had seven bedrooms and three attics, and six rooms for public and private club use. The farm buildings next to it included several stables, wagon lodge, cow houses, piggeries and a barn[8]. The
property was not sold in the 1879 Sale but the inn and land round
it came back on the market in 1880[9]. In 1887 ownership was in the
name of W.G. Bradley, William Battle being the landlord[10].

There was a malthouse business at *Merry Hall* in the 18th century run by the Syms family who lived there. This may have supplied Ashtead with malt for its staple drink, ale and porter, drunk
with meals before the arrival of the water mains in the 1880s.
Agates Lane was called Brewhouse Lane at one time[11]. The property was bought in 1835 by the King family, formerly of West Farm,
and brewing may have ceased. In 1839 there was a beer shop at the
junction of Common Lane (Woodfield Lane) and The Street, the site
of the future *Brewery Inn*[12]. In mid-century brewing began in or
behind this shop, George Sayer being the brewer in 1851, employ-

Fig. 21.   Ashtead Brewery and Brewery Inn, c. 1870. LDLHS Collection

ing five labourers in 1871 and supplying 'genuine ale and porter to the Trade and Families'. His son George followed him, the brewery manager and owner in 1891[13]. Hops were grown on the southern border of the parish in 1839 but the quality was sometimes poor[14].

The *Woodman*, a rival beer shop to the brewery, grew up near the Woodfield during the century. In the early years it was a house in an orchard but successive occupants may have supplied the locals with a brew. The navvies who built the railway in 1857–9 were partial to their beer, which they obtained from a mobile store until a magistrate's licence was granted for the beer house. The second group of navvies of 1866 were better served. In 1887 it was in the hands of the same Bradley who bought the *Leg of Mutton*, Smithers being the publican[15]. In 1906 the owners were Page and Overton, the firm which still owned it in 1954[16]. The Public Houses had thus been restored from the Howards to ownership by private individuals or companies by the end of the century. The growth of beer shops from the middle of the century may have been accompanied by more drinking by the labouring classes, the well-to-do drinking wines and spirits at home.

THE LAST 25 YEARS OF THE CENTURY
In common with the nearby metropolis, drunkenness increased in Ashtead in the 1880s, evoking a strong response from Victorian

Fig. 22. Quoits players, c. 1885. LDLHS Collection

society and the church. An Ashtead branch of the Church of England Temperance Society was formed in 1884 by the Rector, the
Rev. Adamson. Regular well-attended meetings were held at which
eminent speakers drove the message home, often from personal
experience, that alcoholism was the cause of degradation and
poverty. The *Parish Magazine* periodically carried a recipe for
'stokos' as an alternative to alcohol: '$\frac{1}{4}$lb or more of fine oatmeal,
6oz sugar loaf, and $\frac{1}{2}$ lemon, sliced. Mix in pan with a little warm
water; add 1 gallon of boiling water; stir thoroughly; drink hot or
cold. Costs 3d (old pence) a gallon.' This drink was claimed to be
particularly suitable for drinking in warm weather, for example, by
labourers in the fields[17].

The Working Men's Club, founded in the 1880s as a social club
for men, had its premises in The Street. The first President was the
Ashtead Rector, the Rev. F.G.L. Lucas, who held the office for many
years. Open at midday and during the evening, it provided bagatelle
boards, tables for cards, chess and other games, daily papers and
periodicals, for members who paid eight old pence per month.
Smoking was allowed; smoking concerts were held; biscuits, ginger
beer, etc. were available but no liquor. Entertainments were held in
the Church School room. In 1888 a very popular Nigger-Minstrel
concert was given, and in 1896 a successful concert helped provide
funds for a second room at the club. The church also ran a coffee

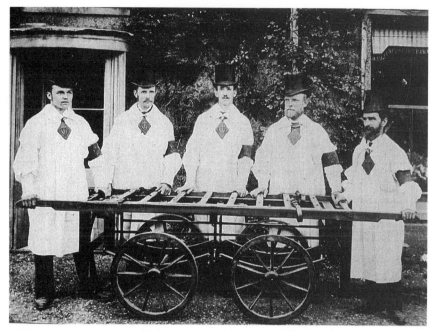

Fig. 23. Ashtead Burial Guild, 1895, outside the Old Rectory. Left to right: G. Chitty, George Lisney. T. Goldsmith J. May and John Fowler. (Courtesy, the Rector of Ashtead).

room in The Street in the 1880s in another attempt to provide alternatives to the public houses.

In 1893 the Ashtead Burial Guild was formed with J. Fowler (of *Fowler's Cottage*), a leading member of the Temperance Society, as its secretary. Its purpose was to provide an alternative to the use of non-churchgoing bearers, to provide a service for the poor and to avoid drunkenness after funerals. The coffin was to be conveyed on a bier, the wheels of which were without tyres for several years. The bearers wore smocks which are said to have been cruder than those normally seen in Surrey[18].

The Excursionists

The Woodfield and the Common attracted many day visitors brought by the railway from London and its growing suburbs. Many gypsies, costermongers and undesirable travellers saw in them an easy source of income. In 1889 the Steward of the Manor forbade swings, stalls, vehicles, donkeys etc on the Common; tents were not to be erected without permission. The editor of the *Parish Magazine* supported this action but was sorry to spoil the children's

fun. The profits of the tea rooms on both sides of the railway continued to come in. The Rector deplored the drunkenness that was
rife on the Common; the magistrates turned down an application
for the conversion of the *Woodman* beer house into a fully licensed
public house. Another group of recreation-seeking excursionists
were the cyclists, a great many of whom passed through Ashtead
on their way to the country towards the end of the century. Some
patronised the hostelries, while others availed themselves of the
water at the drinking fountain in The Street. This had been erected
by parishioners in 1879 in memory of Mary Howard.

Local entertainments

Entertainment for the community outside the home was provided
by a round of concerts held mainly in the Church School room and
in the summer by excursions and outdoor events. These were usually well-attended, both children and adults being catered for. A
favourite in the 1880s had been the annual evening concert on Boxing Day, arranged as a wholesome alternative to the drunkenness
and disorder prevalent on this evening. There were frequent concerts in the 1890s which usually consisted of the rendering of songs
by local and visiting talents and of other musical items. At one such
in April 1895 the Crampshaw Works brass band made its first and
very successful appearance and the Rector sang Harrow school
songs. In 1898 the Christmas season was particularly notable. At
the two performances on Boxing Day two very amusing farces entitled *Number One Round the Corner* and *My Lord in Livery* were
given in the Church School before a large audience including Mr
and Mrs Ralli. Four gallons of coffee were consumed, with plenty
of buns and bread and butter. On the following day, the Rallis gave
their annual school treat, also at the Church School. The smaller
children were prevented from going that year because of rain but
those who did go enjoyed the antics of 'A Musical Clown' who had
a special line in drawing outline sketches in charcoal. After tea every
boy and girl went home with a new sixpence and a bag of sweets.

On 2 January 1899 an Old People's dinner was given to the over-
60s by the churchwarden, Hue Williams, and his wife at the *Rosary*,
Mr Curwood's tea-rooms south of the railway beside the Woodfield.
Traps were sent to fetch those unable to walk and a company of
eighty sat down to the meal at 1.45 pm. The oldest there was 90,
a child when Napoleon Bonaparte was the bogeyman, and an exam-

ple to all of how to enjoy the party. Speeches, songs and fun went on all afternoon, the house being brought down by *The Old Man's Darling*. Carriages summoned for 4.15 were kept waiting for an hour while tea was served.

Every opportunity was taken for such amusements by many different groups. In November 1898 the choirboys were invited to Downsend, the home of S. Johnson, for fireworks. Beautiful wheels, a 'flying pigeon', excellent rockets, a fine balloon and a blazing bonfire, with squibs, crackers and coloured lights gave the boys a great time. Concerts were held to raise funds for the Church School, the church building, the Working Men's Club, the Cricket Club and many other causes.

Every summer from 1890 Pantia Ralli gave a party in the Park for the domestic staff and others who were in his service; usually over a hundred were present.

Outings were arranged each summer for the choirboys and the choirmen separately, sometimes with the bell-ringers, and for members of the Temperance Society, frequently shared with groups from Leatherhead, Epsom and Ewell. The railway sometimes put on special excursions, destinations including Brighton, Hastings, Eastbourne, Portsmouth, Dover and the London Zoo. The railway sometimes failed to come up to expectations: unpunctuality in 1888 threatened the return journey of one outing to Dover and the train, it was said, would have been later but for the 'judicious application of an accelerating coin in the palm of the guard and engine driver'! An adult outing often meant an early start at 7.00am and a late return to Ashtead at 10.15pm or 11.00.

Sport

If the church provided all the best entertainments and outings (and we have no record of any others) it was also to the fore in the development of village sport. The Rev. Francis Lucas, son of the Lord of the Manor, was a cricketer of some repute and the *Parish Magazine* carried full reports of each cricket match in which an Ashtead team played between 1886 and the mid-1890s. In the earliest recorded match, played in the Park on 31 August 1886 between Ashtead teams, Mr Lucas scored 102 runs and took three wickets. At that time he was curate of St. Margaret's Church, Westminster, and the following year he brought a team from there which beat the Ashtead village team by an innings and 23 runs. This game was played on the new ground in Woodfield Lane lent to the newly-constituted cricket club by Sir Thomas Lucas "our worthy Squire" in time for the 1887 season. As Rector of Ashtead in the 1888 season and onwards, the Rev. Francis Lucas played for Ashtead, as also did two successive curates, the Revs. Milne and Green Price. In 1892 the latter topped the batting averages with 438 runs in twenty innings, average 25.7, while Mr Lucas was third with 325 in fourteen innings, average 23.2. In July Mr Lucas took 9 wickets for 8 runs against Downside, Cobham. Hue Williams, churchwarden, and three other members of his family also played for Ashtead that year.

In 1891 the land used by the cricket club was owned by the Ashtead Land Company which required improvements to be made in the pavilion. Pantia Ralli, Lord of the Manor from 1889, had hired the land but in 1899 he gave it up to the company. The club arranged a seven-year lease at £10 per annum and a year later issued an appeal to members for a new pavilion. The club thus gradually became independent of the church and manor. A football club had been formed in 1894, players wearing dark and light blue colours in halves. The club had difficulty in finding a field but in 1898 was using the cricket club ground in winter. A lawn tennis club was formed in 1896. There was also a golf club for which the subscription was 15 old shillings (75p) per half year and to which a silver bowl was presented for competition in 1900. There were racehorse owners and jockeys in Ashtead. Derby Day was a great attraction to the local inhabitants. The children were sent home early during Derby week to avoid the crowds. An annual tea was provided by Mrs Denshire on the Friday after the race for those children who had attended school and had not gone to the races.

Queen Victoria's Golden Jubilee was celebrated by everyone in 1887 and her Diamond Jubilee in 1897. On the first occasion a huge bonfire was lit in the King's Grove field in Crampshaw Lane on the night of the Jubilee but the main local celebration took place a week later as authorized. The parish church was crowded for a service, processions were led by the Leatherhead band, and teas were served in tents in the cricket field. This was followed by games, illuminations and fireworks. Donations were made to the proposed new Epsom Cottage Hospital to be built to commemorate the occasion. In 1897 the day of the Jubilee was made a public holiday and many residents went to London to see the procession. Those who stayed behind were treated to tea, with sports, dancing, fireworks and another huge bonfire at the top of Crampshaw Lane after dark.

Notes

1. Paget, op cit. (see p. 49)
2. Sale Catalogue, 1879.
3. Census Abstracts.
4. 'Ashtead Past and Present' in *Ashtead Parish Magazine*, April 1903.
5. Wyburd Survey, 1802.
6. SRO/4/11a; R.A. Lever, 'Leg of Mutton & Cauliflower Inn in 18th century', *Procs LDLHS*, 4(6), 1982, pp. 165–6
7. D. Robinson, 'Crime and punishment in Surrey', *Surrey History* 4(5) 1993
8. Sale Catalogue, 1879
9. Plan with Estate Sale Catalogue 1880 (courtesy T. Devitt)
10. Altered Tithe Apportionment, 1887: PRO IR 29–34/6; Society records
11. Wyburd Survey, 1802; & G.J. Gollin, *Bygone Ashtead* (1987) p. 117
12. Tithe Apportionment, 1887.
13. Census abstracts
14. Wyburd Survey, 1802; & SRO/203/28/21
15. Tithe Apportionment, 1887
16. *Ashtead Parish Magazine*, Feb 1906; Ashtead PCC papers 1954/5
17. The information in this and subsequent paragraphs is taken mainly from the *Ashtead Parish Magazines*.
18. Mary Alexander "An Ashtead Funeral Smock" *Procs LDLHS*, 4(10), 1986, p. 267

Chapter 14

THE EDWARDIAN PERIOD AND THE PRELUDE TO WAR (1901–14)

The new century, which was to change the look of Ashtead so much, was just over a year old when Queen Victoria died and Edward VII came to the throne. The whole village joined in a commemorative service on the day after the Queen's funeral and muffled bells were tolled[1]. The mood was quite different in the following year when the Boer War ended, the church bells sounding a victory peal on 2 June 1902[2]. This was soon followed by the celebrations for Edward VII's Coronation on 9 August that year: to mark the occasion, Ashtead was en féte, with sports on the Cricket Ground and a bonfire on the Common at nightfall[3]. The next day there was a special service at St. Giles' Church. Not long after this, the local 'returned warriors' of the Boer War were entertained to dinner, 170 of them, in Woodfield Hall close to the Common; the ceremony was chaired by Pantia Ralli, the owner of Ashtead Park[4]. In church affairs, the most important event was the building of St George's Church, consecrated in 1906 (see p. 167). Close to the end of this pre-war period, the Coronation of George V in 1911 gave Ashtead another opportunity to display a festive mood like the rest of the country.

In the years before 1914, a string of government decisions affected Ashtead's everyday life. The 1902 Education Act[5] made the County Council responsible for the village schools, leading in 1906 to the building of Ashtead Council School (see p. 184). In 1908, pensions for the old were introduced while three years later Lloyd George's Insurance Act created the doctor's panel and the insurance stamp, protecting the poor, disabled and aged from hardship through illness or unemployment. This Act looked forward to the

Welfare State of the 1940s. The Shops Act in the same year granted a weekly half-day holiday for the first time to all shop workers.

At the local level, the Ashtead Parish Council frequently debated the deficiency of its fire brigade, the performance of the street lighting and the quality of the water supplies, though there was general approval that since 1900 the village had had a fully adequate water drainage and sewage system. The Ashtead Fire Brigade, so much talked about by the Council, had been formed in October 1901 with eight members, a hose cart, some small items of equipment and two hydrants (five more on order); the cart and appliances were first held at the *Leg of Mutton & Cauliflower* inn but in 1908 they ended up being kept at Haynes' Stables in Agates Lane. Alan Hicks was the Captain at this time, to be succeeded late in 1912 by Aubrey Marshall, the son of the Chairman of the Parish Council. There were long discussions as to whether a motor fire engine should be purchased but no decision was reached and the outbreak of war in 1914 closed the matter until peace came. Policing of the village was also very much a Council concern, heightened by the spate of burglaries in the district. There was, it seems, only one policeman regularly on duty and the Council asked for the number to be increased[6].

The postal services were still run from a counter in The Street as they had been in the Victorian period. Mrs Mary Stewart took over the post office in 1908, running it from a stationer's shop at 51, The Street. She handed over the counter to H.B. Johnson in late 1911/early 1912 who moved it the following year to his printing premises a few doors away. A sub-post office was established in Barnett Wood Lane in 1906 at Charles Gibbs' saddler's shop, moving in the next year to Tom Steer's grocer's shop at the west corner of Glebe Road.

The Growing Village

Ashtead's population grew rapidly during this period, from 1,881 in 1901 to 2,921 in 1911. New housing was to change the village over these years. Much of the building work was in the west of the parish where Edgar Littlewood and his brother Lionel erected substantial middle class houses around Skinners Lane, Ottways Lane and The Mead. They also worked in Oakfield Road where a rival builder, Joe Curwood, built some large villas. Curwood was active as well in Highfields and was responsible for the cottages close to

Fig. 24.   Ashtead Post Office Staff, October 1911 (Courtesy, Mrs G. Mooring). Mary Stewart, Postmistress, stands in the centre, with Postmaster Berry of Epsom seated to her left. Behind him is Charlie Putland, a senior postman. LDLHS Collection

the Woodfield Pond. Another prominent builder was George Baker, who concentrated on small houses in Church Road, also building the hall there. Other parts of Ashtead were not neglected by the developers. By 1914, there were several new houses, with spacious gardens, along Leatherhead Road, Ermyn Way and Grange Road, as well as along Woodfield Lane, Meadow Road and The Marld[7].

Many of the new residents were professional men, commuting daily to London, including barristers, solicitors and civil servants. However, some of these made their living in Ashtead: in 1907, there were no less than six doctors who had surgeries in the village[8]; two were in Oakfield Road, three in The Street and one in Woodfield Lane. A dentist practised in Barnett Wood Lane. Ashtead's health was therefore in good hands, but for hospital treatment the villagers had to go to Epsom or to the newly-opened Queen Victoria Memorial Hospital (now Victoria House) in Leatherhead.

Farming and New Industries
Despite the influx of so many people from outside the district, Ashtead for a few more years retained its farming traditions and

occupations closely linked with the land. Even so, there were now only three farms compared with at least twice that number in the mid-19th century, Woodfield Farm in Woodfield Lane, West Farm in Harriotts Lane and Park Farm (or Home Farm), associated with Ashtead Park. Cereal production at the farms continued to fall as it had done since the early 1880s, but with more arable land turned to pasture the farmer could look to dairying with increasing success. Small-scale industry, which had started late in Queen Victoria's reign, continued into this century[9]. Sparrow's brick-works was doing well in the early 1900s but fell on bad times and ceased trading in 1909. Photographic plate and paper were manufactured by Cadett & Neall at the Victoria Works and the Crampshaw Works; though success-ful, the firm was bought out by the Eastman Kodak Company in 1903 and five years later the plant was moved away from the dis-trict. Electrical accumulators were made by Peto & Radford Ltd at the Greville Works. Another firm, Swabey & Saunders, were leather manufacturers in premises now occupied by Woodfield Close. In 1912, the Victoria Works was being used for making private cars.

Road Transport
The first motor bus through Ashtead was on one of the Sunday ser-vices developed by the London General Omnibus Company before the First World War, which gave Londoners the opportunity to make excursions into the countryside. The earliest vehicles were of the solid-tyred, double-deck, open-top type. Travel on these was not without hazard, as is shown by the need of excursionists to the Derby in 1913 for first aid to remove particles of tar which had been thrown up off the roads and had lodged in their eyes[10]. In May 1914 the weekends only service, Route 107 between Clapham Com-mon and Epsom, was extended through Ashtead to Dorking, on Sundays only. This became a daily service in May 1916.

Long-distance carriers continued to operate to and from London despite powerful railway competition although, in the rural areas south of Dorking, most carriers operated short journeys. In 1904 services ran twice weekly from Dorking to London, and from South Holmwood to London, via Dorking. Ten years later these two ser-vices to London stood out from others which were of a predomi-nantly local character. In 1914, the service from South Holmwood was shown as being routed by way of Leatherhead and Epsom, and would have passed through Ashtead.

Fig. 25.   Junction of The Street and Rectory Lane, early 20th century. (Courtesy, Bob Gibb).

Fig. 26.   Crampshaw Works c. 1900, built by Cadett & Neall Ltd on land between Parker's Lane and Rectory Lane. (Courtesy, Worsfold family).

Fig. 27. A coursing meet at Ashtead, off Park Lane in Edwardian times. Second from left, Ralph Steere, Reddick with Sharp behind. Ralph Sayer and far right, Goldsmith. (Courtesy, Mrs G. Mooring).

Fig. 28. Matten's Tea Gardens, Rectory Lane. This was an attraction for Edwardian cyclist visitors to Ashtead. The photograph is thought to date from about 1910. (Courtesy, John Gent Collection).

Road transport has always produced characters and one of these was the American multi-millionaire, Alfred Gwynne Vanderbilt. He exercised his penchant for stage coach operation, and often acted as the driver of his own coaches, dressed as for Ascot races, complete with grey top hat. He had been active on the Brighton (via Reigate) and Portsmouth runs from London since 1908. He operated on the route to Brighton through Epsom, Ashtead and Dorking between 1910 and. 1914. On the run to Brighton, lunch was taken at the Burford Bridge Hotel. Vanderbilt died at sea in May 1915 when the *Lusitania* was torpedoed.

Ashtead's Railway: Edwardian Changes

On 2 February 1901 at least one Ashtead observer stood at Lady Howard's Crossing and saw the late Queen Victoria's funeral train pound up the gradient from the direction of the station en route from the Isle of Wight to London (Victoria). It was late and the driver of the 4-4-0 locomotive No 54 *Empress* was desperately trying to make up time with his royal cortège, six royal saloons and two other coaches. Then Ashtead's railway settled down into its accustomed operations.

In 1902 and 1903 the Joint Companies – the London, Brighton & South Coast Co. (LBSC) and London & South-West Co. (LSW) – spent nearly £12,000 renewing the track between Epsom and Leatherhead. As far back as 1872 an Inspector had expressed his concern at its condition. While platelaying, a ganger named Silver was awarded £1 for saving the life of a child who fell out of a passing train into the path of another. A footpath off Ashtead Woods Road named 'Sleepers' Alley' was fenced with old railway sleepers which were being sold. In 1903 Ashtead's platforms were extended again to take longer trains which were taking the increasing number of passengers from the suburbs to London. This entailed moving the points which had led into the single siding in the yard since 1859. A second line was laid into the yard and in 1907 the roadway in the yard was made up, the trader's rents being raised. In 1904 a new crossover on the Epsom side of the level crossing was built, enabling locomotives on 'Up' goods to put wagons in and out of the yard without the use of horses and tow rope.

Few goods trains called at Ashtead: one LSW stopped for five minutes about 7.45 a.m., and briefly in the evening. Two 'Down' LBSC goods called after the mid-1880s if required and one 'Up'

Fig. 29. Alfred Vanderbilt's stage-coach 'The Venture' driving through Ashtead in 1914. LDLHS Collection

goods at 4.5 a.m.. Several other goods trains passed through Ashtead without stopping, all LBSC, many of them at night.

Many travellers cycled to the station and to meet their increasing numbers the cycle sheds were extended in 1907. Two years later the second footbridge was built and in 1911 the station was renovated. A long standing dispute with the Rural District Council was at last settled about the road leading to the station: the railway agreed to pay for kerbs and the making up of the paths, with a small annual sum for maintenance. When the war broke out in 1914, the government took over the railways, and in 1923 the Epsom & Leatherhead Joint Committee disappeared in the amalgamation of the LSW and LBSC and other companies to form the new Southern Railway.

Village Life

The Coronation celebrations at Ashtead for Edward VII in 1902 and for George V in 1911, already mentioned, were days to remember by everyone but year in year out there were plenty of other occasions, sporting and convivial, to keep the spirits high. Every year, many flocked to Epsom on Derby Day and some were probably there when Edward VII's horse, Minoru, won the race in 1909. More people were now taking day trips by train to the country and coast and some used the new motor buses, whilst the wealthy flaunted their motor cars.

Football and cricket were popular in the village and both clubs, formed in the late 19th century, had full fixture lists with neighbouring towns and villages. In May 1902, the two clubs played each other at cricket in a match called 'Flannelled Fools' v 'Muddied Oafs', won, not surprisingly, by the cricketers; and in the next month there was a 'Married' v 'Single' cricket match, won easily by the married men[11] The cricket and football clubs continued to have friendly relations, dining together early in 1909 at the Woodfield Hall[12]. Tennis and golf were also played. Many of the large houses had tennis courts in their gardens. A golf course, begun as part of the planned Warren Estate development, was advertised in 1912 but it was never completed[13]. Ashtead's 'Country Cinema', in the hall along Church Road, was advertised in 1912/13 as 'the only picture palace in the district'; it was also used for dancing and roller skating[14].

The Village Fête was the highlight of the year in 1907, the first year that it had been arranged. It was held in late July on the Cricket Ground, with flags and bunting round the ground, sporting competitions and dancing after dark. In the winter months, a successful series of University Extension Lectures often took place in the Parish Room. The novelist, E.M. Forster, came here in 1909 to give a number of lectures[15].

Notes

1. *Parish Magazine* (*P.M.*), Feb. 1901
2. *P.M.*, July 1902
3. *P.M.*, Aug. 1902
4. *P.M.*, Dec. 1902
5. D. Robinson, *Surrey Through the Century, 1889–1989* (1989), p. 13
6. *P.M.*, Jan. 1912
7. Alan A. Jackson (ed) *Ashtead: A Village Transformed* (1977) pp. 101–4
8. Kelly's Directory, 1907
9. Alan A. Jackson (ed) (1977) op. cit.
   pp. 98–9
10. *The Southdown Story: A History of Southdown Motor Services, 1915–65*, p. 47
11. *P.M.*, July 1902
12. *P.M.*, March 1909
13. *P.M.*, Feb. 1901; advertisement for Warren Estate in *Where to Live in Rural London's Southern Side*, (1912/13)
14. *P.M.*, March 1913
15. *P.M.*, Nov. 1909

Chapter 15

THE FIRST WORLD WAR

Eight months before the outbreak of the First World War, William Batstone, an 87 year old veteran of the Crimean War, was laid to rest in Ashtead churchyard, his coffin escorted to the church by seven men of the East Surrey Regiment[1]. Another war was soon to come and this was the Regiment or its Territorials which thirty-four Ashtead men joined in 1914, out of a total of 130 who enlisted to serve their country. They ranged in rank from Surgeon-General H.A. Whitehead and Major F. Gascoigne to F. Pritchard, a stoker on *H.M.S. Bristol*. The women and children of the parish, through the Waifs and Strays Society, made special efforts to provide clothing and funds for service families in need. The Aldershot C.O. acknowledged the receipt of 101 blankets collected by Ashtead in October 1914 for the troops. Later, the Victoria Works was taken over to serve as an Army clothing depot.

During the first months of the war, Ashtead was the base for the 21st Battalion of the Royal Fusiliers (University and Public Schools Brigade). Several hundred men, some fresh from school, were billeted in the village[2]. One cottager wryly remembered two young men coming from an exercise digging trenches on the Common, flinging themselves with their dirty boots on the white counterpanes of the beds prepared for them. Church parades were held at St Giles' or in the open fields and on 13 October 1914 King George V came to Ashtead to inspect the Battalion. At first, the companies marched back and forth through the village in civilian clothes and when their uniforms arrived they were asked by the parishioners to donate their suits for jumble! The Battalion helped to build a Convalescent Hospital in Woodcote Park just outside the parish boundary, which was

Fig. 30. New recruits, October 1914. They are marching past Felton's refreshment rooms and Woodfield House, beside Ashtead Common. LDLHS Collection

soon filled with wounded from the Front and was visited by the King and Queen.

Many of the young men from Ashtead and the neighbouring districts who had volunteered so eagerly to answer Kitchener's call to arms at the start of the war were killed or wounded in its early months. Every week the local papers were filled with accounts of heroic deeds and of lost or wrecked lives. These stories brought home to everyone that the early cry of 'over by Christmas' was not to happen. Although Ashtead's life in the fields and at home no doubt continued as best it could, the seriousness of the war, leaving aside the news of casualties, was brought home to them by lighting restrictions imposed early in 1915, soon after the first Zeppelin raids on London[3]. Householders who showed too much light at night were fined and special constables who had been appointed in January that year watched over this as well as the conduct of troops billeted in the village[4]. There were said to be about 1,500 soldiers based in Ashtead at this time[5]. The army commanders were sufficiently aware of damage by ill-disciplined troops to issue an Order saying that 'Great care is to be taken by troops of all arms when training to avoid doing damage to wheat and young seeds and they must also keep at a distance from sheep folds and lambing pens'[6].

Local papers in 1916 were fuller than ever with details of the heavy casualties of the war and the general sombre picture they gave was made more so when on 11 March there was published a Defence of the Realm Instruction in the Case of Invasion: this stated that 'if a state of emergency were announced the people of Ashtead who wished to move to safer places should assemble at the Cricket Field'[7]. Many more Ashtead men had by now been called to the colours, since early in 1916 conscription was introduced for all men between eighteen and forty-one. There was still, however, a Surrey Volunteers Regiment and its Ashtead platoon was reported to be in camp at Headley in August 1916[8].

There were food shortages in 1917, though Ashtead farmers had considerably extended their normal crop-growing areas on orders from the Surrey War Agricultural Committee[9]. In February that year there was a serious fire at the British Film Stock Company's works in Crampshaw Lane, dealt with efficiently by the Ashtead Fire Brigade, with help from the Epsom and Leatherhead Brigades. Food rationing was introduced early in 1918[10] and a National Kitchen was established in Ashtead. Its later accounts showed how popular it had been[11]. When coal soon became difficult to get the Parish Council recommended that the timber and bracken of the Common should be used to meet fuel needs[12].

Thanksgiving for the end of the war was celebrated at St Giles' Church on 17 November 1918. A peal of bells – Grandsire Triples with 5,040 changes lasting three hours – had been rung here a few days before by the Surrey Association of Change Ringers. This was the first unmuffled peal of bells in Ashtead since the declaration of war in 1914.

The Rector, the Rev. R.A. Waddilove, maintained worship at the two Ashtead churches throughout the war. Open-air services were held on Sunday evenings in summer after the Summertime Act came into force in 1916. There were memorial services to those killed in action, including one for Capt Kenneth J. Maples on 30 May 1915, another for George Taylor of the Royal West Surreys on 27 Feb. 1916, and a third, on 13 June 1916, for Lord Kitchener. The Rector was single-handed in 1918, the services alternating between St Giles' and St George's. Canon Hunter, former Vicar of Christchurch, Epsom, gave much assistance as did many other visiting clergy.

The British Legion Roll of Honour recorded the names of sixty-two Ashtead men who gave their lives in the First World War. Seventeen of these were 1914 volunteers, including ten privates and

Fig. 31. Peace celebrations at Ashtead Cricket Field, 4 August 1919. LDLHS Collection

four officers. In 1934, the names on the Roll inscribed in the Golden Book were placed in a case in the chancel of St Giles' Church. A War Memorial was erected in 1920 close to the north-west corner of St George's Church.

Notes

1. Except where otherwise stated, information on church matters is taken from the *Parish Magazine*, also the Worsfold Collection and the St Giles' Service Registers
2. *The History of the Royal Fusiliers, 'U.P.S'.* (1917) pp. 48, 52–64
3. A.J.P. Taylor, *English History, 1914–45* (1965), pp. 43–4
4. *Leatherhead Advertiser, (L.A.)* 9 Jan. 1915
5. *L.A*, 9 Jan. 1915
6. *L.A*, 13 March 1915
7. *L.A*, 11 March 1915
8. *L.A*, 26 August 1916
9. *L.A*, 29 Jan. 1916
10. A.J.P. Taylor (1965) op. cit. p. 95
11. *L.A*, 2 Feb. 1918
12. *L.A*, 26 Oct. 1918

Chapter 16

THE INTER-WAR YEARS

Between the First and Second World Wars there were many changes in Ashtead, especially after the sale of the Ashtead Park estate in 1924 on the death of its owner, Pantia Ralli, and in the 1930s with the rapid expansion of suburban type housing estates. Ashtead was to lose much of its rural aspect in these years, becoming more and more a commuter village.

The Aftermath of War
At the end of the First World War in November 1918 there was a natural anxiety in Ashtead, as elsewhere, concerning the future. After the excitement of the return of the soldiers home it soon became clear that there would be many hardships to face. The cost of living had increased since 1914, affecting all those with small incomes. Concerns about the future, however, were put aside for a while in the midsummer of 1919 when everyone took part in the nation-wide Peace Celebrations. These were arranged for 19 July in London, but Ashtead held theirs on August Bank Holiday Monday[1]. A Grandsire Triple peal of bells was rung at St Giles' Church and later that morning 250 service men sat down to a 'splendid repast' at the Council School in Barnett Wood Lane, with Maj-General J.W.G. Tulloch as special guest. After this, the band of the 2nd Battalion The Queen's (Royal West Surrey Regiment) led the way to the cricket field, which was beflagged and garlanded with laurels and evergreens. The day finished with sports, fancy dress displays, an open-air concert and fireworks.

THE TWENTIES

During the early 1920s, unemployment and low wages for those at work promoted the fledgling Labour Party's interests in the Ashtead area. The Labour candidate for Epsom, Dr Somerville Hastings, was a frequent visitor here, but despite much local support he was defeated at the General Election by the Tory candidate, Sir Rowland Blades[2]. Ways to relieve unemployment continued to be discussed by party activists and by the Parish Council, which in October 1922 recommended that 'road improvements could provide work in the winter months'. In late November, the Council advised the setting aside of land for new allotments, some 'adjoining the main Leather-head Road'[3]. As in the past, Friendly Societies provided help for those in need; the 83rd annual meeting of one of these took place at the *Leg of Mutton & Cauliflower* early in February 1925[4].

A substantial village hall had long been wanted and in the early 1920s there were many fund-raising events to support the project. The foundation stone of the Peace Memorial Hall was laid on 21 June 1924. Sir Rowland Blades officially opened the building at a

Fig. 32. The Peace Memorial Hall Committee, 1920, outside Ashtead Park House. Front row sitting L to R: Miss Denshire, Revd R.A. Waddilove (Rector), Mr & Mrs Pantia Ralli, Mr M.W. Marshall. Standing L to R: Mr Aclam, Capt Slater, Mr Bissiker, Capt (later Col) Hughes, Mr S. Wilcox (with button hole), Mr Andrews, Mr Dyer and Mr Winteridge, builder. (Courtesy, Worsfold family).

Fig. 33.   John Wyatt, blacksmith, at the Forge, Rectory Lane, 1920s. LDLHS Collection

ceremony on 3 November that year[5]. It soon became an important centre of village life. The long-established Village Club continued to be popular in these years, arranging competitions and many other events.

By the late 1920s, Woodfield Farm was the only working farm in Ashtead after West Farm had been lost to developers, though there was a model dairy at Park Farm in 1927. In the same year, Farrant & Hoyle were continuing as grainers and the Wyatts were still pursuing their long-established business as wheelwrights and smiths in Rectory Lane[6]. Many of the villagers were employed in a variety of shops, also in light industries. These included, apart from a number of builders, the Brifex Company at the Crampshaw Works, making leather cloth and other goods; Foster's Machine Tool and Engine Company in Woodfield Lane; and Ashtead Potters Ltd, which was established in 1923 and soon to become well-known as a producer of fine pottery (see p. 206)[7]. The Rayon Manufacturing Company opened its works at Ermyn Way in 1928, but production difficulties forced it to close down four years later.

Fig. 34.   Woodfield Farm c. 1925. LDLHS Collection

Ashtead's normally quiet working life was disrupted by the General Strike of May 1926 which, though it lasted for only just over a week, brought much of the country, including the trains, almost to a standstill. Since Ashtead had many commuters who travelled daily by train to work in London the effect was disturbing, but limited rail and bus services were run by volunteers[8]. It took some time for the day-to-day life to get back to normal after the strike ended, but business soon recovered.

Population and Housing

At the 1921 Census, Ashtead had a population of 3,226 which increased to 4,783 in 1931, nearly 50% in ten years. As in the immediate pre-war decades, Ashtead was continuing to attract commuters. After the end of the First World War, builders were quick to acquire land where they could erect houses for purchase by outsiders, mainly Londoners. George Baker, who had been active in Ashtead for some years, soon filled-in the gaps in his Church Road estate and, when land from West Farm came on the market, he sold plots for housing in Harriotts Lane and Barnett Wood Lane; he was also offering building land for sale along Links Road. The Warren

Fig. 35.   Ashtead Fire Brigade, 1920, outside Gayton House. LDLHS Collection

Fig. 36.   Jesse Killick, fishmonger, and Bill Gardiner outside No 4 Rectory Lane. (Courtesy, Mrs Dorothy Chitty).

Estate was another area developed at this time, mainly for large houses, one of the finest being *High Warren*, completed in 1922, the home for many years of Sir Arthur and Lady Duckham (of Duckham Oils)[9]. A small group of houses was built in the 1920s in Howard Close, each containing bed-sitting rooms for single women and widows on modest incomes. In 1926–29, bungalows were erected on large plots in Grange Road and Leatherhead Road.

Other specialized housing developed in Ashtead around this time included that by the Ashtead Potters Housing Society Ltd, which was registered in April 1925, to provide housing for the disabled ex-service pottery employees. Houses in Park Lane and Purcell Close were developed for this purpose, to commemorate Kathleen Purcell, Lady Weaver, one of the founders of the pottery company. The houses were taken over by the trustees of the Haig Memorial Homes in 1930.[10]

Break-Up of the Ashtead Park Estate – the sale of 1924

A major housing development occurred when, following the death of Pantia Ralli in February 1924, the Ashtead Park estate was offered for sale by his widow on 8th October of the same year. The sale covered some 1,300 acres (including manorial rights) in Ashtead and adjacent parishes, a far smaller area than was offered in 1879 (see p. 62). At the time of the sale, apart from Newton Wood and manorial rights over Ashtead Common, the estate lay chiefly to the south of the main Ashtead-Epsom road (the present A.24) and to the south and east of Ashtead village.

The sale catalogue stressed the overall suitability of much of the land for immediate housing development, and described roughly half the lots as building land[11]. The development potential of such land had been anticipated at the time of the 1879 sale, but the parkland fronting onto the main road remained undeveloped, until safeguarded under planning legislation.

The estate did not reach the reserve price, but it was sold in its entirety for £51,500 to an anonymous purchaser on whose behalf it was offered immediately for resale in the same lots. Of the total of 52 lots, 31 were withdrawn, including the *Mansion* and its parkland which were subsequently purchased by the Corporation of London and occupied since 1926 by the City of London Freemen's School.

The manorial rights, including the control of Ashtead Common, were purchased in the 1924 sale by A.R. Cotton, acting in a private capacity rather than in his role as Clerk to the Epsom Rural District Council. Cotton retained these rights until selling them to Lord Barnby in 1962 (see p. 11). Although Newton Wood, adjoining Ashtead Common, was withdrawn from the sale, it was purchased subsequently by A.R. Cotton and remained in his possession until he sold it to P.J. Houston of Epsom in 1980.

Of the 21 lots sold, ten were recorded initially as having gone to Major Chance of Dorking, who was to play a significant part in subsequent housing development in Ashtead. The anonymous purchaser of 1924 was acting, however, on behalf of the Landed and General Investment Company. A Conveyance of 1925 detailed the transfer of 19 lots, totalling almost 125 acres, from Mrs Ralli and the Company to Major Chance[12]. This included the areas of parkland which had been withdrawn the previous year, when the *Mansion* had failed to find a purchaser. Of the lots purchased by Major Chance, only five were specified as suitable for building. Apart from those within the Park, areas which he purchased included land in Park Lane and Walton Road, as well as Park Farm. The Conveyance transferring the land to Major Chance stipulated that on the land between the main road and Rookery Hill, and on plots in Farm Lane, Pleasure Pitt Road, and Walton Road, only detached or semi-detached houses (of a given minimum price) should be built, except that business premises might be erected on the frontage to the main road.

Crowded Roads

Cars and buses often packed the streets at holiday times, so much so that in July 1925 the Ashtead Parish Council proposed to complain to the Surrey County Council about the 'diabolical' noises of motor coach parties passing through the village at weekends[13]. This congestion was later to lead to the talk of by-passes. Some tourists came to Ashtead to potter round the Common, visit the tea-rooms near the station and, while walking through the woods, have a look at the excavations of the Roman villa, discovered in 1925.

Excursion traffic from London by motor-bus was promoted by a poster entitled 'Ashtead by Motor Bus' (see Fig 38). A London Underground guide featured Ashtead as 'one of the favourite and most famous excursion resorts around London – a place which caters especially for excursionists'[14].

Such was the demand for these bus services, that independent operators were attracted to the Epsom-Ashtead-Dorking road on

Sundays during the summer. These included in 1924 *City, Choco-late Express, New Times* and *Peraeque*, and in 1925, *St George, C.H. Pickup* and the *Shamrock Traction Company*. These three latter companies continued to provide a service until 1933, and introduced some weekday journeys. There was even a horse-drawn coach passing through the village around this time. A former student of Parsons Mead School recalled that "Every afternoon we had games in the field. At mid-afternoon we changed-over teams and this took place when the London to Brighton coach and horses went southwards along the road from Ashtead to Leatherhead – this was the best clock!"[15]

Railway Improvements

Soon after the formation of the Southern Railway Company in 1923, electrification of the line through Ashtead began, using the direct current (DC) third rail system rather than the alternating current (AC) system with overhead wires. The first electric trains in service arrived in Ashtead on 12 July 1925, running from Waterloo to Dorking North and Effingham Junction, but it was not until 3 March 1929 that suburban trains from London Bridge and Victoria were also electrified. Steam still mingled with electric until 3 July 1938 when lines beyond Dorking, to the south coast, were electrified. Goods trains continued to be worked by steam engines.

With electrification, trains ran at regular intervals during the off-peak period, with a much more frequent commuter service in the rush hour as more people settled in the outer suburbs, including Ashtead, but worked in town. Southern coaches were painted green, often being operated in multiples of three.

The station and yard remained mainly unchanged from pre-First World War days but in 1930 the signal box was moved from the middle of the 'Up' platform to its new position on the Epsom side of the level crossing, the gates being controlled from the box.

Public Services

Ashtead's water was supplied by the East Surrey Water Company from the Leatherhead pumping station. Its gas was provided by the Wandsworth, Wimbledon & Epsom District Gas Company, at Epsom[16]. For its electricity, Ashtead depended on the Leatherhead District Electricity Company, though street lighting at this time was all by gas.[17]

Fig. 37. Village Club outing by charabanc, 1920s. (Courtesy, T.H. Devitt).
    Front seat: Tom F. Devitt, Bill Peters, driver Chris Taylor; 2nd row: Bert Ottway, Bob David; 3rd row: Frank Bromfield, —, Joe Felton; 4th row: Mr & Mrs A. H. Marriott; 5th row: Fred Bailey, Bill Bailey.
    Rear seat: Reg Bromfield, Florence Bromfield, Humphrey sisters.
    At back, L to R: Mrs Coleman, Mrs Ottway, Albert Munday, Hector, Mabel, Len Marriott & in front of them Jim & Ann Marriott.

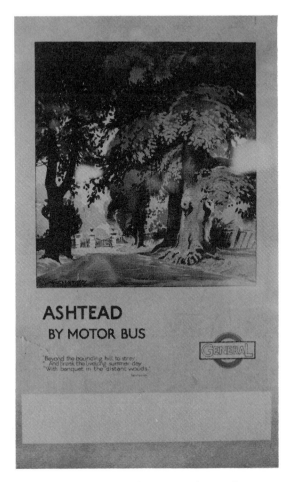

Fig. 38. Poster published by the London General Omnibus Co in 1921, based upon a painting by W. E. Spradbury, showing the entrance to Ashtead Park from Dene Road. (Courtesy, Alan A. Jackson)

Fire services were the responsibility of the Ashtead Fire Brigade which had been a successful and independent unit since its founding in 1901, but moves for a merger with Leatherhead surfaced in the early 1920s. It was not Ashtead's efficiency which was in doubt, and water pressure at the highest points was effective enough to justify the purchase of a 'steamer' or motor fire engine. This was, however, the issue which in 1926 led to the decision to merge the two brigades. Early that year a fire station was built in Emlyn Lane, Leatherhead, to house a new Merryweather motor fire engine, and on 6 October 1926 the Ashtead Brigade was disbanded.

THE THIRTIES

Although the 1930s started with hardship and unemployment as severe as in the years after the war, the growth of Ashtead continued unabated, its population nearly doubling in size from 4,783 in 1931 to 9,336 in 1939[18]. Few could have forecast this during the Depression years early in the decade when the Ashtead Parish Council and local government officials were taking urgent steps to help the needy, especially those without a job. At a Council meeting in early April 1932 there were said to be three organizations in the village working for those in distress: the Sick & Poor Fund of the Church of England, the Free Church Fund and the British Legion Fund. Appeals were made to all in the village to 'do their utmost to give employment wherever possible'[19]. Unemployment continued to be a major concern, accentuated later in the year by the closing down of the Rayon Factory in Ermyn Way, throwing another 78 people out of work. There were over 100 villagers unemployed and the Council suggested that road work might be found for some of them, while others might clean out the Rye Brook. In December 1932 the press reported that the unemployment scheme had made a good start with money coming from the various funds to pay for the activities being undertaken.[20] Despite the Depression, an end-of-the-year press report noted that Ashtead had been 'growing appreciably'; and earlier in the year there had been high spirits at the opening of the new Ashtead Recreation Ground off Barnett Wood Lane. An Ashtead resident, R.H. Davis, was knighted in the 1932 Birthday Honours for his invention of deep-sea and other breathing apparatus.[21]

In the mid-1930s, the Silver Jubilee of George V and the Coronation of George VI were celebrated. On Jubilee Day, 6 May 1935, there were street parties in Ashtead, with sports in the afternoon and a bonfire in the evening. Two years later, on Coronation Day, 12 May 1937, a carnival procession of decorated cars passed through the village and there was a sports fête in the Recreation Ground.

Housing Developments

The number of houses built in Ashtead greatly increased in the 1930s, helped by the improved railway service to and from London and by the recent extension of sewers along the principal roads.[22] A 1932 town-planning scheme, though restricting the density of new developments, allowed building over a wide area of the village. There were proposals for Ashtead to increase its population to 30,000, far more than it is today. Although these plans did not materialize, large numbers of new houses were built, especially on former Woodfield Farm land north of the railway, where in 1935–39 E & L Berg laid out and developed the Ashtead Woods estate, comprising Overdale, Culverhay and Broadhurst. Other builders erected mostly semi-detached houses south of the railway in Craddocks Avenue, St Stephens Avenue, Chaffers Mead, Newton Wood Road, Loraine Gardens, Petters Road, Cray Avenue, Bagot Close and Forest Crescent. In February 1937 the Leatherhead Urban District Council reported that 152 houses had been built in the Woodfield area and development of the Links Road area was also mentioned[23]. A new block of flats and shops was built in 1938 at the west entrance to Craddocks Avenue on the site of the former Woodfield Farm; an hotel was proposed for a site near here but it was not built. House building took place at this time in and near Barnett Wood Lane, also along the Leatherhead Road at Stag Leys, Old Court and south of the Warren Estate[24].

Houses were being built by W. Robinson in the Farm Lane area, but financial stringencies forced him to cancel contracts and refund deposits. He was left with unfinished houses on his hands, having to discharge the majority of his workforce and to contemplate closing down altogether. Like other builders, however, he was to resume activity after the war[25].

Shops and Businesses

Much of Ashtead's character at this time can be gathered from a look at the Directories dating from the 1930s[26]. Because of the demand for new houses, it is not surprising to find a number of estate agents listed (Osenton & Co and Arnold & Sons, both in The Street,) and many builders – the well-known E. Littlewood in Ottways Lane, E. & L. Berg in Overdale, Sydney Darton in Woodfield Lane, S. King in Barnett Wood Lane, Bowring & Gower in The Street and W. Robinson in Chaffers Mead, to name only a few. Most of the shops were in The Street, though there were others in the north of the village near the railway: the butchers, Grimditch & Webb, were in Barnett Wood Lane and there were also two grocers here (A.H. Golding and T. Steer), as well as a newsagent (E. Follett). Shops in The Street included two butchers (Baldwin Bros and Page & Clatworthy) three fruiterers and florists (D. Lisney, A. Whitehouse and Pullen & Co), several grocers (J. Gadsby, Heywood Stores and the International Stores), a tailor (A.H. Marriott), a watchmaker (H. Richards) and a cycle dealer(Mrs E.M. Snow). Rectory Lane had a fishmonger (J. Killick), a confectioner's shop (A. Marshall), a draper (H. Large) and a laundry (Miss Prosser). A riding school had been established recently in Ottways Lane.

Other businesses included four boot and shoe makers, three cabinet makers, a large joinery works and four garages. Thirsts could be quenched at the *Brewery Inn*, the *Leg of Mutton & Cauliflower* and the *Woodman*; or at the tea-rooms on The Street and Rectory Lane, with others on the Common. Care for the ill and needy was in the hands of several doctors all but one of whom had been practising here for a long time; there was also a dentist and two District Nurses. Ashtead Potters Ltd, successful for many years, had to close in 1935 (see p. 206). The Goblin Company, makers of vacuum cleaners and other household utilities, opened its works at Ermyn Way in 1938. A small silk-making factory was set up near The Warren by Lady Zoe Hart-Dyke and her husband after the success in the early 1930s of their silkworm farm at Tyrells Wood in Leatherhead. The factory had to close after a short time when Lady Duckham, a neighbour, complained of the unpleasant smell emanating from it[27].

The Last Years of Peace

There were perhaps few in Ashtead, and in the country as a whole, who believed that the late 1930s would end in war. Some were worried no doubt by the black news from abroad and the discussions on air raid precautions at Ashtead in January 1937 made the threat of war seem more real[28]. However, daily life carried on more or less as usual. Older residents recalled that in the pre-war days there were as many as four posts a day, with daily deliveries to the home of freshly-baked bread, meat and groceries of all kinds. In winter, if the roads were unfit for vans, groceries were delivered by sledge. New Ashtead residents were presented with a gift of farm produce by Prewett's of Leatherhead. On Sundays and school outing days children were to be seen playing on a helter-skelter by the railway bridge close to the Common[28].

With its new and growing housing estates, Ashtead was primarily a residential area in 1938 and 1939, though some of the village atmosphere survived. In the Ashtead Woods area, cows grazed in the fields and there were sheep around the Thirty Acres Barn in the south. Although Woodfield Farm, the last of the farms, had been taken over by builders in the early 1930s, dairying at Park Farm brought back memories of the rural past.

Notes

1. *Leatherhead Advertiser (L.A.)*, 9 Aug. 1919
2. *L.A*, 18 Feb, 15 July 1922
3. *L.A*, 14 Oct, 18 Nov. 1922
4. *L.A*, 7 Feb, 1925
5. Peace Memorial Hall pamphlet (1984)
6. Kelly's Directory, 1927
7. Kelly's Directory, 1924
8. Edwina Vardey (ed) *History of Leatherhead* (1988), p. 232
9. Alan A. Jackson (ed), *Ashtead: A Village Transformed* (1977) p. 106
10 E.H. Hallam, *Ashtead Potters in Surrey, 1923–1935* (1990) p. 11
11. Sale details taken from the Catalogue: SRO 448/4; and from *L.A. and Epsom Times*, 11 Oct. 1924
12. Conveyance of freehold hereditaments...in Ashtead and Walton-on-the-Hill, 11 March 1925. Mrs Pantia Ralli to Major Chance.
13. *L.A*, 11 July 1925
14. Alan A. Jackson (ed) (1977), op. cit. p. 201
15. *L.A*, Feb. 1993
16. F.H. Chown, *House Hunter's Guide to Ashtead* (1926)
17. *L.A*, 7 Feb. 1925
18. Census Reports: see Chapter 20
19. *L.A*, 1 April 1932
20. *L.A*, 23 Dec. 1932
21. *L.A*, 10 June 1932
22. Alan A. Jackson (ed) (1977) op. cit. p. 109
23. *L.A*, 12 Feb. 1937
24. *L.A*, 1 Oct. 1937
25. Alan A. Jackson, *Semi-Detached London* (1991), p. 256
26. Kelly's Directory, 1938; Surrey Trade Directory, 1939
27. Edwina Vardey (ed) (1977) op. cit. p. 234
28. *L.A*, 22 Jan. 1937

Chapter 17

THE SECOND WORLD WAR

In the months before the outbreak of war in September 1939 the gloomy news from abroad did not deflect Ashtead from holding its May Day celebrations and the traditional Whit-Monday fête. In March, members of the Ashtead British Legion had borne one of the standards for the Guard of Honour at the French President's state visit to London[1]. The threat of war was, however, being brought to everyone's attention by the newspapers and radio, further by the anti-gas lectures in the village as early as mid-April. In July, there were combined exercises of the Auxiliary Fire Service and the Air Raid Wardens. At a local Council meeting in August billeting arrangements for evacuees was discussed[2], pointing all too clearly to the imminence of war.

The Council's plans for billeting were soon put to the test, since children from Streatham and Dulwich schools arrived in Ashtead just before the declaration of war and were billeted on local householders. One of these remembers vigorously washing a little girl's hair to rid it of nits and to prevent them spreading to another child. The Peace Memorial Hall opened its doors daily to the evacuated mothers and children[3]. Apart from billeting worries, everyone in the village now had to ensure that they knew how to put on and use their gas masks and to cope with the black-out regulations, risking a fine if they showed a light after dark. They also had to get used to soldiers in their midst, since a unit of the Royal Norfolk Regiment was stationed in Ashtead for a time early in the war, as well as a fair number of Canadians[4]. Dances and concerts were given to the troops at the Peace Memorial Hall; partners for the dances were provided by 'lady employees' from the Goblin Works and other local establishments. The Canadians married several of these Ashtead young ladies.

Wartime restrictions soon became the constant bane of everyday life, though after a time they were accepted. Dark curtains or shutters had to be put up to meet the black-out provisions, petrol was in short supply, and good clothing hard to obtain. Food rationing began early in January 1940, first affecting butter, bacon and ham and a little later sugar was reduced to 8 oz a month per person to be followed by many other daily foods. When tea was cut down to 2 oz per person per week in July of that year the local press believed this to be 'a devastating blow to the Home Front morale'[5]. The Ministry of Food's 'Dig for Victory' campaign encouraged many Ashtead people to grow their own vegetables and 'War Allotments' were set up on land off Craddocks Avenue[6]. Pigs were nurtured on vacant building sites in Overdale. The local farmers were exhorted to grow more wheat and potatoes; some areas of the Common were converted to arable fields. This work was partly done by the newly formed Women's Land Army, some of whom lived in a hostel in Farm Lane; they were often to be seen on the Common in their distinctive large felt hats and brown corduroy

Fig. 39. Members of Ashtead Home Guard, with sprocket mortar, June 1943. L to R: Ron Main, Arthur Kemp and John Thorpe. LDLHS Collection

Fig. 40. Ashtead Section Special Constabulary, 1939. (Courtesy, Worsfold family). Photographed in the garden of The Old Bakery, Section Leader, Fred Goldsmith's home. L to R: Fred Goldsmith, George Cook, Harry Barrows, Harry Chitty, ? Davidson, Bert Goldsmith, E. Gritt, H. Edwards, H. Pateman, W. Ayliffe, Jack Worsfold.

breeches. The opening in October 1941 of a British Restaurant in the Ashtead Recreation Ground off Barnett Wood Lane proved popular, offering 'an appetising and sustaining meal at nine pence a head'[7].

Ashtead formed a Company of Local Defence Volunteers soon after Sir Anthony Eden's broadcast appeal for these on 14 May 1940. This was a fortnight before the evacuation of British troops from Dunkirk, at a time when there was an increasing threat of a German invasion. The L.D.V's, as they were first called, soon became known as the Home Guard, later (in peacetime) fondly nicknamed 'Dad's Army'. The Ashtead Company consisted of 60 men under Major Aitken and had their headquarters in The Marld. They trained on the Common, made route marches to Burford Bridge and carried out night patrols[8].

The War comes to Ashtead (1940–41)

Ashtead suffered bomb attacks from late August 1940 onwards. Fleets of German bombers protected by fighters appeared over S.E. England and were opposed by R.A.F squadrons in what was to become known as the Battle of Britain. The first bombs fell in Ashtead on 26 August when 35 houses were damaged and 500 windows smashed; one of the bombs dropped close to Ashtead Park[9]. Surprisingly enough, the one casualty from this attack was a tame rabbit. Only a few days later there was a second and larger raid, this time in daylight. Five people were killed and many were injured, but casualties were fairly low because the majority of people had taken refuge in their garden shelters[10]. Gaywood Road, St Giles' School and the windows of St Giles' Church sustained serious bomb damage at this time.

The German attacks, especially their increasing threat to London, led to many more evacuees being sent to Ashtead and surrounding areas. Invasion seemed so likely at this time that an 'imminent invasion' notice was sent out to all counties on 7 September[11] and the Ashtead Home Guard, like all others, stood to arms, but though nothing happened the London Blitz was soon to begin.

Almost daily bomb alerts continued at Ashtead after these first raids with more bombs dropped, and shelters were planned to be erected in Craddocks Avenue, the Berg estate and The Street[12]. Early in 1941, sticks of incendiary bombs set fire to several houses and in March that year St Andrew's School was largely destroyed by a landmine. Incendaries continued to be troublesome during much of the year.

Two Quiet Years (1942–43)

There was a long respite from bombing after the rash of incendaries late in 1941, life in Ashtead settling down into a routine again, although personal tragedies affected many families. The *Parish Magazine* of July 1943 conveyed sympathy to the friends and families of two men killed in action, three more reported missing, and another in an army hospital in North Africa. There were many others for whom life would not be the same.

Although there was palpable relief at the cessation of bombing, everyone followed the twists and turns of the war's fortunes, especially feeling the loss of the two battleships, the *Prince of Wales* and the *Repulse* in Singapore waters in the last month of 1941, since so many Ashtead people had readily joined in Leatherhead's recent Warship Week. In 1942, housewives felt the pinch even more with flour and bread becoming scarcer, owing to the loss of so many supply ships through enemy action. Coal was more difficult to buy in this year, though rationing it was avoided. Spirits were lifted late in the year when news was broadcast of the British success at El Alamein and a few days after this, the Ashtead church bells, and others all around the country, were rung to celebrate the victory[13].

The Bombs return (1944)

Soon after the excitement of D-Day and the invasion of Normandy in June 1944, Ashtead's life was again disturbed by enemy bomb attacks in the form of pilotless doodle-bugs or V-ls. Sixteen of these fell in the Ashtead and Leatherhead areas, one landing at Chaffers Mead and another at Newton Wood[14]. The last of the bombs, a V-2 rocket, exploded in Park Lane damaging 50 houses, but there was only one minor casualty. From then on it was all quiet in the Ashtead skies and within a few months the war was over.

Dame Sybil Thorndike lived in Ashtead for a period with her husband, Lewis Casson, in a corner house on Ottways Lane near Parsons Mead, looking after her daughter-in-law and children when their father was in a Japanese prisoner of war camp. She was a regular attendant at the dim, candle-lit 8 a.m. service at St Giles' and was seen at the altar rail still wearing the grease paint of her

Saturday night performance at a London theatre after a late journey back to Ashtead.

Victory Celebrations

The end of the war was marked by a special service at St Giles' Church on 8 May 1945, celebrating VE or Victory in Europe Day. On the following Sunday afternoon a Thanksgiving Service was held with the British Legion, the Home Guard and other organizations taking part. The names of the 70 Ashtead men who fell in the war were added to the British Legion Roll of Honour and to the Ashtead War Memorial.

Notes

1. *Leatherhead Advertiser (L.A.)*, 24 March 1939
2. *L.A*, 25 August 1939
3. *L.A*, 29 Sept. 1939
4. Peace Memorial Hall pamphlet (1984)
5. *The Home Front, 1940–45 (L.A.)* (1989), p. 7
6. *The Mole Valley at War (L.A.)* (1989), p. 11
7. Society Records, L.W. 299
8. *The Home Front, 1940–45 (L.A.)* (1989) p. 14
9. *L.A*, 30 August 1940
10. *L.A*, 6 Sept. 1940
11. A.J.P. Taylor, *English History, 1914–45* (1965) p. 499
12. *L.A*, 4 Oct. 1940
13. A.J.P. Taylor (1965) op. cit. p. 560
14. Edwina Vardey (ed), *History of Leatherhead* (1988) p. 249

Chapter 18

MODERN ASHTEAD

Introduction
At the end of the Second World War the population of Ashtead was about 9,500 as compared with over 13,300 in 1995[1]. The increase was much less than that of the previous half-century, when Ashtead changed from being partially a farming community with some light industries to a commuter village with new, large housing estates, and only a sprinkling of industries, most of which were soon to disappear. The transformation, which took place principally in the 1920s and 1930s, would have continued after the war but for the disciplines recommended by Sir Patrick Abercrombie's Greater London Plan of 1944, imposed by the Town & Country Planning Act, 1947. This created a Green Belt around Ashtead, which has managed therefore to retain a semblance of its old rural aspect, helped over the years by a vigilant Residents' Association, founded in 1945. Virtually all new development since the war has been restricted to in-filling of the existing built-up area. New buildings like St Michael's Catholic Church (1967), the Library (1968), the Youth Centre (1970) and the Hospital (1984) have added appreciably to Ashtead's amenities and architectural interest. The closure of the Goblin Works at Ermyn Way in 1984 was followed by the discovery of Anglo-Saxon graves (see p. 21) during the construction of the new Esso headquarters, opened in 1990.

The Early Post-War Years (1945-60) There were street parties in Ashtead on 8 May 1945, VE Day, when the war in Europe ended and everyone welcomed the lifting of the blackout. Two months later, street lighting was restored. The expected better times of peace, however, were long delayed[2]. Rationing of food and clothing continued and a close watch was kept on wrongdoers; an Ashtead man was fined in 1946 by the Epsom magistrates for receiving and selling extra clothing coupons[3]. A coal shortage soon added to everyone's difficulties. Despite these worries, the returning soldiers helped to make family life normal again for many, the *Woodman* giving a special party for ex-service men in June 1946[4]. A month later, bread was put on ration for the first time, so feeding the family became even more difficult, though many, as exhorted to do so by the government, grew their own vegetables. Food stocks were boosted by the large number of gift boxes from Australia, distributed to Ashtead and other villages by the Leatherhead & District Food Control Committee[5]. New cars could not be bought for some time after the war, luxuries were scarce and foreign travel curbed by currency restrictions. The talking point in 1948 was the government's introduction of the National Health Service and National Assistance, launching the Welfare State. This coincided with a slight easing of rationing, heralded by the freeing of bread and, in early 1949, of clothing, though nylon stockings were considered a luxury for some time after this. Shortages continued until the early 1950s.

As the shadow of the war years lifted, Ashtead grew in population, trading prospered and social life revived. The Peace Memorial Hall was the centre of much of this new social activity, as it had been in the 1920s and 1930s[6]. The churches were concerned to help the young and others adjust to the post-war world (see p. 173). During the Festival of Britain in 1951, Ashtead decorated its streets with bunting. Two years later, on Queen Elizabeth's Coronation Day, 2 June 1953, there was a fancy dress parade, with dancing in the evening, a bonfire and fireworks[7].

Ashtead since 1960 There are many things Ashtead people will recall in the years since 1960, not least the heavy rains of 1968, the drought of 1976 and the storms of 1987 and 1990 (see p. 5). Ashtead received acclaim (and a cup) in 1971 for having done most to brighten up the village, better it seems than all others in the Leatherhead Urban District Council's area[8]. On the Queen's Silver Jubilee Day, 7 June 1977, Ashtead had its own special celebration, over 1,000 of all ages attending a fête in the grounds of the City of London Freemen's School. There were Morris Dancers, many side-shows, and music was played by the Mole Valley Silver Band[9]. Since then, the celebrations in the village have been mainly locally-inspired, like the annual Village Day in summer and the fêtes devised by societies and schools. Several Ashtead war veterans attended the D-Day remembrance ceremonies in June 1994[10]. There were flags in Ashtead streets on VE-Day, 8 May 1995.

Post-War Planning

Post-war legislation, as mentioned earlier, produced a greater density of development but no significant expansion of Ashtead's built-up area. This arrested the continuous outward development of London that was threatening to engulf Ashtead.

Abercrombie's Greater London Plan of 1944 made specific recommendations about Ashtead, speaking in particular about the need to preserve the narrow belt of open country between Ashtead and Leatherhead[11]. Ashtead Park was mentioned as being partly developed with fairly large houses and a recommendation was made that further development should not take place here. This view had a notable affect on the then current building plans for the parts of Ashtead Park not occupied by the City of London Freemen's School.

The builder, W. Robinson, active in Ashtead before the war (see p. 133), purchased the land between Rookery Hill and the Epsom Road from Major Chance and design work on the roads and sewers was started late in 1946. In October 1947, however, the Mid-Surrey Joint Planning Committee spoke against these plans, quoting the provisions of the Greater London Plan, and in July 1948 Robinson's scheme for 114 houses was turned down. The land was acquired by the Surrey County Council in March 1957 and later transferred to the Leatherhead Urban District Council; the aim was to preserve the land as a natural park for the benefit of the public.

In November 1978, when discussions were taking place on the draft Structure Plan for Surrey, the Ashtead Residents' Association was the only voluntary local organization in the county to be invited to the sessions on the Green Belt. Similarly, when the Leatherhead area Local Plan (covering the former Urban District including Ashtead) was in draft in 1983, the Association was in a position to call attention to the danger of trying to accommodate housing demand in full within an island in the Green Belt.

The Mole Valley District Council in 1988 designated three conservation areas under the 1971 Town & Country Planning Act, giv-

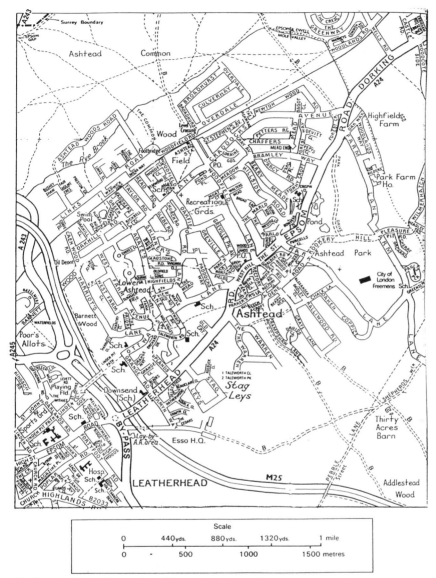

Modern Ashtead. Reproduced from the Surrey County Street Atlas, courtesy of George Philip Limited. © Crown Copyright

ing the local authority greater powers to control demolition and tree felling and to seek good design in new development[12]. One of these areas included the west side of Woodfield Lane where the houses fronting the service road represent a good example of Edwardian development. The second area chosen was the land around the junctions of Rectory Lane, Dene Road and Crampshaw Lane, including the *Old Rectory* and The *Old Bakery*. The third area lay around *Ashtead House*, the *Headmaster's House* of the City of London Freemen's School and the lodge just inside Ashtead Park. It was thought that the high, brick walls and the lack of pavements in the second and third areas gave them a village atmosphere.

Local Government
Ashtead has never been its own master since the start of statutory local government in 1894, just over 100 years ago. It has, however, always been able to elect one or more representatives to speak for it. The following table shows the responsibilities at various times during the past century, the dates each authority took charge and how many councillors represented Ashtead electors:

Date	Authority covering Ashtead			Councillors for Ashtead		
	County level	District level	Parish level	County	District	Parish
1888 (Local Govt. Act)	Surrey CC	—	—	1*	—	—
1894 (Local Govt. Act)	"	Epsom RDC	Ashtead PC	"	1	?
1933 (Surrey Review Order)	"	Leatherhead UDC	—	"	4	—
1946–74	"	"		1 (1952)	Successive increases to 8	
1974	Surrey CC†	Mole Valley DC		1	7 (3 Wards)	

Notes   * For an area wider than Ashtead.
        † Some functions transferred between county and district levels.

Local Councils are responsible for administering a vast range of services and the following table shows those most affecting Ashtead:

Surrey County Council	Mole Valley District Council	Shared or overlapping responsibilities
Consumer protection	Allotments	Arts and leisure
Education	Food hygiene	Emergencies
Fire Service	Housing	Footpaths
Highways and traffic	Planning (Local Plans and control of development)	Gypsies
Libraries	Public conveniences	Land drainage
Planning (Structure Plans)	Recreation grounds	Litter
Police	Refuse collection	Parking off-street
Public transport	Registration of electors	
Refuse disposal	Tax collection for county and district services	
Registration of births etc.		
Social services		

Some other services, like sewers and sewage disposal, are now the responsibility of Thames Water plc in conjunction with the East Surrey Water Company.

This framework has operated for twenty years and its forerunners were recognizable in the earlier legislation. The practices and achievements of local government have been significantly changed by several background trends and influences. Probably the most pervasive of these has been the increasing centralization of financial control, which has limited the scope for local councillors to choose policies to meet the needs of their area. One example among many is the limited re-investment in new housing permitted by the government following the sale of council houses (typically 3-bedroomed) to tenants causing a shortage of houses to rent. There has also been a trend towards decentralization. Before 1990 most of the financing and organization of schools was carried out by the Education Department of the Surrey County Council but during the next three years this was largely transferred to the school governors, leading to reductions in the Council's staff and the creation of new office units in each school. A third widespread trend, and one in which Ashtead has been to the fore, is increased public participation in local decision-making, which has received official encouragement since the 1960s[13]. Although the decisions may have been delayed sometimes, they have proved more likely to be acceptable to local people and the results have been seen as more enduring.

Ashtead has for long achieved an increasingly special position regarding politically sponsored councillors. Instead of following the trend elsewhere, it has staunchly maintained the benefits of independence, focusing on the good of the district without the distractions and point-scoring of national party politics. Perhaps this has been the most significant factor of all in the recent history of Ashtead's government. Almost all of Ashtead's District Councillors (at least since 1945) have been elected on the basis that in Council affairs he or she would be independent of national political parties. For a long time this has also been true of the County Councillor. There can be few places which for fifty years have so consistently bucked the trend towards partisan representation. Other wards, like Leatherhead and Bookham, have had independent councillors yet their numbers tended to dwindle over the years. The factor making the difference was the strength and consistent backing of the Residents' Association, which has maintained close liaison with all branches of government and administration.

The organization of local government described earlier in this chapter was under reconsideration recently for nearly two years. Initially the government favoured the abolition of county councils and the transfer of most of their functions to the district level, thus forming 'unitary' authorities: there might also be boundary changes and in many cases two or more districts would be combined. A Local Government Commission was appointed to advise on the best arrangements, county by county.

The Commission began its study of Surrey on 15 December 1993, and invited local opinions. Many people expected that the Mole Valley District would be split between neighbouring areas, and there was some support for Ashtead to be amalgamated with Epsom. However, a public meeting called by the Residents' Association favoured retention of the existing county and district arrangements. The final recommendation of the Commission also came to this conclusion, and the Secretary of State for the Environment announced in the House of Commons on 2 March 1995 that he accepted their advice.

Housing since the war
New housing in Ashtead after the war was restricted to in-filling, the developers taking over, where possible, the large Edwardian and Victorian properties with their spacious garden plots. Most of the housing growth occurred before the end of the 1960s, although some small pockets have been filled-in since then. The Span housing estate was built on the site of *Westfield* in The Marld.

Council housing was started in Ashtead by the Leatherhead Urban District Council in June 1946 when 50 pre-fabricated bungalows were built on the Green Lane site. Most of the tenants were ex-service men or war widows and their families. The 'pre-fabs' at Brooker's Close remained until they were replaced in the mid-1950s by 87 flats and bungalows and an old peoples' home. Bramley Way was the Council's other major post-war project, totalling (on completion) nearly 300 homes, built in stages from 1946 onwards. E & L Berg were awarded the contract to build the first 24 homes, but other builders were engaged on the remainder of the scheme, each contracted to build a few houses. By November 1948, the first phase was completed and 138 houses, including a few old peoples' bungalows, had been built. Sixteen houses were added in 1951 on land fronting Bramley Way and Cray Avenue, repeating types already built. Finally, in 1953, after more land was purchased, a second major phase of 113 houses and bungalows was built along both sides of Berry Meade and extending into Stonny Croft, thus completing Ashtead's largest ever housing development.

Private house building restarted very soon after the end of the war. Plots which had remained undeveloped during the war were built on. This happened in Broadhurst and Overdale, part of the 1930s Ashtead Woods Estate, and also in Stag Leys, West Farm Close, Petters Road, Newton Wood Road and part of Craddocks Avenue. In the south of Ashtead, housing development in the early 1950s followed the old bridleways of Crampshaw Lane and Grays Lane, whilst the nearby Ralliwood Road was laid out on virgin land. For some years after the war the government limited the size of houses and today there are some small houses on sizeable plots in Grays Lane and Ralliwood Road whose owners have now extended their properties by adding double garages and other rooms. Recent housing development is well shown by comparing a current street map of Ashtead with one published in 1958: the modern map gives about fifty additional street names, most of them cul-de-sacs. Links Road now has nine cul-de-sacs leading to developments in the once lengthy gardens behind the original houses and bungalows. Other cul-de-sacs represent development of the sites of demolished old houses or groups of houses, or of gardens where the original houses remain but now look oversize for their sites. Oaken Coppice is the most notable exception to the fashion for cul-de-sacs in that it is a through road from Chalk Lane to Park Lane. All these developments suggest that the in-filling of Ashtead has been completed, but opportunities are still found. Houses with large gardens continued to disappear and be replaced by three or four new houses, even during the recession years of the early 1990s.

Housing for special needs The long-established almshouses in The Street have been administered in recent years by the trustees of the Ashtead United Charities. They were named *Feilding House* after their founder and in 1975 a block of four flats, called *Maples House*, was built in the grounds, in memory of a long serving secretary of the trustees. In the same year, *The Haven* in Ottways Lane, comprising four cottages for retired domestic servants founded in the 1880s, was taken over by the Ashtead United Charities as another almshouse. Ashtead played a full part in the Leatherhead Old People's Welfare Committee when it was set up in 1953, its name later changed to Age Concern. The Forget-me-Not Club and the Ashtead Day Centre were founded, further helped by services such as Meals on Wheels and Home Care. The Mole Valley District Council recently provided two residential centres for the elderly, *Griffin Court* at the entrance to The Warren and *Lime Tree Court* on West Hill.

Housing associations and the private sector have also provided homes for the elderly. Mole Valley Place, off Ottways Lane, consisting of bungalows linked by covered walkways, was developed in 1966–68 by the Leatherhead (Mole Valley) Housing Association. More recently, a small block of four flats was built in Oakfield Road by the Mount Green Housing Association. In 1983–4, building by a private firm took place off The Marld, behind St Michael's Church, and more recently another site was similarly developed in Greville Park Avenue. *Milner House* in Ermyn Way has been a home for the elderly since 1987. For those with special needs other than the elderly, the two largest post-war housing schemes have been Paul's Place and Alexander Godley Close, both developed in similar style in about 1950–1 by Haig Homes, for ex-service men or their widows and families.

Today's Roads
Although there have been many minor changes in the road pattern within Ashtead since 1945, the main roads have remained largely

unchanged for a considerable period. The A24 London-Worthing road has always been the chief feature. Attempts to improve the lot of pedestrians included the provision of a footbridge at the junction with Grange Road/Ermyn Way, where traffic lights were also installed, and of pedestrian controlled lights in The Street and at West Hill. The junction of Woodfield Lane with The Street was improved in 1978, but this was only a partial solution to a long-standing problem. The need for traffic lights was recognized immediately after the war[14]. The matter has been raised many times, and was the subject of a speech by Lord Moynihan in the House of Lords in 1959 when he cited Ashtead as an example, in arguing the general case for traffic lights in similar locations[15]. What should be done here remains to be resolved. A lay-by in The Street, which had been used for parking, was removed in 1992 to aid road safety, but this action may have contributed to the closing of shops in the area. A mini-roundabout was constructed in 1985 where Woodfield Lane joins Barnett Wood Lane and Craddocks Avenue. The east-west road here was planned as a through-route in the 1930s to link Lower Ashtead with Epsom and to provide an alternative to the A 24. When the area came to be developed with housing, Craddocks Avenue was made wider and stronger than normal to take through traffic.

Fig. 41. Woodfield Lane, looking north in 1964. The last vestiges of Woodfield Farm are seen on the right. LDLHS Collection

Fig. 42. The Street, 1989, north side, looking towards Epsom. LDLHS Collection

The Ashtead By-Pass, first mooted in 1948, was a project which threatened the southern part of Ashtead for almost 30 years. It was planned to run from the Epsom Road near the Ashtead boundary through a corner of Ashtead Park, along the line of Dene Road, to rejoin the A 24 near The Warren with a roundabout at each end. In 1954 there were suggestions that as an alternative The Street should be widened, but this was quickly rejected on the ground of cost. Pressures to build the by-pass mounted and in November 1965 the Residents' Association called a special meeting to set up a fund to pay for lawyers to fight the proposal. Notwithstanding these submissions the by-pass remained as a long-term plan until its final abandonment in 1977[16]. There are six houses facing Dene Road which are set back well from the road and have their own service road off Grove Road, a curious planning feature which acts as a reminder of the by-pass that never materialized[17].

The Motorway Arrives When the M 25 (London's orbital motorway) was at the planning stage much controversy was engendered over whether it should pass east or west of Leatherhead, and the decision to take the east route meant that it would pass quite close to Ashtead. This happened despite strong local opposition against the proposal. A major though partial success was the lowering of

Fig. 43.   Craddocks Parade. Photograph by Mrs E.C. Hudson.

the motorway into a cutting below the A 24. The M 25 was eventually opened on 6 October 1985. Although there had been many reservations about the motorway most people soon adjusted to it. In 1986, a coach link between Heathrow and Gatwick was instituted after the Ministry of Transport revoked the licence for the helicopter service between the two airports. This service, operating since 1978, had raised public protests because of the helicopters' intrusive noise when flying over Ashtead.

Motor Buses and Coaches
Public road services have had to adapt to changing conditions. The main services through Ashtead in 1994 were Route 408 from West Croydon to Guildford (which originated in 1921 when it started in Epsom); and Route 479, between Kingston and Bookham, with some journeys extended to Guildford. In 1978, this latter route had replaced Route 418, introduced in 1927 as the first bus serving Ashtead Pond and Barnett Wood Lane.

For many years, Route 470 provided another vital link in the local service. This was introduced in 1938 between Warlingham or West Croydon and Dorking, passing through Epsom, Ashtead and Leatherhead, and its origins may have stemmed from excursion services, such as Route 107 which had run from Clapham Common to Dorking and Epsom since before the First World War. Route 470 ran daily until 1980 and, after various subsequent changes, by 1994 formed part of a composite service, Route 465 between Kingston and Horsham, via Leatherhead, no longer serving Ashtead.

Under the Transport Act of 1985, the state-owned National Bus Company was privatized and London Country Bus Services was sub-divided into four subsidiary companies, Ashtead being served by London Country Bus Services (South-West) from October 1986.

The same Act required bus companies to register those services which they were prepared to operate on a commercial basis. It was left to County Councils to offer for contract and fund those other services which they considered to be socially necessary. Of the routes through Ashtead, those not registered passed to Epsom Coaches – operating as Epsom Buses. A new fleet name, London and Country, was adopted by London Country Bus Services in April 1989; the corresponding change in the Company name was delayed until spring 1993.

Following deregulation, many changes occurred in the bus services, including journeys specially timed to serve schools like St Andrews' and an 'Access' bus for the disabled. During the school holidays in the summer of 1993, a service from Epsom to Weybridge, via Ashtead and Leatherhead, was extended to Thorpe Park. Later, Route 516, linked Dorking, Box Hill and Headley with Leatherhead, and with the Tesco supermarket at Woodbridge. A limited number of the journeys passed through Ashtead, going to and from Epsom.

Green Line services through Ashtead, as elsewhere, had been withdrawn during most of the war years, but in May 1946 Routes 712 and 713 provided a service between Dorking and Luton/Dunstable, via Ashtead, Epsom and London[18]. These were replaced in 1975 by Route 703 between Dorking and London (Baker St), but this lasted only until October 1976 when local authority subsidies ceased; it has not been replaced[19].

London Country Bus Services operated regular summer weekly services from the 1980s to a number of coastal resorts, from Margate to Portsmouth and Southsea, using double-deck vehicles. Not all the routes passed through Ashtead, but the services were available to local passengers at Epsom or Leatherhead.

The relentless growth of car ownership since the late 1950s was reflected both in the withdrawal of Green Line coach services in 1976, and in the progressive decline in bus services over recent years. This latter was particularly noticeable at week-ends when, for instance, on Route 408, an hourly Sunday service was provided between West Croydon and Leatherhead, but only a two-hourly service between the latter and Guildford. By 1994 the main off-peak clientele for the buses seemed to be elderly persons, some housewives out shopping and children when they were not at school. A growing tendency for the elderly and school children to be the chief bus users became generally apparent by the 1990s, not peculiar to Ashtead alone. Most such traffic appeared to be of a significantly local character, people on longer journeys, who might once have used Green Line coaches, now travelling by train or car.

The Railway since 1945

Neither the nationalisation of the railways in 1948 nor the rationalisation programme associated with Dr Beeching in 1963 had much effect on suburban services through Ashtead. The goods yard was closed at the end of 1961, all siding connections being removed in December 1963. The passenger train siding on the 'Up' side built to accommodate excursion trains also disappeared as did the last rush hour train to start at Ashtead, the 8.15 a.m. to Waterloo. These changes made it possible to extend the platforms.

Ashtead's 1885 station buildings were replaced in 1969 by a factory-built 'CLASP'* model which had been developed for school buildings. At the same time a new concrete footbridge was erected for access between the platforms. The stationmaster's house was also taken down in 1969, the sole building on the 'Up' side being an open passenger shelter and small waiting room. Furniss's offices in the yard were demolished in 1971 and the car park extended to cover the whole of the former station forecourt and freight yard.

A pole barrier level crossing replaced the gates on 14 December 1975, controlled at first from the adjacent signal box. Colour light signals had replaced semaphores in 1964 and the Ashtead Woods intermediate signal box had been closed in 1963. The operation of the signals and the control of the barrier were transferred to a central control centre at Wimbledon. Closed circuit television cameras were installed overlooking the crossing in December 1978; the

* Consortium of Local Authorities Special Programme

Fig. 44. The concrete footbridge is lifted into place in 1969. The old and new station buildings can be seen. Photograph by H.J. Davies.

Fig. 45. The former signal box and level crossing gates with wickets for passengers, 1975. Photograph by H.J. Davies.

redundant signal box was demolished in 1979. Mirrors were erected on the platform later to enable the train driver to take on the role of guard and platform attendant. As road traffic grew, the crossing became an increasing source of frustration to the inhabitants north of the line, and in spite of protests the 1897 central footbridge was removed in 1981.

Although the railway was well used, especially by commuters to work in London, season ticket issues declined and the frequency of service was gradually reduced, both in peak and off-peak hours. The station's passenger traffic remained buoyant throughout the day, with some 1,200 boarding trains daily in 1991, 63% bound for Central London. The four coach 'slam door' suburban units in use after the Second World War were gradually replaced from the late 1970s by four coach open seating central corridor units with electrically-operated sliding doors. The Thameslink service which was in operation between 1988 and 1994 did not call at Ashtead (except for the occasional train) and was responsible for the suspension of off-peak Waterloo to Effingham Junction trains which had formerly called at Ashtead. The year 1994 saw the introduction of separate South Western and South Central services with regular trains to both Waterloo and Victoria, Effingham and Guildford, and Dorking and Horsham. In preparation for privatisation, the pendulum began to swing back towards the smaller operating companies which had existed before 1923.

Post Offices

Ashtead's post office was at 13, The Street after the war, fronting the sorting office and telephone exchange. When William Bean was postmaster in 1950 the posts were still administered from Epsom. In 1972, the G.P.O. decided to return to locating the counter in a shop. 'Debbies', owned by Philip Camp, at 11, The Street became the post office counter, until 1986. The business was then sold to Keith Jackson who moved it in May 1993 to 39, The Street (formerly 'Sweet Things'), thus providing Ashtead with a centrally located post office once more[20].

Sub-post offices were built at various times this century in the areas north of The Street to serve its increasing population. There was a counter at Tom Steer's grocer's shop in Barnett Wood Lane from 1907 to 1950 when it was transferred to Follett's newsagents and confectioner's shop, with the counter managed by Mr. Low.

This was closed down in 1956, but two years later Mrs Jo Underwood opened one up in her Oakfield Road house, the counter being in Dr. Dawson's old dispensary. In 1978 the counter moved to 230, Barnett Wood Lane, under Chris Harris who after four years sold the business to M.G. Patel the current post master. There used to be a sub-post office on the eastern corner of Ottways Lane and Agates Lane, first opened before the last war at Henry Moran's grocer's and general store and held there until the early 1950s. After a short time under A.E. Bowker, it was run by Charles Yellow for ten years from 1957. Mr & Mrs Kemble were its last owners, the counter being closed in 1976. The Craddocks Avenue sub-post office, opened in 1938, was originally at 'Henry's', the newsagents and library, with Henry Binns in charge until 1971. After ten years under Barry Burtenshaw the counter was transferred to 'Knitcraft' on the north side of the Parade, under the supervision of Mrs Elizabeth Webster. When she retired in 1993 the sub-post office was taken over by M.R. Kahn.

The earliest pillar box in Ashtead, dating from Victoria's reign, was in Oakfield Road, now to be seen in Green Lane with the 'V.R.' cipher on its door. Pillar boxes were installed in Craddocks Parade and Overdale during the brief reign of Edward VIII. The box in Overdale is still in place, identified by the 'E. VIII R' cipher, but the one in Craddocks Parade was removed when 'Knitcraft' became the sub-post office, and its present location is unknown.

Ashtead at work

After the war, a large part of Ashtead's population continued to be employed outside the area, mainly in London and its suburbs, also in Guildford, Croydon and places further afield. This is so today. In Ashtead itself, the working population, increasing over the years, took employment in the wide variety of shops, the service sector and other outlets.

No farming of the kind that there used to be survived the war, though a few fields south of the Ashtead Woods Road were used for grazing cattle in the 1970s[21]. The fields in the Thirty Acre Barn area were given over mainly to horses some years ago. Allotments continue to be in use along the Leatherhead Road. Of the pre-war light industrial sites, the Victoria Works on West Hill, now chiefly remembered for its use by the Ashtead Potters (see p. 206) was bought by the Council in 1965 and used for warehousing until the sheltered housing scheme, *Lime Tree Court*, replaced it in the early 1990s. The Crampshaw Works, also on West Hill, which used to house Brifex (see p. 124) was converted to offices in 1972. In the Woodfield area, Astridge's Yard, the haulage and removal contractors, gave way to flats in 1984. Near the new Esso building is *Milner House* at the back of which is Remploy, providing employment for disabled people. Remploy have occupied their building since 1981, which was originally put up in the 1940s as a sheltered workshop to give occupational therapy to the ex-service men who were at *Milner House* (see p. 150) from 1926 to 1987. Before Remploy took over, the workshop was used for many years by Thermega, which made electric blankets.

The largest development of new shops since 1945 has been the Craddocks Parade block on the north side, opened in 1959/60. Four shops were built in The Street in 1955, incorporating a bus lay-by, to be followed later by a block of four shops opposite. In the same year, two lock-up shops, now formed into one unit, were erected in Rectory Lane. Two shops, opposite the entrance to Greville School, were included in the Bramley Way housing estate. Only one of Ashtead's shops bears the same name and carries on principally the same trade as before the war. This is 'Jennifer's Bakery' in The Street although it is no longer a tea shop.

Ashtead's way of life, like that of the rest of the country, was in many ways transformed during the years after 1950 by the coming of television, which soon reached most homes, by the great increase in car ownership offering mobility far in excess of what the railway and motor bus could provide, and by the upsurge of air travel to most places in the world. Although many Ashtead people may have been induced to stay at home to watch TV rather than join local clubs and attend plays and concerts, this did not happen to the extent it might have done, most clubs and societies reporting no great reduction in support. Some effect on Ashtead's cohesion as a village community, however, probably occurred, but despite these pressures the community feeling, albeit perhaps muted, still exists today, helped no doubt by the ribbon of green round the village.

Notes

1. Census Report
2. M. Sissons & P. French (eds), *Age of Austerity* (1963) pp. 35–64
3. *Leatherhead Advertiser (L.A.)*, 21 June 1946
4. *L.A*, 7 June 1946
5. *L.A*, 5 April 1946
6. *Peace Memorial Hall* pamphlet (1984)
7. *The Ashtead Resident*, June 1977
8. *LA*, 20 Oct. 1972
9. *The Ashtead Resident*, Sept 1977
10. Royal British Legion, Ashtead Branch. Richard Butler, a contributor to this book, was one of those who attended the D-Day ceremonies in Normandy.
11. *Greater London Plan, 1944*, HMSO (1945) Ch. 10, p. 156
12. Chief Planning Officer's Report to Mole Valley District Council, Jan. 1988
13. 'People & Planning' *Committee on Public Participation in Planning* HMSO (1969)
14. *The Ashtead Resident*, 1945
15. *Hansard*, 10 June 1959
16. *The Ashtead Resident*, 1977/78
17. Leatherhead Urban District Council Minutes, 1954/55, p. 344
18. D.K. Jones & B.J. Davies, *Green Line, 1930–80* (1980); A. McCall, *Green Line: History of London's Country Bus* Services (1980), p. 23
19. A.G. Newman, 'Bus Services and Local History' *The Local Historian*, 13, 5 (1979) pp. 280–6
20. Leslie Bond provided valuable help on Ashtead's post offices.
21. Alan A. Jackson (ed), *Ashtead: A Village Transformed* (1977) p. 163

Chapter 19

THE CHURCHES SINCE 1800

The Parish Church of St Giles[1]
St Giles' Church at the beginning of the 19th century had changed little since early Tudor times. The interior in 1817 was plain, damp, dark and cheerless, with a flat plaster ceiling, and a minstrels' gallery at the west end, painted blue. The whole space was choked up with high pews[2].

During the century the church building was thoroughly restored and enlarged. The first restoration work was undertaken in 1830–31. A new transept was added on the north side, replacing the former north porch. The new arch was a copy of the arch at the west end of the church and was of Reigate stone. The gallery was taken down and the roof given a new frame supported by plain trusses. A porch and a new entrance were built on the south side of the nave where a former doorway had once been. The high canopied pulpit, with its lower deck for the Parish Clerk who read the service, was moved to a position near the new door. All the pews were removed and replaced by new similar ones of cedar from Col Howard's estate. New pews with medieval poppyhead carvings were installed in the north transept. All the work was paid for by Mary Howard and her husband[3].

A new east window was installed in the chancel, a gift to Mary Howard from her cousin, Sir Charles Bagot, Ambassador to The Hague from 1824. The glass was of the 15th or 16th century and was originally at Herkenrode Abbey near Liège, the abbey having been dissolved after the French Revolution. It is St Giles' greatest treasure[4].

The exterior of the church was also restored at this period, including the removal of earth heaped up against the south wall

Ground Plan

Scale of 30   50   100 Feet.

Fig. 46. St Giles' Church, c. 1822. Sketch by S.T. Cracklow.

Fig. 47. The interior of St Giles' Church, looking east, before the 19th century alterations. Watercolour by E. Hassell, 1827. (Courtesy, London Borough of Lambeth Archives Department, Minet Library).

almost to the window sills and the closing up of the south door in the chancel.

The mid-Victorians, in Ashtead as elsewhere, restored the church building in the Gothic style. By the mid-1860s the nave had been decorated: the roof trusses had been given filials, the timbers concealed by cedar panelling, a frieze carved with the words of the Te Deum, and wooden angel figures placed at the join of the trusses and the walls. The chancel had been embellished. Behind the altar a pinnacled stone reredos and marble tablets, with the words of the Ten Commandments, the Creed and Lord's Prayer in letters of gold, had replaced an earlier simple structure. An altar table with carved 'caryatid' legs had been given by Baron de Teissier from his private chapel at Woodcote Park. The barrel-vaulted ceiling, put up prior to 1831, had subsequently been richly decorated with cusping, angels and a frieze with the 'Holy, holy, holy', the 'ter sanctus' from the Communion service.

Two further extensions to the building had been built. The first was the short north aisle running parallel with the eastern end of the nave. The second was the extension of the north transept which was made to house the fine new organ given by Mary Howard in 1861. The quatrefoil font, which survives and is believed to be of the 15th century, was placed in the crossing at the centre of the nave near the south door and was given a hood which could be raised by pulley and chain attached to the roof timbers. A doorway had been made into a small vestry from the north side of the chancel.

In 1873 the six bells were recast, two more added and the tower restored. The plain glass window above the west door was replaced by stained glass.

In response to the needs of the increasing population and to the desire for improvements in the music, an organ chamber was built alongside the chancel in 1891, entailing a new arch[5]. The church was given new pews. Some of the uncomfortable old pews were preserved at the back of the transept. An unforeseen complication caused the cost of the work to escalate: much of the timber beneath the Horsham slabs on the roof was found to be rotten. The font was moved to the front of the north transept. The completion of the work which included a new choir vestry was celebrated on 13 December 1891, but it took another 18 months to clear the debts! The lych gate was erected in 1902 in memory of Sir Thomas Lucas. Several small stained glass windows were installed in the church. St

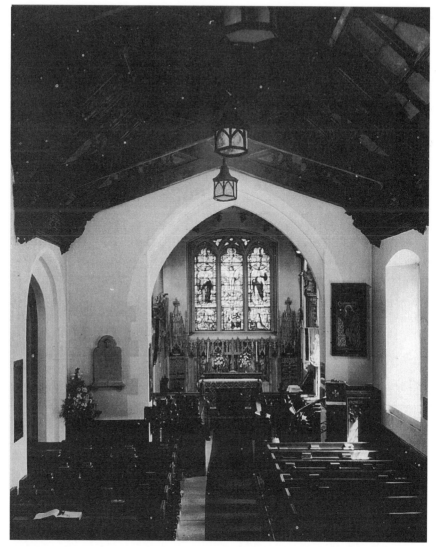

Fig. 48. The interior of St Giles' Church, looking east, in the 1970s. It has been virtually unchanged since 1891. (Photograph by, M.T. Jenkyn A.R.P.S.).

Giles' Church had acquired all the main features which it was to retain throughout the 20th century.

During the Second World War the windows of St Giles' Church suffered extensive damage from the bombing. When the first bombs fell on Ashtead in the night of 26 August 1940, they badly damaged the stained glass west window in the tower and the leaded diamond panes in the window above. The Smith Memorial window in the chancel, otherwise known as the Denshire window, was also damaged. Although the treasured east window was only slightly affected by the blast the churchwardens hastened to board it up. Further damage was done to the west window in another raid on 30 September. The Howard window beside the pulpit was also destroyed. The windows were repaired between 1946 and 1949, the cost being borne by the War Damage Commission. The east window was more badly damaged than expected and had to be taken away for repair. The Howard and Denshire windows were beyond repair and were replaced respectively by a figure of St Giles with a hind, and a roundel, both set in plain Nailsea glass. The value of the west window was disputed by experts but it was eventually repaired with matching coloured glass.

On 14 December 1957, the 300th peal on the bells was rung, 5,040 Grandsire Triples, this being the first peal ever rung by a band of Ashtead resident service ringers. The bells were removed in 1961 for general overhaul by John Taylor of Loughborough and rededicated by the Bishop of Guildford in January 1962.

A new and enlarged clergy vestry was erected in 1966 in memory of Mrs Peggy Halsey, the Rector's wife, who had died the previous year. This and the internal front entrance doors to the church were constructed through the initiative of the Sanctuary Guild. A church hall was erected in 1973/4 in the dell, on land given by the Corporation of the City of London in 1929.

Major restoration work was carried out on St Giles' Church in 1994. The roof was repaired, stonework and buttresses renewed, and extensive work carried out on the tower. St Giles' was ready to enter the 21st century in substantially the same form as it entered the 20th.

St George's Church

In 1882 a small Iron Church, given by Sir Thomas Lucas, had been built in the north of the parish for the growing population there. It was described as a pretty little church but it suffered from extremes of temperature. The ceiling was sometimes covered with a coat of ice which gradually thawed when the stove was lit and dripped on the congregation.

Although the building of a permanent church in its place had been discussed as early as 1890, it was not until 1899 that a fund was established for the purpose. In 1900 Frederick Peake gave land for the church on the corner of Oakfield Road. After generous contributions from one or two leading members the response to the Appeal was very slow. In January 1905 a Building Committee was set up and Arthur Blomfield, son of Sir Arthur Blomfield, was chosen as architect. The parish engaged in fund raising activities. Lily, Duchess of Marlborough, opened a large-scale bazaar in May held in a field opposite the Old Rectory. Ashtead's many young ladies were out in force manning stalls and running a hat trimming competition. The Duchess said it was the first time she had opened a bazaar in a parish where two churches could not contain the congregations.

Because of the shortfall in contributions, the architect modified the specifications, resulting in what was feared would be a plain church, seating only 300 people. The south aisle, organ chamber and vestries were excluded. A north transept was included but no 'lady chapel' was mentioned. The ceremony of laying the Foundation Stone in the wall of the Baptistry by Lord Ashcombe took place on 18 November 1905 after work had already begun on the site. The weather was so bad that the large congregation had to crowd into the Iron Church for the service. A glass jar was buried in the wall containing various documents, including the November *Parish*

Fig. 49.   St George's Church soon after it was built in 1906. The old *Woodman* can be seen in the background. LDLHS Collection.

Magazine. The Ecclesiastical Commissioners agreed to the dedication of the new church to St. George.

The Iron Church, which was standing on the same site, had to be removed, Mr Llewelyn Smith offering a portion of his garden for its new site on the opposite side of the road. In bad weather and over uneven ground, the church was slowly but successfully moved on rollers and reopened after only 10 days. The building was used as a parish room, later becoming the scout hut. Only five months after building started the main part of the church was finished. On 21 April 1906, two days before St. George's Day, the church was consecrated. A temporary wall was built on its south side. Furniture and furnishings were generously given by parishioners and others, from a wooden altar to umbrella stands. The clergy reading desk was given by past clergy in the parish and the pulpit given in memory of Sir Thomas Lucas's late widow by members of the family. Although the finished church was plain it was generally felt to be 'charming' by most contemporaries[6].

In 1908 an organ chamber was built to house an organ given by Mr Garlick who had also given the altar and bell. A vestry was added behind the organ on the south-east side of the church. The new organ, described as excellent, was dedicated on 29 September and a recital given by Dr Alcock, organist at the Chapel Royal and assistant organist at Westminster Abbey. After the First World War, changes were made in the chancel sanctuary as a succession of curates moved St George's in an Anglo-Catholic direction.

The first building project after the Second World War was the construction of a church hall in 1954. The hall fitted neatly into the site abutting the east end of St George's Church. There had been plans for a hall in the mid-1930s on the south side of the church but lack of funds held up the project then. The hall was designed for use both by the church and the community and was licensed for music and dancing.

Between 1959 and 1964 St. George's Church, which had been left incomplete before the First World War, was enriched and enlarged, while retaining its essential character. A formerly dark building was transformed into a light and spacious place of worship, although without a proper entrance or circulation area.

A new east window was installed in 1961, in place of three former lancet windows, the shafts of light from which had obscured the rest of the sanctuary. The new window was designed by Christopher Webb on the lines of a window he had designed in 1957 for the Commonwealth Chapel at St. Lawrence Jewry in the City of London. The area to the north of the chancel, which had been used as a children's corner for many years, was converted to a Lady Chapel in 1950. In 1962 a pastel-shaded open metalwork screen was erected between the choir stalls and the chapel in memory of the Rev. A.W. Douglas, a retired clergyman who had assisted at St. George's.

A south aisle was added in 1964. The temporary south wall built between the brick pillars in 1906 was removed and space for 120 seats provided. The aisle was given large windows and a low pitched roof with a blue and white ceiling. New clusters of pendant lights were introduced, suspended from steel bars, and concealed lighting in the side windows of the chancel. The single vestry of 1908 was divided into clergy and choir rooms behind the organ, with a new bay window on the south. The new work was dedicated on 20 October 1964.

In the 1980s a dais was constructed between nave and chancel covered with gold-coloured carpeting. A portable font was introduced, with a light oak pedestal, the work of church member, Graham Laird, with a stainless steel bowl, processed to resemble hammered pewter, made at Richard Quinnell's forge in Leatherhead. The old stone font was removed to St. Giles' churchyard and placed in the children's section, filled in the summer with flowers.

After several years of planning, the decision was made in 1995 to proceed with the St George's Project, the re-ordering of the church building and other buildings on the site at the corner of Oakfield Road.

Clergy and People

The two most notable and long serving Rectors in the 19th century were the Rev. William Legge (1826–72) and the Rev. Francis Lucas (1887–1906). The former was a relative of Mary Howard and the latter the son of Sir Thomas Lucas. Mr Legge was personally responsible for many of the changes in the church building and gave generously.

The Rector was required to count the congregation at the Parish Church on 30 March 1851 for the unique Ecclesiastical Census[7]. On that Sunday 260 adults attended Morning Service and 245 Afternoon Service, there being no evening service. Mr Legge estimated that at least 200 different persons attended, some going to both services. There were also 57 children called 'Sunday Scholars' in the morning and 62 in the afternoon, and a Sunday School class of about fifteen. The total population was 684 in 124 households. The total number of sittings was reckoned to be 380, including places for children. At least 80 of these were described as 'free', the rest being appropriated or 'booked' for named individuals or households. There were no pew rents in Ashtead as there were in many parishes.

The churchwardens in the earlier years of the 19th century were often farmers but at the end of the century were professional people, solicitors and the like. Until 1894 they, the Rector and the Lord of the Manor, formed the body known as the Vestry and were responsible not only for church matters but also civil. The development of new local government bodies in the last decades of the century led to the transfer of civil responsibility from the Vestry to the Parish Council. Unfortunately, the records of the Ashtead Vestry have been lost. After 1894 the church continued to minister to the poor and needy, to be the source of entertainment and the centre of much social activity, and to manage the Church of England School.

During the time of the next two Rectors, the Rev. R.A.W. Waddilove (1907–28) and the Rev. E.J. Austin (1928–42), the Anglican Church in Ashtead declined, but the evidence for the period from 1915 to 1946 is scanty because of the loss of the *Parish Magazines*. W. Maples, M.W. Marshall and J.W. Grove were leading laymen in the earlier part of the period. Parochial Church Councils were introduced by legislation in the 1920s. Names familiar in the post-1945 church, E. Graham, J. Symonds and L. Gowdey, for example, were active just before the Second World War, during the curacy of the Rev. W. Curtis.

There have been five successive Rectors and many curates since the Second World War. The Rectors were the Revs W.H. Alan Cooper 1942–51, G. John Halsey 1951–66, John F.W. Watson 1966–72, Richard G. Askew 1972–83, and Christopher C. Hughes from 1983. Each made a distinctive contribution to the growth and development of the church in which there has been an increasing involvement of the laity in recent years.

The people of Ashtead responded well to the Christian message after the war, put to them by Mr Cooper. This was helped by a succession of special events and by notable speakers, the Rev. Jack

Winslow, Gordon Guinness, J.B. Phillips, O.K. de Berry, Hugh Redwood and others. The number of Easter communicants in 1950 had risen to 900 and children's groups were formed in private homes to meet the bulge. The parish joined in a Diocesan Mission in 1956, when Mr Halsey was Rector, St George's Church being filled to capacity. In the late 1960s Mr Watson's ministry was marked by a challenge to individual members to witness to their faith. A campaign, 'Who Cares?', followed in the 1970s and the Rt Rev. Cuthbert Bardsley led a mission in 1981. The main evangelistic thrust in Mr Hughes' ministry from 1983 has been directed towards youth and young families, full-time youth workers being appointed.

The youngest Rector to fill the pulpit for 50 years, Mr Cooper, immediately appealed to young people, running youth camps every summer and forming active youth groups. Later Rectors continued to make youth work a priority and this has been a feature of the parish ever since. Mission at home and abroad has been generously supported by the parish and several young people have worked overseas. The annual Missionary Sale, later the Parish Fair for Christian Mission, has been held each November since 1947 in the Peace Memorial Hall. Since Refugee Year in 1960, when shacks were erected in the village and a mile of pennies collected, an annual Christian Aid Week has been held.

The Ashtead Branch of the Mothers Union, MU, was inaugurated following a visit by the Bishop's wife, Mrs Sumner, on 1 November 1890 and has flourished ever since. Church and family life were much strengthened by the MU and in 1970 the members accepted new and more inclusive aims. Ashtead women took an important part in the affairs of the church from the 1920s and in the 1990s three former Ashtead women were ordained priest.

There have been many changes in the church's worship. Minstrels played from the gallery in St Giles' in 1800. They gave way first to portable and then fixed organs. In the last quarter of the 20th century groups of musicians returned in some services with piano and keyboard! Robed choirs processing to choir stalls were introduced in 1887, unrobed worship leaders with microphones in the 1980s at informal services. One of the striking features of the 20th century has been the growth of the Christmas services which hardly existed in the 1890s.

The 700th anniversary of the first known Rector of Ashtead was celebrated in 1982 shortly before the departure of Mr Askew. There was an historical exhibition and a flower festival to mark the event.

Ashtead Free Church

Throughout the 19th century there had been little evidence of non-conformity in Ashtead. In 1895 the Ashtead Gospel Mission had been set up in an iron church in Barnett Wood Lane (later to become the Constitutional Hall). The congregation was composed initially of cottage folk, working people and servants from the newly-built large houses. Under Pastor Harris, a business man from Camberwell, who became its honorary leader in 1913, the name was changed to the Ashtead Free Church. A new building was erected a few yards to the west in 1924 on land belonging to Mellish of Woodfield Bakery. A hall was built by Jack Worsfold and members at the rear of the church in 1934, by which time the church had a flourishing congregation and Sunday School.

After a period of ill-health Pastor Harris retired in 1947; a plaque was put up in the church in his memory when he died in 1957. Miss E.F. Richardson who had served as church secretary since Edwar-

Fig. 50. The opening of the Ashtead Free Church in April 1924. (Courtesy, Worsfold family).

dian times retired in 1958. Pastor Harris was succeeded by the Revs. Roland Meyer and Hugh Robinson, the secretary being W.E. (Eddie) Hawker. Under the Rev. Neville Swain who became pastor in 1961, the church flourished with a thriving youth work. A manse was provided in Rectory Lane in 1957, to be replaced later by a new house in Glebe Road. A new church room was built in the 1980s. The last two ministers were the Revs. Philip Craig and Chris Searle. The church has been without a pastor for some years.

Other non-conformists from Ashtead have attended churches in Leatherhead and Epsom and elsewhere.

St Michael's Catholic Church

St Michael's Catholic Church celebrated its Silver Jubilee in 1992, having been officially opened for worship in October 1967. Until 1942 Catholics, who lived in Ashtead, could attend Mass only by travelling to a church in Leatherhead or Epsom. That year arrangements were made to use the Constitutional Hall in Barnett Wood Lane for the celebration of a weekly Mass for members of the growing Catholic population, Ashtead still being counted as part of Leatherhead parish. In 1944 the Roman Catholic Diocese of Southwark purchased a bombed property, *Mawmead Shaw*, which stood

Fig. 51.   St Michael's Catholic Church. Drawing by Betty Eldridge.

at the junction of Woodfield Lane and The Marld. Its large garage then became the local Mass centre. The house was demolished and the present church stands on its site. As the curate from Leatherhead who had the care of this centre was Fr Michael Costello, the Bishop suggested the embryo parish be dedicated to St Michael.

In 1947 the adjacent property, *Rushmere*, was purchased and an ex-army hut erected to act as a chapel in place of the garage. The house was used as a parish centre and provided a residence for a priest; in 1948 Fr St Clair-Hill was appointed as Priest-in-charge. The parish began to grow but in 1955 Fr Hill was moved to Kent. After a year's interregnum, during which Mgr Wall, the Diocesan Chancellor, cared for the parish, Fr Edward Maxwell was appointed. Under his ministry plans were made for the building of a permanent church but sadly he died before these materialised. He was succeeded by Fr Bernard McGrath. In that year the parish became part of the newly-formed Diocese of Arundel and Brighton. Regulations issued by Vatican II and rising costs necessitated the revision of the original more elaborate plans and a modern octagonal building with walls of timber and glass was designed. Building commenced in 1966, the church being completed in the following year. Behind the church is a priest's house with a parish hall added in 1983.

Fr McGrath retired in 1977. He was succeeded by Fr Richard Veal, who was later succeeded by Fr John Healy. The parish priest in 1995 is Fr Robert Davies. As the population of Ashtead has grown, so has the number of Catholics and the average weekly attendance at Mass is about 400.

Moving towards unity

After the war, Mr Cooper established 'Towards Fellowship', twice-monthly meetings aimed at bringing together people of all the churches and the community. Outstanding speakers were obtained and an annual Harvest Supper was celebrated. This event continued after the demise of 'Towards Fellowship' in 1963, with clergy, ministers and leading lay people from church and community seated together each year at top table. In 1963 much time was devoted to the abortive Anglican-Methodist unity proposals. Since 1966, Anglicans, Roman Catholics and some members of the Non-Conformist churches have joined together in the Week of Prayer for Christian Unity. By the 1970s an annual joint service was being held by the churches on Good Friday near Ashtead Pond and on several occasions united services were held in the Recreation Ground. Ministers, priests and clergy continued to exchange pulpits and lead a combined mid-week service once a year during the Week of Prayer. Many inter-church activities take place in Ashtead, including the Women's World Day of Prayer, house visiting, Christian Viewpoint meetings and the support of the needy and homeless through, for example, Christian Aid.

Notes

1. Much of the information in this chapter is taken from the *Ashtead Parish Magazine* and the records of the Ashtead Parochial Church Council.
2. 'Some Records of the Ashtead Estate and its Howard Possessors' (1873) pp. 179–80. Unpublished work attributed to the Rev. Francis Paget.
3. SRO 203/19/2 5 & 7
4. For a description of the glass see *Archaeologia,* vol. c.viii, 1986, pp. 215–18
5. SRO PSH/ATD/GIL 11/2 & 3
6. SRO/PSH/ATD/GEO 5/3 & 4
7. Ecclesiastical Census, 1851: PRO: HO 129/37

Chapter 20

POPULATION

Since the first Census was taken in 1801 Ashtead has experienced a dramatic increase in population*. In common with Surrey as a whole, the greater part of this increase has occurred since 1901. The growth in Ashtead's population since 1801 is illustrated by equating the figure for 1801 to 100, and by adjusting the other figures accordingly:

Year	Actual Population	1801 Population equals 100
1801	552	100
1841	618	112
1851	684	124
1871	906	164
1901	1,881	341
1931	4,783	866
1971	12,950	2,346
1981	12,805	2,320
1991	13,363	2,421

The figures up to and including those for 1931 are for the civil parish, subsequently for Ashtead ward(s).

The adjusted figures demonstrate the relative rates of population growth over different periods, but it is important to appreciate the actual changes, which have reflected the influence of London, par-

* For Ashtead's population before 1801 see pp. 24, 35, 44, 50 and Alan A. Jackson (ed) *Ashtead: A Village Transformed* (1977) pp. 164–6

ticularly during the middle decades of the present century. The increase between 1931 and 1971, for instance, was of over 8,000 people.

The figures in the table show that during the first century for which Census records exist (1801–1901), the population of Ashtead increased by almost 250% of its original size (552 to 1,881). Over the next 30 years, up to 1931, it more than doubled (1,881 to 4,783). There are particular difficulties in tracing the growth of Ashtead's population between 1931 and 1951 due to the effects of the Second World War. These included the cancellation of the Census which otherwise would have been taken in 1941. The figure from the National Registration of 1939 (9,336 persons) although not directly comparable, gives some indication of population growth up to the outbreak of war in that year.

In the four decades to 1971, the population increased to 12,950 – almost three times as large as that in 1931. During the century 1871–1971 the population of Ashtead showed an increase of more than 13-fold (906–12,950). The contrast in the rates of growth 1801–1901 (552–1,881) and 1871–1971 underlines the most significant feature of Ashtead's demography and illustrates the extent to which Ashtead has been affected by London; particularly since the turn of the century.*

By 1971, however, the rate of population growth was slowing-down, to roughly seven per cent (12,109 to 12,950) during the previous decade. This slowing-down of the rate of increase was due probably to strict planning controls, imposed in support of Green Belt policy. The following ten years, up to 1981, were to show a decrease in the population of Ashtead of roughly one per cent (12,950 to 12 ,805). This is the first indication of any decrease in the population since the first decade of the 19th century, when Ashtead was among 21 Surrey parishes to show a small decrease. By 1991 the decrease had been reversed and an increase of 4% (12,805 to 13,363) had taken place during the previous decade.

A comparative approach to Census data for Ashtead and the three neighbouring parishes of Epsom, Headley and Leatherhead is shown in the following table.

The figures show that, apart from a fall in the population of Headley between 1851 and 1871, the population of all four parishes

---

* See E.C. Willatts, 'Changes in land utilization in the South-West of the London Basin, 1840–1932' *Geog. Journ*, LXXXII (1933) pp. 515–28

RELATIVE GROWTH OF ASHTEAD
AND NEIGHBOURING PARISHES

	ASHTEAD	EPSOM	HEADLEY	LEATHERHEAD
1801	552 (100)	2,404 (435)	217 (39)	1,078 (195)
1841	618 (100)	3,533 (572)	317 (57)	1,740 (282)
1851	684 (100)	4,129 (604)	363 (53)	2,041 (298)
1871	906 (100)	6,276 (693)	337 (37)	2,455 (271)
1901	1,881 (100)	10,915 (580)	394 (21)	4,694 (249)
1931	4,783 (100)	27,092 (566)	487 (10)	6,916 (146)
1971	12,950 (100)	32,820 (253)	758 (6)	9,591 (74)
1991	13,363 (100)	28,879 (216)	709 (5)	9,718 (73)

(Figures in brackets indicate the population, taking that of Ashtead as 100)
The figures up to and including those for 1931 are for the civil parishes and subsequently for wards, except for Headley where the figures relate to the civil parish throughout. For Epsom, College, Court, Stamford, Town and Woodcote wards are taken as equivalent to the civil parish

increased at least until 1971. The population of Epsom grew relative to that of Ashtead until 1871. Epsom had been a spa town and market centre and, probably by 1871, was beginning to fall under the influence of London as a place of employment. The railway had reached Epsom, via Sutton, in 1847 and, via Wimbledon, in 1859. It is apparent from the figures, however, that Ashtead has grown at a higher relative rate than Epsom during the present century. In the case of Leatherhead, the decline in its rate of growth, relative to that of Ashtead, is apparent from 1851 and is more marked than that of Epsom, during the present century. These comparisons demonstrate further the rapid growth of Ashtead.

There has been a steady overall decline in the rate of population growth at Headley, as compared with that at Ashtead, which is of far greater significance than the figures suggest. It emphasises the chief factors which have influenced Ashtead's growth. Headley, a downland village, has lain off the main communication routes throughout its history, and has not changed greatly. By contrast, Ashtead has been sited upon lines of communication; first track, then road, and then railway, which have influenced its growth and fostered eventually the suburban character of its present-day community.

ASHTEAD CENSUS TABLE

Year	Total Population	Percentage Increase	Males per 100 Females	Inhabited Houses	Average House	Persons per Family
1801	552	—	99	91	6.07	5.31
1811	548	−1.0	100	88	6.27	5.27
1821	579	5.6	93	94	6.16	5.22
1831	607	4.8	102	111	5.47	4.90
1841	618	1.8	106	124	4.90	n.a.
1851	684	10.8	102	124	5.52	n.a.
1861	729	6.6	98	124	5.88	n.a.
1871	906	24.3	104	150	6.04	n.a.
1881	926	2.3	99	160	5.79	4.95
1891	1,351	45.9	87	278	4.86	4.79
1901	1,881	39.2	89	379	4.96	4.71
1911	2,921	55.3	78	n.a.	n.a.	4.52
1921	3,226	10.4	78	680	4.74	4.21
1931	4,783	48.5	82	1,193	4.01	3.77
1939	9,336	95.2	n.a.	n.a.	n.a.	n.a.
1951	9,852	5.5	85	2,906	3.39	3.25
1961	12,109	22.7	86	3,824	3.16	3.06
1971	12,950	6.9	89	n.a.	n.a.	2.89
1981	12,805	−1.1	91	n.a.	n.a.	2.72
1991	13,363	4.4	91	n.a.	n.a.	n.a.

Notes

1. The table is derived from the published Census reports. The figures for 1801–51 have been taken from those included in the 1851 report.
2. For the years after 1951 the figures are for the constituent ward(s) rather than for the parish.
3. The figures for the National Registration, 1939, are not strictly comparable with those for the Census. They serve only as a guide to the extent of population growth up to the outbreak of war.

Chapter 21

THE SCHOOLS OF ASHTEAD

It is difficult for us to imagine a world in which the state provided nothing, but this was the case until the late 19th century. The prevailing view had always been that a man should be independent and proud, taking no 'charity'. For most children the only schooling in Ashtead and elsewhere had been at home. The gentry were tutored privately by clergy, governesses or tutors, frequently impoverished gentry themselves. Some went to the few old public or grammar schools, and Oxford or Cambridge universities thereafter, for which the entry criteria were social rather than academic. The ordinary person's only access to learning was, with few exceptions, parental, or after the later 18th century from Sunday Schools. A rector would tutor a bright child, but in most families every child was needed to earn its living as soon as possible. This view was still prevalent in the Ashtead Church of England School one hundred years ago.

'Dame schools' existed in Ashtead, as elsewhere, and the cottage in Rectory Lane, *Applebough*, had a schoolroom behind it. Often these schools had a reputation for too many children huddled in a room with an old woman teaching for a few pence, while chickens ran in and out. However, there was certainly a schoolmaster in Ashtead from the mid-18th century onwards.

National sentiment was changing, and in 1725 David White, a Ewell bricklayer, left £9.10s.0d. annually for the education of poor children in Ashtead. There was no application for these funds until a school was established by the Howards in 1815 behind the almshouses in Park Lane. This building was shingled with wooden tiles, and about 60 children were taught there, increasing to 100 by 1850.

The Parochial Schools Bill of 1820 called for teaching by the clergy, and when the Rev. William Legge, a young relative of the Howards, became Rector in 1826 he worked with Mary Howard for many years to improve conditions in the village. Under both their wills provisions were made which still continue[1]. The Ashtead Howards owned other estates in England, and James Penny came to Ashtead from Levens Hall near Kendal as schoolmaster. He later combined this with being Postmaster. The schoolmaster and mistress received a joint annual salary in 1846 of £114 10s 0d. The monitor, or pupil teaching system, was used throughout the century, with the older children teaching the younger. Slates and chalk were used, and the provision of books would have been minimal. Learning 'by rote' or recitation was the usual method. By the middle of the century, the majority of people signing the Parish Registers still signed their names by a cross. These were chiefly the farm labourers, who made up the bulk of the Ashtead population.

Compulsory education was first introduced by the 1870 Act, but this was not popular because the average fee for schooling was 3d a week. For a farm labourer to pay so much when his weekly wage could be as little as 10 shillings must have been an effort. School attendance was a major problem at this time, since many parents expected their children's help at home or on the farm. The unpopularity of fees led to their abolition in 1891 and eleven years later the schools came under the management of Surrey County Council[2]. Free education at all levels was introduced by the 1944 Education Act, and important developments since the mid-1960s were 'comprehensive' education, the 'three-tier' system of First, Middle and Secondary schools and the return in 1993 to Infant, Junior and Secondary schooling with the change in the age of transfer[3]. More flexible teaching methods have been introduced with increased freedom and responsibility for school governors, especially since the 1988 Education Act.

Church and State Schools

Ashtead Church of England School (St Giles' Primary)
This school dates from 1852 when Mary Howard, owner of Ashtead Park, had a new school built in what became School Lane and later Dene Road[4]. It replaced Park Lane School which was used for housing teachers and is now a private house. In 1856 Mary

Howard gave the school and land to the Rector and his successors for the education of the poor of both sexes in the principles of the Christian religion. In its early days the school was in three parts: infants, boys and girls, each with its own teachers. Slates were used for writing and taking dictation, arithmetic and drawing. Poems were recited and learnt by heart, and needlework of the highest quality was taught to the girls. Children entered at any age from two years upwards. Some came to the school from Epsom Common, Headley and Langley Vale, walking all the way when the roads were often poor and muddy. There was no street lighting, and in cold, wet weather the numbers attending understandably dropped. This was of great concern because the school grant depended on attendance. Medals were presented to encourage children to go to school each day, and the Attendance Officer visited parents of truants. Older boys were often in trouble (whether for absconding or even riding sheep) and in 1895 cottage gardening began to be taught on part of what is now the school field, which improved attendance greatly. The boys' and girls' schools were amalgamated in 1900 after the retirement of the girls' school mistress.

The gentry and clergy frequently visited the school. Mrs Denshire of *Ashtead House* arranged for the infants to strew rose petals at her daughters' weddings, and for the whole school to have a day off. A Christmas treat was given by the owners of Ashtead Park, and in Derby week Mrs Denshire would provide a tea only for those attending during the whole week. Absence during the Derby was a recurring problem throughout the village until the 1950s.

At the beginning of this century the school was heavily overcrowded, owing to the increase in Ashtead's population. In 1904 there were 317 children at the school and some had to sit seven or eight together on benches made to hold five. This overcrowding led to the call for a new school which later became Barnett Wood School. In the mid-1900s sickness was particularly rife in the village, with epidemics of measles, scarlet fever and diphtheria. Many children died and the school had to be closed for fumigation. From 1908 onwards, and for many years thereafter, the Ashtead schools celebrated Empire Day together, which entailed saluting the Union Jack, a tea and a concert. On one day in 1911 the school's opening was delayed 'to witness the interesting sight of aeroplanes flying over this locality'. Six planes were seen by the pupils, a rare sight in those days.

Fig. 52.   Class at St Giles' School c. 1911/12. (Courtesy, Janet Goldsmith).

Soldiers were billeted in the school during the First World War, and extra land was provided by the Rector for 'war plots'. School attendance was poor and there were great problems with staffing. In the early 1920s the number of pupils had fallen to 167, especially following the opening of the Epsom Downs school in 1923. The roll declined to 121, with a consequent reduction of staff. The first school cap with badge became available at the end of the decade and gas lighting was installed in 1931. Throughout the years the school allotments were occasionally vandalized, or trampled by cows from adjacent fields, and on one occasion the buildings were severely damaged by intruders; the constable named those responsible later that day.

In the Second World War the school provided accommodation for one of two Dulwich schools evacuated to the area, but most of the evacuees had returned home by 1943. School holidays were cancelled for pupils and staff because of war work. When the school lost its roof in an air raid in September 1940 classes had to be held throughout the village. On one occasion there was no school, due to the church vestry being required for two weddings and a funeral. Air raid shelters were built beyond the playground and electric light installed. During the war a former infants' room was converted into the first staff room. When this later became the boys' toilets the telephone continued to ring in there! The boys' gardens provided

Fig. 53. Pupils of St Giles' School who performed at the May Festival concert 1929 in crepe paper crinolines made by Miss E. Bourne, Infants teacher. L to R: Ivy Draper, Eileen Bailey, Kathleen Beasley, Doris Clatworthy. (Courtesy, Kathleen Davies).

produce for families and staff, but at the end of the war it was decided that a playing field would replace the gardens.

Following the 1944 Education Act, the school opted for 'aided' as opposed to 'maintained' status, and became a Primary School to the age of eleven. The first Parent Teacher Association (PTA) was formed and the name of the school changed to St. Giles, although it had been registered as 'All Saints' initially. In 1949 a school badge was designed, based on Mary Howard's colours of red, gold, silver and white, using a hind from the legend of St Giles superimposed on a cross. The badge was affixed to navy caps, berets and blazers. At this time, there were 215 children at the school. The PTA began a Parents' Day, which later developed into the annual school fair. In the early days, sweets could not be sold at this event as they were still rationed. Some of the PTA funds went towards part-purchasing and forming a level playing field on the land adjoining the school in the early 1950s. Since every part of the school had been in use as classrooms there was no assembly hall, and in the mid-1950s a hall was built behind the existing buildings and joined by a covered walkway. This is now the reception classroom, and the hall is in the original building.

There were celebrations on the centenary of St Giles' School in

1952 but these were clouded by the threat of closure, since the site was deemed unsuitable for modern development. However, after the appointment of Mr Morgan as headmaster, the school began to thrive again. In 1970 there were 170 children in five classes, ranging from five to eleven years of age. In 1975 the school became a First School, with children aged from four to eight, and in 1986 the first female Headteacher was appointed, an internal promotion. In 1993 the school became an Infant School, teaching children from four to seven years of age. There were 128 pupils in 1995. The fundamental principle of hard work within a religious framework, as envisaged by Mary Howard, although modified by a modern outlook, continues to be the basis of this school.

Barnett Wood Infants' School (formerly Ashtead Council School)
At the beginning of this century it was decided to build a new Council School in Barnett Wood Lane. There was severe overcrowding at the Church of England School, and children as young as three years old had to walk to school from the outskirts of the village. The school, built on the site of a tannery, was opened in 1906 for children from the age of eight, who were housed for eight years in temporary accommodation. From the outset, the demand for infant teaching was apparent, and early in 1907, with desks and readers borrowed from the Church School, Miss Bertha Bumpstead began to hold an infant class. The school was recognised for 100 juniors and 50 infants, but by 1911 it was over-subscribed. There were occasional breaks from routine; in 1912, the Headteacher took the 'elder scholars . . . to see the Royal train pass, in which His Majesty George V was returning from his historic voyage to India.'

The present school buildings were completed in June 1914 when there were four classes of mixed juniors and an infants' class. In 1915 the children collected 800 eggs for the Central Fund for the Wounded, and sent Christmas parcels to 22 former pupils in the armed forces. Gardening was an important part of the curriculum, with part of the school field used for the cultivation of crops. The traffic along Barnett Wood Lane was so heavy by the 1920s that the school had to close for most of Derby Day. Over 60 children were absent on that day in 1922 . In 1929 the school became a Junior Mixed Infants' School taking children to the age of 11. Under the new Headmistress, examination results were very good, and by 1938 there were 250 on the roll. The school was not permitted to

Fig. 54. Football team, Council School Barnett Wood Lane, 1922/3. L to R: back row: Mr Dyer, Arthur Haffingden, Tom Newbury, Harold Winteridge, Alf Goodhew?, Fred Etherington, Sir Arthur Glyn. Middle row: Albert Dorling, Frank Frewin, Percy Millman, Jack Fuller, Theo Hoyle. Front row: Reg Lifford, Ken Overington, Alf Cook. (Courtesy, Bob Gibb).

accept any children from the new Berg estate; these had to travel to the Church of England School.

The school initially closed on the outbreak of war in 1939, as there were no air raid shelters, but it opened again when these were built in the playing field. Children from Dulwich were evacuated to the school early in the war. Teaching accommodation for all the Dulwich and Ashtead school pupils had to be found throughout the village. The *Woodman* made its dining room and billiard room available, the children instructed to hide under the tables during air raids. After the Church School was bombed in 1940 it also shared the Barnett Wood accommodation, together with its Dulwich school, for four months. The school participated in the War Savings Scheme: 'Our aim is to raise £100 to buy a machine gun. Our final total was £300.' By 1952 it had been decided to build two temporary extra classrooms to meet the expected increase in numbers coming to the school. In 1954 there were 332 on the roll.

From 1975 the school catered for children from five to eight years old, and to seven years of age from September 1993. Before this happened there were about 120 'busy bees of Barnett Wood School', (100 in 1995) an appreciably smaller number than there had been because many potential pupils had gone to either the Greville School or West Ashtead School.

A play scheme for younger children was opened in 1993 on the school premises.

Greville School

With the increasing population after the Second World War, another infant and junior state school, Greville, was opened at Stonny Croft in January 1958, with 92 boys and girls. The school is believed to have been named after Col Fulk Greville Howard, Mary Howard's husband. There were five classrooms initially, but two others were added in 1962. In 1975 the school became a First and Middle School, with pupils from five to twelve years. There are now over 300 pupils aged from five to eleven.

West Ashtead School

This school, in Taleworth Road, was opened in 1964 as an Infant and Junior state school, with 22 pupils initially, soon rising to 65. In the mid-1970s it increased substantially in size and became a First and Middle School. It now has about 320 pupils, aged from five to eleven.

St Andrew's School

St Andrew's is the secondary school for the Roman Catholic Deanery centred on Epsom, forming part of the Diocese of Arundel and Brighton. The Deanery consists of nine parishes from which children may attend this school, an area stretching from as far as Guildford to Molesey. Over 750 children, aged between 11 and 18, attend the school.

In 1935 the Sisters of the Congregation of St Andrew purchased *Hillfield*, a large house with a lodge on Grange Road. The house stood on the site of the M25, which today effectively divides the various locations of the school buildings as they were through the war years. The school began with six boarders and 13 day pupils, but numbers grew, particularly with the outbreak of war when many children were evacuated to Ashtead. After *Hillfield* had been destroyed by a bomb, together with a new gymnasium/hall, Downsend School lent two classrooms, but the remainder of the school moved to *The Knoll* (now the Elizabeth Ellen Nursing Home) on the Leatherhead Knoll roundabout. The Community of St Andrew's purchased this property, and later *Oversley* (now also a nursing home) on the other side of Epsom Road. This housed the senior school.

In 1945 *The Grange*, adjacent to *Hillfield*, was bought from the Lines family, together with extensive grounds containing a swimming pool, orchards and a kitchen garden. The Community of St Andrew's and the inter-denominational fee-paying preparatory classes moved there; St Peter's Catholic Primary School was later built on one of the fields.

The school became voluntary-aided in 1956, developing into a comprehensive school for girls, aged 11 to 18, and in 1971 boys were admitted. By 1977, the Sisters of St Andrew decided to hand the school over to the Diocese of Arundel and Brighton, and the first lay Headmaster was appointed. The Preparatory School was closed two years later and the Diocese converted *The Grange* into a sixth form unit. Many new buildings have been added over the years, including a library, resources centre and science wing.

Independent Schools

Apart from the schools described below, there were a number of other private schools in Ashtead earlier this century. Among these were Mead School (started about 1918) in The Mead which thrived for a few years and then closed in the 1930s; and another small school in Skinners Lane during the 1930s, which moved to Agates Lane as Bowood School, only to close a few years later. In 1940 there was a school at *Downside* (41 Woodfield Lane) called Nonsuch. It became Woodfield Preparatory School, and had over 100 pupils in the 1950s, but closed in 1961.

Downsend School

The oldest independent school in Ashtead is Downsend[5], noted in the 1871 census as 'Leatherhead Road Boarding School'. At this time it was about three years old, with fourteen boys aged from eight to thirteen, under its Headmaster, the Rev. E.T. Scudamore. The premises were at *Gateforth House* on the present site. By 1890 this had become the Gateforth House Preparatory School under S.H. Johnson, two dormitories, two classrooms and a gymnasium being added at this time. The name changed to Downsend in 1895.

Fig. 55.   Downsend School, original building c. 1870. LDLHS Collection

Although large enough to house 25 boarders and 25 day boys, the school was run down in the First World War and had only one boy when A.H. Linford acquired it in 1918, but by the following year when Linford's son, Cedric, joined the school to help his father the numbers had increased to about 20 pupils. In 1923 the school acquired a sports field and four years later built a swimming pool. There were 50 boys by 1929/30, when a corrugated iron gymnasium was demolished so that new form rooms could be built. These were called 'the senior school'. Numbers had doubled again by 1934 and the 'junior school' was built to accommodate the growth. A house called *Ermyn Way* was bought in 1939 to provide a nursery department, but the war intervened and it was occupied by Canadian troops until June 1944. Destroyed by a V1 rocket, it was rebuilt after the war and is now the school's administrative offices. A.H. Linford retired at the end of the war, but Cedric Linford had run the school for a number of years before that. He had been joined by Denys Straker in 1936. When Cedric Linford retired in 1968 his son, Christopher, became joint Headmaster with Denys Straker, who retired in 1977. At that time Christopher Linford became Principal and Andrew Hooper and Tony White were made Headmasters of the Senior and Junior Schools respectively. The school used to take about 27 boarders but this was discontinued in 1968.

Downsend was one of the first preparatory schools in the country to have science laboratories, built in 1964, and later, in 1983, the school again led the way with the opening of its first computer laboratory. Further improvements to the science facilities took place in 1991, including a new technology laboratory. In 1979 the school founded its first pre-preparatory department when it took over *The Lindens* in Park Rise, Leatherhead. This was renamed Downsend Lodge. Four years later, the school acquired its second pre-preparatory department, Oakfield House School (formerly Ryebrook), calling it Downsend Lodge (Ashtead). By 1987 there were in all four pre-preparatory departments in different locations.

A major reorganisation took place in 1989, when, after the retirement of Andrew Hooper, Tony White became the sole Headmaster, Christopher Linford continuing as Principal. By 1991 there were about 1,000 pupils under the Downsend 'umbrella'.

The expansion of numbers to be accommodated was eased by the acquisition of a corridor of land between the school and the M25 motorway. With the help of the motorway contractors, excellent pitches were created. The school doubled its acreage to 15, and also doubled the number of pitches available for sports. The cricket field off Taleworth Road was sold in 1988 and the funds generated enabled a Sports Complex to be built with a swimming pool and sports hall. These were opened by the Rt. Hon. Kenneth Baker M.P. during the celebrations to mark Downsend's 100th birthday year in 1991.

Parsons Mead

Parsons Mead in Ottways Lane is Ashtead's second oldest independent school, founded in 1897 by Miss Jessie Elliston, who had previously been a governess for twenty years. She was born in 1858, the eldest daughter of a Baptist Minister, and went to school in Leighton Buzzard. Friends made there later taught and helped at Parsons Mead, or sent their daughters to be educated as 'young ladies'. Her last employer was Canon Utterton, Vicar of Leatherhead, who advised her to start a private school in the area. Initially, she rented a house, *St. Anne's* in Woodfield Lane, now No. 11, later renamed *Cranham*. She had two boarders, one of whom, Marguerite Hopkins (daughter of a former school friend) later taught at the school and then became its Headmistress and co-director. A.P. Herbert (later Sir Alan Herbert M.P.) was a day boy at the school in these early days. The daughter of one of Miss Elliston's cousins, Laurette Elliston, came to live with her in 1900 and was informally adopted, devoting a major portion of her life to the school. Parsons Mead soon came to reflect the happy atmosphere which Miss Elliston did so much to promote, supported and assisted by family, friends and former employers.

In 1901 more space was needed for the 16 pupils, and *Claverton*, next to the cricket ground in Woodfield Lane, was rented. Increased numbers led to a move to the present site in 1904, when there were 45 girls, aged 10 to 18. Parsons Meadow in Ottways Lane had belonged to the old parsonage which was demolished to make way for *The Haven* almshouse on Ottways Lane. Opposite was another meadow and pool for the animals farmed on the parsonage lands. This pool later became Littlewood's Pool, and was used for swimming (see p. 213). Captain (later Colonel) Gleig had purchased Parsons Meadow and built a large country house, with stabling and outhouses in six acres. This was the property, now known as Parsons Mead, which Miss Elliston decided to rent for six years at £200 a year. She then went on to purchase it over the next ten years.

The uniform at *Claverton* had been red blouses with long navy skirts, changed to pinafores in 1906. By 1912 the colour was brown, later green.

For the 50 girls then at Parsons Mead Miss Elliston made 'a home from home'. She and her school friend, Miss Rowe (who functioned as bursar and later acting Headmistress) would read aloud each evening while the boarders embroidered or knitted items for charity. Advertisements of the time show the school to be 'A High Class Boarding and Day School for the Daughters Of Gentlemen'. The education was designed to produce good wives and mothers for their station in life. Various properties were rented around the village for the growing school. Miss Jessie Elliston's hearing had progressively deteriorated, and by 1912 she had become profoundly deaf. Being such a vigorous, intelligent woman, she taught herself to lipread. In 1914 Miss Laurette Elliston became co-principal of the School for Domestic Science which was opened in Oakfield

Road[6]. This gave a thorough training in household management for six resident female students, with the facilities of Parsons Mead open to them. Classes were also available to the neighbourhood ladies. Canadian troops were billeted at Parsons Mead during the First World War, as in other village locations.

By 1925/6 all the school resources were concentrated on the Parsons Mead site. Much building and conversion work had been carried out over the years. The gardens had been planted with fruit trees, and bottling and jam making were regular holiday activities.

During the Second World War, one of the classrooms was reinforced and filled with mattresses, while the Juniors had an Anderson shelter in Westmead. Miss Hopkins became Headmistress during the war, and on Christmas Eve 1942 Miss Elliston died. School numbers during this period fluctuated violently, probably due to the unexpectedly heavy bombing. Numbers went down from 110 to 63 over one weekend. This caused grave financial problems. The dining room and study at Westmead were converted to classrooms, and this building is still the Junior School. Miss Hopkins retired, and a former teacher in the school became the new Headmistress. A period of radical change followed. Control was handed over to a voluntary board of governors headed by a former public

Fig. 56.   Parsons Mead School, 1976. LDLHS Collection

school headmaster. An educational trust was established in 1957, with non-profit making charitable status.

Miss N.K. Maude was Headmistress from 1951 to 1963 when the numbers increased to 250, soon rising to over 300. Over the years, the school facilities were improved and expanded to a total of 12 acres, with the addition of an outdoor swimming pool and Junior School Hall in the 1960s, and in the 1990s a sports hall and completely new science laboratory. Part of the buildings were grouped around Elliston Court, in memory of the school's founder, and Gollin Court after Geoffrey Gollin, a former Chairman of Governors. Today, there are about 350 girls at Parsons Mead School, 10 of whom are boarders.

Ryebrook School
A small pre-preparatory school in Oakfield Road, taken over by Miss Winifred Owen in 1948, was renamed Ryebrook School. It had pupils from three to eight years (raised to nine years in the 1950s), and there was a nursery section for the youngest children. The recreation ground opposite the school was available for outdoor games and the annual Sports Day. St George's Church Hall was also used for social occasions. Most of the children went on to local private schools. Ryebrook School was acquired by Downsend in 1983 when it became known as Downsend Lodge (Ashtead). By the 1990s there were almost 100 children at the school, aged from two to seven years of age.

City of London Freemen's School
This co-educational independent school came to Ashtead Park from London in 1926 when the Ashtead Park estate was bought by the City of London after the death of its owner Pantia Ralli two years earlier[7]. The school had been founded in Brixton in 1854 for the education of charity orphans, but its origins date back to the late 17th century when bequests were made to educate the City's children, and in particular the orphans of its Freemen. There were 100 boys and 65 girls in the Brixton school's early years, and its relocation to the country was increasingly debated. On coming to Ashtead, the school was renamed with the word 'Orphan' deleted from its title. The number of orphans of Freemen had declined, and by the time of the move there were approximately 70. Fee-paying board and day boys were taken, but the 'foundation scholars' from

Brixton showed some resentment against the newcomers and one of the Ashtead day boys was found tied to a tree! Classes had been co-educational in Brixton since about 1914, but fee-paying girls were not admitted to the Ashtead school until 1933. In fact, girls had been in the extreme minority for some time, and even by 1939 there were 160 boys in the school compared with 34 girls. The total number of foundation scholars at this time was 43.

The school was confined for many years to the main buildings of the old Ashtead Park mansion. There was teaching on the ground floor, with boys boarding on the first floor and girls on the top floor. A cluster of new buildings has sprung up in the last thirty years, including a boys' boarding house, an Assembly Hall and a large swimming pool. The mansion is now mostly used for administrative purposes and for girls' boarding accommodation. By the mid-1970s, there were about 500 pupils in the school, and by 1993 almost 680, divided equally between the sexes; the number of pupils increased to about 725 in 1995. A new junior school was completed in 1988 to admit children aged eight, and this building has been extended to accept children at seven, in line with Surrey's change in the age of transfer. A new sports hall is due for completion this year and a complete new senior school is planned to replace the older mix of buildings.

Throughout the history of the school the Corporation of London has always been closely involved. The Lord Mayor makes the presentations on Prize Day, and various livery companies give support. Although foundation scholars are not numerous nowadays, there is still help available for them from the City of London. School services are held in St Giles' Church each week, and the school supports many local charities.

Notes

1. The bequests from Mary Howard and the Rev. William Legge, and that from David White, are still paid to the St Giles' School Fund.
2. D. Robinson, *Surrey Through the Century, 1889–1989* (1989) p. 13; C.R. Chapman, *The Growth of British Education and Its Records* (1991), p. 47
3. D. Robinson (1989) op. cit. p. 36
4. St Giles' School, centenary booklet (1952)
5. Downsend School account written by Christopher Linford
6. As M.L. Rowe after her marriage, Laurette Elliston co-wrote the school history with G.J. Gollin, published in 1978.
7. M.J. Kemp, 'The School in the Park' *Ashtead Parish Magazine*, April 1978, pp. 7–9

Chapter 22

THE ARTS

MUSIC AND DRAMA

For its size, Ashtead has been stikingly prolific in its music and drama, since the late 1920s at least. Credit must go to the members of the Ashtead Players, the Ashtead Choral Society and other groups, but Ashtead was lucky in having a few highly qualified professionals who provided guidance seldom available to amateurs. Clara Dow, Dr. Edith Bathurst, Kathleen Riddick and George Pizzey were among those whose contributions to the many artistic productions and concerts were of major significance.

The Ashtead Players

The Ashtead Players as constituted today were formally established in June 1949. They had existed, however, in other forms and under other names long before the war, and the new organisation was to that extent a continuation of the old. 'Ashtead Players' was the revival of a title last used in 1940. A pre-war forerunner was the Ashtead Musical Society which between 1928 and 1936 produced an operetta every year. The productions of 1937 and 1938 were by the Ashtead Operatic Society, but as the same people were involved in both societies this can have been little more than a change of name. On the dramatic side pre-war, there is evidence of the existence of the Ashtead Amateur Dramatic Society but little sign of their activities. In 1921 M.W, Marshall, Chairman of the Parish Council, was President of the Society and a programme of June 1923 showed that an evening of one-act plays was staged in Ashtead Park.

When war broke out in 1939 amateur dramatic activity soon

ceased, but a modest revival took place in 1942 when the Rev. John Ragg, a curate of the Parish, began to produce revues for the church youth group. They were staged at Parsons Mead School and were well attended. By 1946 this group had developed into a company calling itself the 'Ragged Revellers'.

Between 1945 and 1947 two plays and one revue were put on each year by the 'Revellers' and by a musical company re-using the title of the Ashtead Amateur Dramatic Society. After a joint production in January 1949 of *The Mikado,* Frank Plastow proposed that the two groups should be merged and in June that year they took the title of Ashtead Players. Lois Barker and Aubrey Wyatt were the driving forces on the drama side. It was decided that the new company would produce one musical and two plays each season.

The continuing thread between the pre-war musical societies and the post-war Ashtead Players was shown by the high quality of the performances. The presence of Clara Dow and Edith Bathurst ensured the success of the productions both before and after the war.

Clara Dow (1883–1969) lived in Ashtead from 1934 until her death. She trained at the Royal College of Music, joined the D'Oyly Carte Opera Company and was the last leading lady personally trained by W S Gilbert. In 1909 *The Times* wrote 'She is in our opinion the finest leading lady the company ever had. She has a splendid singing voice, great powers as an actress, infinite grace, and delicacy of movement'. Although uniquely qualified to produce Gilbert and Sullivan, Miss Dow produced other operettas with equal success. Between 1928 and 1938 and between 1949 and 1954 she produced an operetta every year, including *The Beggar's Opera, The Vagabond King* and *The Desert Song* as well as most of the Gilbert and Sullivan repertoire.

Mary Illing, the leading lady in most of the post-war productions by Clara Dow, remembers her as being a wonderful teacher of Gilbert and Sullivan. Every last detail in voice and gesture had to be correct: the footwork, the intonation and lilt of voice, the raised eyebrow, the fan drill in *The Mikado,* the position of the little finger. Clara Dow would demonstrate this personally for every role in the opera. She was so steeped in this that one could imagine the instructions were Gilbert's own. The 1954 production of *Ruddigore* was her last: she had then turned seventy.

Equally important to the success of these productions was the high standard of musical direction. The conductor at *Patience* in 1928 was Dr L. H. B: Reed, one-time President of the London Madrigal Society and organist at St John's School. His assistant on that occasion was Dr Edith Bathurst, organist and choirmaster of Christ Church, Leatherhead for many years, who succeeded him the following year and remained Director of Music until 1953. She was also known in the 1930s for her Ashtead Ladies Choir which gave concerts occasionally in the Peace Memorial Hall. When Dr Bathurst withdrew from the Ashtead Players in 1953 Kathleen Riddick took over.

Two of the Players went on to pursue professional careers. Mary Illing achieved the success prophesied by Beverley Nichols after the 1954 production of *Ruddigore*. She went on to sing roles at Glyndebourne, appear in oratorios and to tour with the Arts Council Operatic Group. She sang in concerts with singers from Covent Garden and other opera houses, and appeared in festivals in a number of cities. The other singer from those days to become well-known was Richard Angas, today a principal bass of the English National Opera. He was a member of the St George's Church choir, sang also with the Ashtead Choral Society and more particularly with the St George's Singers whose connections led to his professional career. He made his professional debut with the Scottish Opera in 1966 going on to sing in every major opera house of the world.

Despite the great success of the operatic side of the Ashtead Players, it eventually became impossible to continue the musical productions. The last to be put on was *Salad Days*, produced by Ken Hardy in 1965 and, although an attempt was made to continue, the shortage of musical talent and increasing costs made it impossible.

With the demise of the operatic side additional drama productions became possible and from 1963 to 1984 three plays were put on each year. This was perhaps the dramatic heyday of the Players, when they had the services of two brilliant designers and craftsmen, Chris Groom (whose father Frederick had sung leading tenor roles for Clara Dow) and Neil Pollard. Barbara Chevins, Wendy Sharkey, Alec Mackrell and Ken Hardy were seldom absent from the stage either as actors or producers in those days.

The Ashtead Players have had a long and successful history with a distinguished artistic record equalled by few dramatic societies.

Kathleen Riddick and the Surrey Philharmonic Orchestra

Kathleen Riddick (1907–73), founder of the Surrey Philharmonic Orchestra, lived in Ashtead for much of her life after studying at the Guildhall School of Music[1]. The orchestra, which she founded in 1932 as the Surrey String Players, steadily flourished, and guest conductors included Vaughan Williams and Sir Arthur Bliss. Many talented musicians came to live in Ashtead during the war and joined the orchestra which became in 1944 a fully fledged symphony orchestra with the title Surrey Philharmonic Orchestra. An amateur orchestra, with some professional "stiffening", it soon gained a reputation for excellence.

In 1951 the Surrey Phil, as it was affectionately known, played in the newly opened Royal Festival Hall in London and Kathleen Riddick became the first woman to conduct an orchestra there. Many distinguished musicians performed with the orchestra which gave concerts in many venues, but, like the Ashtead Choral Society, principally in the Dorking Halls. Kathleen Riddick continued to conduct the orchestra until 1972 when ill health forced her to retire, one year before her death. Although subsequent conductors have not been residents of Ashtead, the orchestra has continued its family connections with Kathleen Riddick through her husband, the late George Bixley, their daughter Susan and son-in-law Neil Gilchrist, also both grandchildren, all of whom have been playing members.

Kathleen Riddick also formed the professional Riddick String Orchestra, which later became the Riddick Orchestra, performing on occasions with local societies, particularly the Ashtead Choral Society in its early days.

Ashtead Choral Society

The existence of the Choral Society in Ashtead was due to the enterprise of George Pizzey (1898–1990), the initiator and founder, who came to live in Ashtead in 1944[2]. When he formed the Society, George Pizzey had been a professional singer, chorister, and soloist for some 25 years, during which he had sung with the foremost conductors of the day and with choirs of all ranges of ability. He had been a member of the choir of Westminster Abbey from 1941 to 1946. With his considerable experience he was keen to establish a choir of his own.

In September 1949, encouraged by the response to an Easter performance in St George's Church, he called and chaired the public

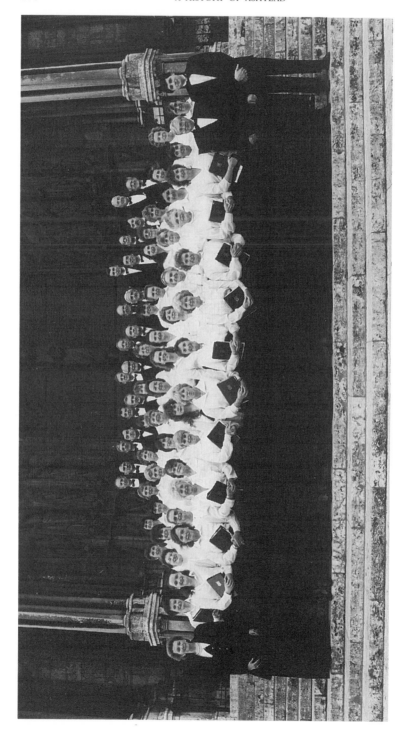

Fig. 57. Ashtead Choral Society on tour in Normandy, on steps of Chartres Cathedral after the concert on 5 June 1993. (Courtesy, H.S. Bayley).

meeting in the Peace Memorial Hall, at which it was resolved to found the Society. Leslie Woodgate, already famous as a BBC Chorus Master, agreed to be the first President. The first two concerts were given at the Peace Memorial Hall: in April 1950 Coleridge-Taylor's *Hiawatha*, and in April 1951 Mendelsohn's *Elijah*.

The Peace Memorial Hall soon proved too small, and the production in December 1951 of *Messiah* was given in the Crescent Cinema, Leatherhead, to a capacity audience. Concerts continued to be given in the Crescent Cinema until 1967 when it was demolished to make way for the Thorndike Theatre. The 1968 performance of Bach's B minor Mass was given at the Dorking Halls, and from then on the Society made the Dorking Halls its 'home'.

At the first concert in April 1950 Dr Edith Bathurst, a principal patron, Deputy Conductor and Honorary Accompanist of the Society, was at the piano. Subsequently the Society has had only two accompanists in its long history. The first was Winifred Boston, present at *Elijah* in 1951, who retired after 25 years. A brilliant musician, forthright, and assertive when necessary, she was a real tower of strength. Seemingly irreplaceable she was in fact succeeded in 1977 by an equally fine musician with the same qualities, Anne Shepherd, who remains the accompanist today.

Orchestral accompaniment was provided from the outset and until 1970 by the Riddick String Orchestra, augmented at first by brass and wind players from the London Symphony Orchestra. There followed collaboration with the Capriol Orchestra and many other well-known orchestras. In 1992 the Society joined the celebration of the Diamond Jubilee of the Surrey Philharmonic Orchestra, with which the Society had also been closely associated over the years. Two years later the Society was particularly pleased to sing at Dorking with the distinguished Hanover Band, an internationally famous orchestra playing contemporary instruments.

From the beginning many well-known soloists sang with the choir, including Heddle Nash, Isobel Baillie, Janet Baker and Owen Brannigan. There were also distinguished instrumentalists, and among the guest conductors were Stanford Robinson and Alan Kirby.

In 1974, the Ashtead Choral Society celebrated its Silver Jubilee and George Pizzey decided it was time to hand over his baton. Fortunately, in the choir there was another talented professional musician, Arthur Diamond, who took over as Conductor, thus ensuring a smooth transition and continuity. Under its new Conductor, the choir began to branch out into some less familiar works and new compositions as well as the standard classic repertoire.

In May 1987 the choir made its first appearance abroad with two concerts in Paris at the church of St Merri and at the Madeleine, both of which were enthusiastically received. Since then the choir has sung in Germany, with an unexpected opportunity to sing in Cologne Cathedral, leading to a friendly association with St Germanus Church, Wesseling. Tours were made also to Belgium – an unforgettable recital was given at the Menin Gate, Ypres – and again to France in 1993 where concerts were given in Lisieux and Chartres Cathedrals.

In London, concerts have been given at the Barbican and for a number of years at the Royal Festival Hall, in cooperation with the Ernest Read Music Association. Local venues have included the Leatherhead Leisure Centre, St John's School, St Martin's Epsom, St George's Ashtead and Polesden Lacey. Since its inception the choir has given over 160 concerts in its many venues.

Arthur Diamond is still the Conductor and Musical Director, and, following the death of George Pizzey in 1990, James Batho, a founder member, became President in his place. The singing membership is about 150 and is supported by some 50 Patrons and Friends as well as by faithful audiences.

St George's Singers

For some 30 years prior to 1976, a small vocal group of usually no more than 15, and trained by Geoffrey Morgan, a gifted amateur musician, gave a number of concerts in village halls and churches in the neighbourhood of Ashtead. The title St George's Singers reflected the fact that at first many were members of the St George's Church choir. The repertoire was broad in scope and ranged from church anthems to humorous part songs, usually unaccompanied, occasionally with piano.

Richard Angas' connection with the Singers has already been mentioned, Mary Illing too was a member. Other members who later followed professional careers were Rosanne Creffield and Margaret Humphrey-Clarke.

The St. George's Singers were sorry to disband when Geoffrey Morgan retired in 1976. It had been an enjoyable and successful time for all.

Ashtead Singers

In 1986 some members of the Ashtead Choral Society, regretful that the choir was inactive during the closed season, decided to form a small mixed choir to continue singing in the summer months. They chose the title Ashtead Singers, and decided to limit the size of the choir to 24 members.

The Director of Music is Paul Dodds, Head of Music at the City of London Freemen's School. Over the years the choir has sung from the classic repertoire of sacred music in Bath Abbey, St. George's Chapel, Windsor, Westminster Cathedral and St Paul's Cathedral. They equally enjoy singing madrigals and folk music in secular, less prestigious, surroundings.

LITERATURE

In recent times there have been a number of Ashtead residents well-known for their literary or artistic pursuits. Of these, perhaps the most notable was the writer, musician and journalist Beverley Nichols, while his near neighbour, Edward MacCurdey, was a leading art historian and an authority on Leonardo da Vinci. The famous author, humourist and Punch contributor, A.P. Herbert (known as A.P.H) spent the first seven years of his life at Ashtead having been born at *Oakfield Lodge* in 1890[3]. He does not seem to have had any contact with Ashtead later in his life. Other writers and artists associated with Ashtead include Eve Williams, a nurse by profession, who is also a writer and photographer, whose first book *Ladies without Lamps* described her wartime experiences; and Geoffrey Fletcher who, apart from much journalistic activity, wrote books on art and exhibited paintings and drawings at home and abroad. Three of his paintings are in the Leatherhead museum.

Beverley Nichols (1898–1957)

Beverley Nichols, a well-known and prolific author and contributor for many years to the magazine *Woman's Own*, was a talented musician and composer and a close friend of many of the theatrical and literary figures of the day. He lived in Ashtead for some ten years from 1946, when he bought the Georgian house *Merry Hall* in Agates Lane. He wrote several of his books here. One of these, *Merry Hall*, was dedicated to A.E. Newby, Nichols' gardener who is referred to in the book as 'Oldfield'. This name is preserved in Oldfield Gardens.

Fig. 58. Signatures of celebrated friends of Beverley Nichols on a door at *Merry Hall*. Photograph by J.R. Clube. (Courtesy, Michael and Alison May).

There are many references in Nichols' books to his guests at *Merry Hall* coming for week-end parties. The panel of the door into the kitchen is filled with the signatures of his famous friends. Now faded, some names are unreadable but many can be deciphered (see Fig 58). They cover the fields of ballet, drama, literature, films and TV and include, for example, Frederick Ashton, the Lunts, Somerset Maugham, the two Hermiones (Baddeley and Gingold), Emlyn Williams and Gladys Cooper, to name only a few.

Nichols' main local interest was in the productions of the Ashtead Players of which he was a patron from 1954 to 1957. He wrote a most complimentary article in *Woman's Own* about the 1954 production of *Ruddigore*, recounting how the cast came to *Merry Hall* after the show, and sang and danced in the music room, repeating most of the opera.

Few local people were invited into the house. One exception was Peter Yorke, a band-leader living in Rookery Hill; another was the Maples family living in *Murreys Court* opposite. As a young girl, Mary Maples (Mary Cree) was intrigued by the bohemian atmosphere of the parties there.

Nichols' household was run by his manservant Gaskin, known to his friends as 'Reg', who had been with Nichols for many years. Gaskin was on particularly friendly terms with Mr Marshall, (known as 'Smiler' and employed by Mr Maples opposite). He would often come across to say that Nichols invited him to join them for a drink. 'Smiler' used to keep a tie ready for such an occasion.

Nichols spent much of his time at the grand piano in the music room, but when working he used an upper room overlooking Agates Lane. Immediately opposite was a field belonging to *Murreys Court* and when Nichols was sometimes disturbed by cows grazing there he would send Gaskin over to 'Smiler' to get them moved away. It is difficult today to imagine cows in Agates Lane.

Although Nichols' presence in Ashtead was, of course, well-known, and he did attend the occasional flower show, he may be better described as a long stay visitor rather than a resident of Ashtead. When he moved away it was to find another house and to write more autobiographical books.

Edward MacCurdy (1871–1957)
If Beverley Nichols was the best known popular writer to live

recently in Ashtead the most scholarly and distinguished resident author was Edward MacCurdy. He was educated at Oxford, had a natural literary talent and wrote essays and poems, serious and light. Above all he was an authority on the works and personality of Leonardo da Vinci.

In contrast to Nichols, who stayed only ten years in Ashtead, Edward MacCurdy spent all his married life here. He arrived in 1907, aged 36, following his marriage the previous year to Sylvia Stebbing. They made their home in *Oakdene*, in Oakfield Road. Here they raised six children: they were thus truly an Ashtead family.

MacCurdy's first work on Leonardo da Vinci was published in 1904, followed in 1906 by a version of the *Notebooks of Leonardo*, and in 1907 by *The Thoughts of Leonardo*. His major work was the issue of a two-volume edition of the *Note Books* in 1938. This was re-issued in 1948 and ran into several editions.

Apart from a spell as a civil servant during the First World War, MacCurdy's place of work was his extensive library in *Oakdene*. For much of his research on da Vinci he was granted access to the papers at Windsor Castle. He was often in close touch with Kenneth Clark, the well-known art historian and da Vinci devotee.

Edward's wife, Sylvia (1877–1976) was a lady of many talents, writing poems and children's books and trained as a bookbinder. She bound many of Edward's books in leather. Bookbinding brought her into touch with Virginia and Vanessa Stephen before their marriages: Virginia to Leonard Woolf and Vanessa to Clive Bell. She enjoyed a life-long friendship with both.

On the death of her husband, Sylvia continued to be active, even in her nineties, travelling alone by train – always walking to the station – to run an old people's club at the Blackfriars Settlement in London. She enjoyed bringing old people by coach to summer tea-parties in her garden, disregarding the fact that she was very much older than her guests. When interviewed at the age of ninety-five she was as independent as ever. It was sad that she failed to make her hundredth birthday by a matter of a few weeks.

Baroness Elizabeth de T'Serclaes

Elizabeth de T'Serclaes, who lived in Ashtead from about 1926 until her death in 1974, was born in 1890. After a brief marriage in 1906, leaving her with a son, she married again in 1916, this time to a

Belgian pilot, Baron Harold de T'Serclaes. They separated three years later. She was a nurse during the war and was awarded the Military Medal, a most unusual event in those days, for rescuing a pilot from near the German lines. She joined up again in 1939 and became a senior Women's Auxilliary Air Force (WAAF) officer.

After the Second World War the Baroness engaged in fund raising for the RAF Association and the Benevolent Fund. She lived in the Earl Haig Homes in Park Lane, Ashtead, a striking figure, tall with a deep voice, flamboyantly dressed with large ear-rings and a voluminous dark cloak. Because of her appearance, she was known as 'Gypsy' but only her special friends were allowed to call her this. She bred chihuahua dogs and was always accompanied by three or four. She was greatly concerned about the welfare of animals and conservation on Ashtead Common. She is remembered as a great character which is well brought out in her autobiography *Flanders and Other Fields* published in 1964.

Peter Hunt (1917–1978)

Peter Hunt, a noted writer on horticultural matters, lived in Ashtead between 1939 and 1954. He was a Fellow of the Linnaean Society, editor and correspondent with several gardening journals, and radio broadcaster. His particular achievement was the setting up of the Garden History Society whose aims were to study all aspects of gardens and gardening techniques. It was on his initiative that a founding group of this Society was set up at the hall of the Royal Horticultural Society in 1965.

ART

Artists who painted in Ashtead included J. S. Cotman who sketched Ashtead churchyard in 1799. But it is Peter de Wint (1784–1849) who is the artist most associated with Ashtead[4]. His meeting with the Howards of Ashtead Park led to a close association with the family in the course of which he gave lessons to Mary Howard (1785–1877), an accomplished artist herself. Henry Edridge ARA (1769–1821) also sketched in Ashtead churchyard.

An artist of a different type and more recent age was Frances Kitchener, a niece of Lord Kitchener, who lived in Ashtead early this century[5]. She had a special interest in the design of coinage: the Wembley Exhibition medal of 1924 was her work, and in 1936 she was involved in designing the twelve-sided three-penny piece.

John Payne Jennings (1843–1926)

John Payne Jennings was a photographer of the late Victorian era, a long-time resident of Ashtead who died here aged 83 in 1926[6]. He arrived in Ashtead about 1890. As a professional free-lance photographer he was active in the period when photography was regarded as an art-form akin to painting. He took many panoramic and scenic views of various parts of England for use by railway companies in encouraging tourism, and was expert in producing coloured versions for exhibiting in railway carriages and stations. He also produced photographs to accompany the works of famous poets such as *The Works of Alfred, Lord Tennyson* (1889).

The Ashtead base for this commercial activity was the Greville Works where he built his own studio. He became a considerable owner of property and land, including the entire Greville Park Estate. He was still living in *Gayton House*, in the Estate, at the time of his death.

Apart from his professional responsibilities Jennings was active in local affairs. He became a member of the Ashtead Parish Council when it was established under the Local Government Act and served from 1894 to 1897. He returned to the Council in the 1914 war and was instrumental in introducing the National Kitchen to Ashtead.

Jennings was described in an obituary notice as being of striking appearance and fine physique. In later years his long white hair gave him a venerable appearance.

Ashtead Potters Ltd

The Ashtead Pottery, in business in Ashtead from 1923 to 1935, was an artistic success and sold its products in major stores, but in the Depression of the mid-thirties was unable to survive[7].

The origin of the Company lay in the First World War, or rather in its consequences, for the purposes in establishing it were not only to engage in the manufacture and sale of its products, but to employ and train disabled ex-servicemen and their dependents. The driving force behind the enterprise was Sir Lawrence Weaver, Vice-Chairman of the Rural Industries Board, supported by his wife, Kathleen Purcell, Lady Weaver, and other persons of note. The company, Ashtead Potters Ltd, was registered in December 1922 and run by a committee of volunteers.

The Pottery itself was established in an old building, the Victoria Works in West Hill, and the work began modestly with four men in April 1923. Production soon developed and souvenirs and commemorative articles were put on sale in the Pottery's own shop in the British Empire Exhibition at Wembley in 1924.

When the enterprise began Sir Lawrence recognized that such a venture could in no way compete with the long-established companies in Staffordshire, nor did he expect it to try to do so. He envisaged rather the production of ware unique to Ashtead much as other small potteries in Britain were doing.

Over thirty of the workforce – there were never more than forty – have been identified by name. They comprise all the skills – throwers, mouldmakers, casters, kilnsmen, artist/decorators and glaziers. Most of them came from outside Ashtead and few had any previous experience of pottery. Some had been diamond workers. Most were housed in accommodation in Park Lane and Purcell Close, later to become the Earl Haig Homes.

The work was carried out on traditional lines without much mechanisation. The clay arrived at Ashtead Station, glazes and colours probably coming from Staffordshire firms. Outlines for decorations were often made by a form of stencilling through metal foil. Designs were sometimes taken from magazines and suchlike. There is no record of transfer printing at Ashtead; the Guinness ashtray for example may have been printed elsewhere. All decoration was by hand painting. In some cases, pieces were bought in from Wedgwood and other potteries in the biscuit stage for glazing and decorating at Ashtead.

The output was prolific, with well over 300 items in the catalogue. Wares could be bought in a variety of colour glazes and decorations which vastly increased the range. Some had a certain 'cottagey' style of the 1930s, but were really based on brightly coloured 'art-deco' styles of the Potteries. The decorators were believed to have looked at ancient artefacts in the V&A in search of inspiration for decoration.

The range of products ran from the well-designed utilitarian articles of domestic use through souvenirs, plaques, advertising goods, lamp bases, vases, to a variety of ornaments, figures and sculptures of unique artistic quality. In the latter, the Pottery was fortunate in having the support of many contemporary sculptors and artists. Most were contacts and many were friends of Sir Lawrence and Lady Weaver and they permitted reproductions of their own work to be made at Ashtead. For example, Phoebe Stabler designed cherubic children; Sir William Reid Dick allowed Ashtead to copy his design for the lion at Menin Gate; Donald Gilbert designed Kipling's Jungle Book figures; Percy Metcalfe, his Wembley Lion; Joan Pyman, her Madonna and Child; and there were many others.

The company enjoyed significant Royal patronage. Queen Mary was presented with the first copy of a plaque *Prince of Wales, Prince of Sportsmen* in 1933. The Duke and Duchess of York visited the factory in 1928 and were presented with a Winnie the Pooh set for Princess Elizabeth, now Queen Elizabeth. Many other royal personages were introduced to the Ashtead shop at the exhibitions, mainly by Sir Lawrence who lost no time in mentioning Ashtead in any conversation.

Nevertheless it would be wrong to assume that the artistic success of the enterprise was largely due to patronage – the quality of the products spoke for themselves. It is no doubt for this reason that many are found in museums today, including the V&A.

The Victoria Works were eventually demolished and *Lime Tree Court*, sheltered accommodation for the elderly, was built on the site. A plaque in the entrance marks the existence of the Ashtead Pottery, but the true memorial is the Ashtead ware itself.

Ashtead Art Group
The Ashtead Art Group was formed in 1967 by Thomas Parr who trained at Epsom Art School. The aim was simply to bring together those who enjoyed painting, and at first they met in the Constitutional Hall. As numbers grew they transferred to the St George's Hall. Exhibitions and demonstrations are held, and painting trips organized.

Notes

1. C.P.C. Martin, *The Story of an Orchestra* (1984)
2. G. Pizzey & A. Diamond, *The Story of the Ashtead Choral Society* (1989)
3. M.L. Rowe & G.J. Gollin, *Parsons Mead, 1897–1977* (1978)
4. G.J. Gollin, *Bygone Ashtead* (1987) p.132
5. *Evening News*, 15 March 1937; Society Records (AX 195)
6. Judith Steinhoff, *Seminar re. Jennings* (1981), Princeton Univ.
7. E.H. Hallam, *Ashtead Potters Ltd in Surrey, 1923–1935* (1990), 41, The Kingsway, Ewell, Surrey

Chapter 23

SPORT AND LEISURE

In Ashtead, as elsewhere, there has been a remarkable growth in sport and leisure activities during this century, helped over the years by the introduction of the five-day week and by longer holidays. The Mole Valley District Council regularly publishes a list of Ashtead's sporting and leisure pursuits and, though only a glimpse of these can be given here, enough is included to show how much Ashtead as a community gains from them.

Sports Clubs

Cricket   The Ashtead Cricket Club was founded in March 1887, though the game had been played before then in Ashtead Park, on the Common north of the railway and on fields near Dene Road (see p. 106). Early this century there were many ups and downs in the Club's fortunes and its funds were boosted by letting out its ground on Woodfield Lane for football in winter while part was laid out for tennis courts in summer. In the early 1930s hockey, lacrosse and archery were also played here. It was at this period that the Club was host to a number of England players in a match which was fully reported in *The Times* of 25 September 1931. Those playing included A.P.F. Chapman, G.O. Allen, M.H. Page of the New Zealand Test XI and the distinguished Indian cricketer, F.S. Duleepsingjhi. The visiting team, captained by Lord Ebbisham, won but Ashtead put up a good fight. Other notable cricketers who played on the Ashtead ground over the years included Trevor Bailey, Alec and Eric Bedser, Richie Benaud, Denis Compton, Wally Hammond, Sir Jack Hobbs, D.R. Jardine and Jim Laker, a star-studded assembly indeed.

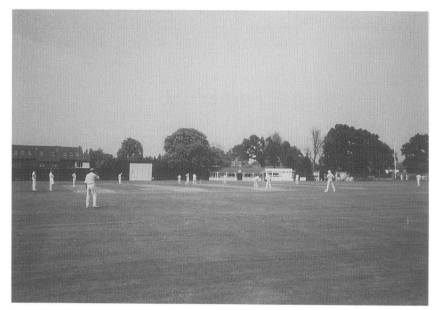

Fig. 59.   Cricket on Woodfield Lane ground, 1995 Photograph by J. C. Stuttard

During the Club's centenary year, 1987, Colin Cowdrey, ex-Capt. of Kent and England, spoke warmly of Ashtead's picturesque playing field and its convivial atmosphere, also saying that the ground was the very first he had played cricket on, as a ten year old. Brian Johnstone, the radio and TV commentator, sent an accolade referring to his many happy memories of playing cricket at the Club on President's Day. A Centenary Dinner was held at the R.A.C. Club when no less than 241 members attended.[1]

In the 1990s the Club continued to flourish and the summer sound of bat on ball will certainly be heard here into the next century.

Football   There has been an Ashtead Football Club since 1894 but games not organized on club lines were likely to have been played before this date. By 1898 the club had successfully negotiated with the Ashtead Cricket Club to be allowed to play on its ground in winter for an agreed rent, and this agreement continued for many years. Football activities were necessarily much curtailed during the First World War, but the Club flourished again when peace came, a fixture list for the 1921/22 season showing a full programme of games against clubs in Surrey, including Epsom, Sutton, Banstead

Fig. 60. Ashtead Football Club, 1921/22. Winners of the Sutton & District Charity Cup. LDLHS Collection

and Carshalton. This round of games, with varying degrees of success, was to continue until the Second World War brought curtailment again.

The Club was reformed after 1945 and since then games have been regularly played on the Ashtead Recreation Ground in Barnett Wood Lane. There were many successes, for which the Club had every reason to be proud: these included becoming top of the Surrey Senior League (1st Division) in 1968 without losing a game, twice winning the Surrey League Cup and in 1992/93 being awarded the Surrey Intermediate Cup for the first time.

Tennis   There are references to tennis being played here in the late 19th century and in the early years of this century (see p. 119). It probably continued to be popular over the years since then, especially in private gardens and public recreation grounds. After the Second World War, four courts were in regular use at the Ashtead Recreation Ground. They were taken over in 1974 by the Mole Valley District Council. In 1981, local residents felt that the courts were not being properly maintained and might fall into disuse. To obviate this, the Ashtead Tennis Players Club was formed in April 1981 and a lease was obtained from the Council giving the Club full responsibility for the courts. The lease also included a small adjoining area of waste land on which a clubhouse was built and opened in 1991, with financial backing from the Lawn Tennis Association and the Sports Council. In 1992, the Club successfully applied for admission to the Dorking and Leatherhead Tennis League. Membership has expanded to an annual average of 150 and the Club is an established part of the local sporting scene.

Squash Rackets   The Ashtead Squash Rackets Club, almost hidden away off Skinners Lane nearly opposite Highfields, was formed in 1937 with two squash courts and two tennis courts. It had difficulties in keeping going in the early days, especially during the war years and in the 1950s. However, in 1966, under the chairmanship of Denys Straker, the freehold of the Club's land was bought, together with some adjoining land, which enabled the Club to expand in the next few years. Two more squash courts were built, also a bungalow for the stewards and an extension of the clubroom. The Club has always maintained a good standard of squash, playing in the Surrey Cup, Division 1 for some periods. There is a thriving junior section.

Fig. 61.   Ashtead Squash Club. Photograph by J. C. Stuttard

Bowls   The Ashtead Bowling Club was formed in 1920, using a green on the north-east corner of the Ashtead Cricket Ground in Woodfield Lane, on the site of some former tennis courts. Club competitions were soon instituted and some of the more expert bowlers entered the Surrey County tournaments. In the early years, the Club had some financial difficulties because of the increasing cost of maintaining the green and during the war this deteriorated so badly that in 1946/47 it had to be wholly relaid. Ladies were admitted as Club members for the first time in 1953 and this proved a popular step. In 1965 a new pavilion was built which was extended and refurbished during the Club's 1971 Jubilee Year. In 1977 and again in 1982 the men won the 'Time Herald' trophy, reaching in 1987 the Nat-West Double Fours quarter final, out of 600 clubs from all over England. The men have won the Mole Valley Cup several times since its inception in 1983. A lady member became the County Four-Wood Singles Champion in 1990, and the Herald Ladies Cup was won in 1991, 1993 and 1994.

Other Sports

Swimming   There used to be good swimming facilities in Ashtead earlier this century when Henry Weller, a nurseryman, developed the old clay pit of Sparrow's brickworks into the Floral Pool, with steps and diving board, as part of his Rose Garden. The pool was used by local swimmers and by many who came by train from London to enjoy the country air and pleasant surroundings. Since the pool was deep and unsafe for poor swimmers, many parents, and children too, must have been greatly relieved when about 1930 Edgar Littlewood built swimming pools in the garden of his house *Littlewoods* in Ottways Lane, opposite Parsons Mead School. There were two pools – a small one for young children and learners and a large one with diving boards for those who could swim. Parties of children came from the local schools to be taught to swim by Littlewood's daughter, Mrs Brooker, and to take part in school swimming galas. During the long, summer evenings, at weekends and in the school holidays Littlewood's Pool was a popular meeting place for Ashtead's young people.

These pools disappeared in the 1950s to provide land for housing, though a small part of the Floral Pool can still be seen today between The Chase and the railway line. While some schools have

Fig. 62. Floral Pool in Henry Weller's Rose Garden, Green Lane, late 1920s, showing Links Rd houses in background. LDLHS Collection

built their own pools, the swimming baths at Epsom and Leatherhead supply the facilities which Ashtead now lacks.

Golf Ashtead had a golf club in late Victorian and Edwardian times, but little is known about it nor how long it survived (see pp. 109, 119). Today, Ashtead golfers play on one or another neighbouring courses in Leatherhead and Epsom and perhaps further afield.

Polo Early this century polo was played on a ground between the Leatherhead Road, where Parker's Hill joins it, and Parsons Mead School. The polo ground has long been built over.

Social Clubs and Societies
The **Village Club** (known as the Working Men's Club until 1910) was founded in 1887 at a Coffee Room on The Street, but in the following year the Club moved to its present site a little further along The Street nearly opposite the Howard Memorial. A corrugated iron building, which had once been two old huts, formed its premises. A licence was obtained in 1911 when ale was a penny a pint and whisky three pence a glass. At that time and for many years

afterwards, the Club was for men only, but since 1959 women have been admitted as associate members. The Club was badly damaged by bombing during the last war, but it kept open. Many famous snooker and billiard players, including Fred and Joe Davis, Lee, Inman and Lindrum paid visits to raise money for wartime charities. Rebuilding of the Club started in 1951, further alterations being made three years later. The present Club premises were opened in 1968 and there has been a steady growth of membership since then. The snooker and billiard teams have won the Oxshott District Snooker League more times than any other club, and have also been holders of the Glyn Cup and the Trinder Cup. Many local organizations use the Club's rooms for their meetings. The Club's centenary year in 1987 was marked by a special dinner and other celebrations.

The **Ashtead Centre** in Barnett Wood Lane, more commonly called the Ashtead Youth Centre, was built by the Surrey County Council and opened in 1970, as a place where young people could meet in an informal atmosphere and participate in a varied programme of sports and social activities. The building is also used by local groups for fitness training and by a well-established play group for children of pre-school age.

Ashtead Branch of the Royal British Legion   This dates from 1924 and ever since then it has helped ex-service men and women, raising money for all manner of causes. These have included the renovation of the war memorial in 1926 and 1948/49, as well as its refurbishment in 1990/91. Many social activities have been arranged over the years, with dinners, bully beef suppers (one of these was broadcast by the B.B.C.), dances, whist drives and bazaars.

Rotary Club   This was formed in 1980 and its members, like Rotarians everywhere, soon showed an active interest in charity work, helping old people and disadvantaged children, and among other things, supporting one young person each year to serve with Voluntary Service Overseas. They completed the Water Park at the Leatherhead Leisure Centre in 1981 and in 1993 arranged a party of young people, with special needs, to visit Euro-Disney near Paris. The Club organises the popular Ashtead Village Day, which is so much enjoyed every year by young and old.

Horticultural Society   This Society was founded in 1875, at first mainly to organize an annual village flower show, which, except for the war years, was held in Ashtead Park until the estate was sold in 1924. The show was then moved to the fields adjoining Parsons Mead in Ottways Lane, and in the 1950s to *Murreys Court* in Agates Lane. In 1963 the Summer Show was transferred to its present venue, the Peace Memorial Hall, where the Society had already established an annual Autumn Show of chrysanthemums and dahlias. Evening lectures, started after the Second World War during the winter months, are still continued today.

Other Ashtead groups actively involved in the Horticultural Society's shows include the Allotments Association, formed in 1931, and the Flower Arrangement Group, dating from 1955. The latter is today one of largest of its kind in Surrey, holding shows and demonstrations, and frequently decorating Guildford and Southwark Cathedrals. The Group has been awarded several medals at the Chelsea Flower Show, with a gold one in 1992.

Other Social Groups

Ashtead has two Townswomen's Guilds, an afternoon one and an evening one. The Afternoon Townswomen's Guild (A.T.G.), the older of the two, was formed in 1933 and its sixtieth birthday was celebrated in fine style at the Peace Memorial Hall in October 1993. The Evening Townswomen's Guild (E.T.G.) was formed in 1945. Both guilds meet regularly, have a wide range of speakers at their meetings, and support charities.

Another popular and well-established meeting group for Ashtead women is the Women's Institute (W.I.). This meets at the St George's Hall in Barnett Wood Lane.

An active Chess Club, founded about fifty years ago, has its meetings at the Peace Memorial Hall.

Scouts and Guides

There have been Scouts and Guides in Ashtead since the early years of this century. Their success since the last war has been greatly influenced by the continuing support of the Ashtead Scouts and Guides Supporters Association (SAGSA), founded in 1947 by E. Chater, A.E. King and C. Cockram. Michael Gale, an enthusiastic member of the Association from its early days, was its Chairman from 1981 to 1991 and Vice-President from then to his death in

1994. The Association's annual Garden Fête in summer has become part of Ashtead's social calendar.

Scouts

A small Scout Troop existed here in 1911, a few years after Baden Powell had founded the movement which swept the world. The Troop soon became well-known because of the bravery of one of its members. In July 1911 Frederick Hampton, one of its young members, saved two boys from drowning in Weller's Pool (see p. 213), for which he was awarded a bronze medal of the Royal Humane Society and a Certificate of Life Saving, presented to him by Mrs Pantia Ralli at Ashtead Park; a little later, he received from the Earl of Rosebery at *Durdans*, Epsom, a medal of the Boy Scouts Association and a Certificate sent by Baden Powell.[2]

After the outbreak of war in 1914 scouting ceased, but the scout spirit lingered on to be rekindled in June 1920 when the 1st Ashtead Scout Troop was formed. Ten years later, the name 'Pelham' was added to its title after its first leader, Pelham, Douglas Maitland, and at this time the pelican became the official badge.[3] For many years, the scouts used as their headquarters the former Iron Church, a green corrugated iron building facing eastwards across the Common, which they called 'Pelham Hut'. This was replaced by the present headquarters in Woodfield, opened in October 1957 by Ralph Reader of 'Gang Show' fame, then a Chief Scout's Commissioner. To this day, the original church bell from the old Iron Church is used as a rallying call at Scout Troop camps.

During the early years of the Second World War, G.J. (Geoffrey) Gollin came to Ashtead and, though much involved in war work, was soon co-opted as Group Scout Master, a post he held for almost a quarter of a century. Before his arrival the Group had been kept going by the efforts of George Bonner, assisted by older scouts.

Soon after Geoffrey Gollin left his Scout post in 1963, Lord Barnby accepted the appointment of President of the Group which he held until his death in 1982. He permitted the scouts to have their own camp-site in Ashtead Woods and followed the affairs of the Group with interest and enthusiasm.

Following a report in 1967 on the future of scouting, the Senior Scouts and the Rover Scouts of the Ashtead Group were amalgamated and became known as Venture Scouts. The reputation of the Group was reflected that year when at the National Parade of

Queen's Scouts on St George's Day at Windsor Castle four of the five Venture Scouts making up the Colour Party were provided by the Ashtead Pelhams. Since then the Group continued to expand, trebling its early membership.

Two new Scout Groups were founded in the early years after the end of the war. One of these, the 2nd Ashtead Group, was formed in 1949 at the City of London Freemen's School, supported by the then Headmaster, Eric Fielden. In its early days Geoffrey Gollin and Michael Gale helped to establish the group which undertook rock climbing, sailing ventures and camping in Wales and Scotland. When M.J. Kemp became Headmaster, he instituted a Scout week-end each term. The Group was forced to close, however, in 1987, mainly because the School was finding it more and more difficult to staff it adequately. After this, the uniform with a blue scarf and the City of London emblem was no longer to be seen.

In the 1950s when the School Group was becoming popular and with the Pelhams over-full, there was clearly a need for another Scout Group to cater for the many boys living at the south end of the village. So the 3rd Ashtead Group was founded in 1954. This began with only a small Cub Pack, but a Scout Troop was soon added; St Giles' School in Dene Road was used in the early days, though eventually a new headquarters was erected for them on the east side of the entrance to The Warren. Arnold Gardiner assisted in the foundation of the 3rd Ashtead Scout Group and was its President for many years. The Group benefited from the use of a small camp-site on Ranmore Common and camping also took place at Boidier Hurst, adjoining Headley Common, this being used by other Scout Groups as well. A group of Beavers (6–8 year olds) was introduced to Ashtead scouting in the early 1980s.

Guides

The 1st Ashtead Girl Guide Company was formed late in 1918 and was registered in January 1919, though there are believed to have been two small units of 'Girl Scouts', as they were then called, some years earlier than this.[4] A Brownie Pack was started in 1921 by Miss Hope-Freeman. Parsons Mead set up its own Girl Guide Company in May 1919, becoming the 2nd Ashtead Group, which also had a Brownie Pack. A Ranger Company was started in 1923. The School Group had its meetings at Parsons Mead, but the 1st Ashtead Group shared the old Iron Church for a while with the scouts, also meet-

Fig. 63. 1st Ashtead (Pelham) Scouts in camp at Hay on Wye, 1985. (Courtesy, Tony Cutler).

Fig. 64. Two members of 1st Ashtead Girl Guide Company 1919, Myrtle and Ivy Chapman. (Courtesy, Mrs L.I. Crimble).

ing at Barnett Wood Lane School and at the nearby Constitutional Hall. Since 1933, these meetings have taken place at the Guide Headquarters behind the Hall. By the mid-1930s, a further Company was added, the 3rd Ashtead, also a Ranger Company. Another Brownie Pack was formed in these years.

In the early days of the war, Stella Cunliffe, Capt. of 1st Ashtead, founded and ran a Guide Company for the City of London School when it was evacuated to the City of London Freemen's School. A 4th Ashtead Company was formed by Margaret Wingfield in 1942 and she also arranged for the Freemen's School to have its own Guide Company (the 5th Ashtead), seven years before the School's scouts were founded (see above). Some of the older girls helped in the war-time allotments and in the British Restaurant in the Ashtead Recreation Ground off Barnett Wood Lane.

When the Diamond Jubilee of Guiding was celebrated in 1970 at a pageant in Twickenham, 120 guides from Ashtead took part. In 1985, Mrs Gasling, then a Ranger Guide, carried the Surrey Standard at the march past on the 75th anniversary of Guiding at Crystal Palace. The Girl Guide Movement has recently been reformed, 'Girl' being omitted from its title and other changes made. There are now three Guide Companies and Rangers, five Brownie Packs and a Rainbow unit (for five to seven year olds).

Boys' Brigade
The Ashtead Boys' Brigade was started in 1939 by W.G. Treagus. Five years earlier he had also been involved with a similar group, associated with St George's Church calling itself the Knights of St George. The Boys' Brigade was known as the 17th Mid-Surrey Company. There was a junior section, the Life Boys, first under Mrs Treagus (helped by Miss Deacon) and then run by Miss Stainer from 1946 to 1976, John Barnett then taking over. Staffing difficulties after 1987 forced the brigade to close.

The Boys' Brigade used to meet regularly at the Barnett Wood Lane School. The bugle band was a great attraction for the boys and was well to the fore in church parades. They enjoyed a variety of activities and both sections went camping in summer, the Company under canvas and the Life Boys generally in church halls.

Notes

1. Astead Cricket Club (1987)
2. *Parish Magazine*, Dec 1911
3. Pelham Scouts Jubilee (1970)
4. Andrée Hicks, *Guiding in Ashtead* (1985)

Chapter 24

BUILDINGS OF INTEREST

Ashtead has a number of fine buildings which are of special interest for historical and architectural reasons, some large like *Ashtead Park House* (now the City of London Freemen's School), *Ashtead House*, *Ashtead Lodge* and the *Park Farm House*, others more modest in size and several hundred years old, like the houses and cottages in Rectory Lane, Agates Lane and Ottways Lane. These are described in the following pages, with notes on their architecture and on some of the Ashtead families that lived in them.*

Ashtead Park House
This house was built in 1790–92 Richard Howard on the site of the 1684 mansion. Successive Lords of the Manor lived here until 1924, when the house was taken over by the City of London Corporation to become a school. The house, designed by an Italian architect, Bonomi, and built by Samuel Wyatt, is a square building of white brick with a shade of yellow with stone dressings[1]. The main entrance is from a terrace on the south side, through a portico into a well-proportioned hall. This leads into a circular saloon with pillars. The dining room was originally on the left and the drawing room, with a beautiful piece of white statuary marble, on the right. The house has three stories and a basement. Each floor has seven windows facing north and five west, but the ground floor has a north porch in place of the central window. Two wings were added by Sir Thomas Lucas in the 1880's. Inside and out, the house gives the impression of dignity and grandeur. Many alterations have, of

---

*For the churches in Ashtead, see Chapter 19.

Fig. 65.   Ashtead Park House. Photograph by J. C. Stuttard

course, been made to allow for its conversion into a school, but the structure of the house remains substantially as it was.

Ashtead House
The house stands near the north-east gate of Ashtead Park, its grounds bordered by a 17th century red brick wall in Farm Lane. It has survived other former nearby houses such as *Newstead House*, long since demolished. Built of mellow red brick and formerly colour-washed, it has an overall Georgian elevation with an attractive shallow bay on the south-west façade[2].

After the death in 1939 of Miss Denshire, the last Ashtead descendant of Capt. Nathaniel Smith (see p. 42), the house was used during the war to billet Canadian troops. After the war, the property was converted into three separate houses, at which time the original kitchen was extensively altered and evidence of the earliest period of the house was lost. However, a great deal still remains to be seen of the successive developments from its modest beginnings into the large house of today. No. 2 contains a late 17th century staircase with a seven metre newel post, and many shuttered windows, ceiling beams and pine panelling. There is also an elegant Georgian staircase in the southern part of the house, where a ballroom was added. This room was reputedly built for the celebration of the King's visit to the Epsom races in the early 19th century.

There are many fine specimen trees in the garden, including a massive tulip tree over 200 years old. Beyond the coach house, in the north-east and now in the grounds of *The Pines*, there is an ice house situated near the pond and possible source of the Rye Brook.

Ashtead Lodge

This brick-built house in Parker's Lane dates from the 18th century, but lies not far from the site of a large house called *Penders*, which was first mentioned in 1476. It has two storeys with attics under a tiled roof and there are three bays, the centre one projecting slightly. The house has a string cornice and sash windows, with pelmets probably for sun blinds. The pedimented porch was probably added later. Much of the original panelling remains in the house and there is a fine staircase. At one time there were stables behind the house and a horse-worked pump; some of the water not required for the house was fed to a tap in Rectory Lane that was used by the villagers.

Ashtead Lodge once had extensive grounds stretching back to Rectory Lane and surrounded by a brick wall, parts of which can still be seen. It was owned by the Beckford family in the mid-18th century. Not long ago, a pump was found in the basement, bearing the date 1765 and the initials 'F.B.' (Francis Beckford). From 1922 to 1953 the house was the home of General Sir Frederick and Lady Gascoigne[3]. The house is now divided into flats.

Park Farm House

This handsome, L-plan brick house in Farm Lane probably dates from the second half of the 17th century, but it was largely rebuilt after a fire in 1731. It is enclosed by a high wall, and has three rooms on each of the two floors, and a cellar. The façade is symmetrical, with six windows to the first floor. The back kitchen has its own chimney stack, and there is a stair turret. In the early 18th century, after the fire, a further storey was added and the roof was raised; at the same time, the stair was replaced with elegant, slender banisters, three to a tread, though the old 'bottle' banisters to the upper stair remain.

The bailiff of the Home Farm belonging to the Howards used to live here, which explains its name. In its early days it had been known as *Hilder House*, after the family of that name[4].

Fig. 66. Ashtead House. Drawing by Mary Cree.

Fig. 67. Ashtead Lodge. Drawing by Gillian Wilson.

An old granary adjoins the house. It has a two-bay 18th century square plan, with a pyramid roof, central king post and butt purlins.

The Headmaster's House

This early 18th century house on Rookery Hill, occupied by the Headmaster of the City of London Freemen's School, is brick built with a slated roof. There are two storeys with casement windows, those on the ground floor having arched heads. The house has a string course, and over the front door there is a sundial dated 1734.

The house was built on or near the site of *Blake's Close*, one of the many properties leased or owned by the Beckford family in the 18th century[5]. In the early 1790's it was occupied by the Howards during the building of their new mansion. It was said to have been a laundry at one time, and for many years the Head Gardener to the Howards lived here.

Other Old Houses and Cottages (arranged by street)

Rectory Lane

Rectory Lane, together with Crampshaw Lane and Woodfield Lane, forms part of the trackway that led from Headley through Ashtead to the Rye Brook. This is the original axis of Ashtead, so it is not surprising that most of the oldest buildings in the village lie along these roads; the other ancient buildings are mostly the scattered farm-houses. These buildings were timber-framed, and the larger were constructed in 'bays', which lay between major vertical timbers, and which each originally contained a room running the depth of the house. In larger dwellings the main reception room, or 'hall', rose the full height of the building, to the under side of the roof.

Applebough Cottage is shown on Lawrence's map of 1638 and could date from the second half of the 16th century. It is a two-storey building of three bays, the narrow central bay containing a chimney with three flues[6] – a type of cottage that is rare in Surrey. There are two main rooms on each floor. It was converted many years ago into two small dwellings that were known as Barton Cottages, but these were reunited in 1954. At the rear is an old school house (see p. 179), which was converted to a hand laundry by the Prossers, who lived in the cottage until the 1960's.

Fig. 68. Headmaster's House, Ashtead Park. Photograph by J. C. Stuttard

Fig. 69. Applebough Cottage, Rectory Lane. Photograph by J. C. Stuttard

Wistaria Cottage and Forge Cottage result from the division of a four-bay medieval hall-house, which was built by a wealthy yeoman farmer c. 1500 and is therefore the oldest house in Ashtead. It is timber framed, with straight wind braces. Normally, the hall occupied the centre two bays of such a house, and those bays were untiled, so that the smoke from the central fire escaped between the rafters, which therefore became soot-blackened. However, this hall-house is unusual in that only one of the two central bays shows this soot-blackening, indicating that the other bay was divided into upper and lower floors from the beginning. Later, c.1550, the smoke was confined to a smoke-hood, and this was replaced by the chimney c.1600, and the original wattle and daub walls were replaced by Tudor brick.

Parts of the original building are now concealed by later, single-storey extensions. *Wistaria Cottage* comprises the lower service part of the original hall, which would have included the pantry and buttery, while *Forge Cottage* includes the original family rooms and parlour. In the early 19th century, there was a blacksmith and wheelwright's forge on the adjacent part of Rectory Lane, and the cottages were bought by the smith, Robert Wyatt, in 1880 and sold by his sons in 1931. The smithy was in use until 1950, and became derelict in the 1970's.

Fowler's Cottage is a mid-17th century two-bay cottage, with straight wind-bracing to its timber frame and a gabled roof with three queen posts. The entrance was into the service bay. Later a back wing was added, and a hearth and an outside chimney were built in the front room, which also includes the stairs.

The Old Rectory is a three-storey brick building dating from the 18th century, with curved bays to the wings on the road and garden side, except that on the north-west; the roof has a fine dentilled cornice below.

The Old Bakery in Crampshaw Lane is a three-bay boarded house, part 17th and part early 18th century, which originally consisted of two small cottages, extended in the late 17th century. From about 1720, the premises were used as a bakery and shop. Though the oven has been removed, its chimney can still be seen on the south side of the house. An area once used for storing flour now forms a gallery over the main lounge, and the crane and pulley for hoisting sacks, with wooden cogs, still survive.

Henry Harman and his daughter Ann carried on the bakery business for 50 years, 1841–1891. It was then taken over by A. Sheath, who continued the business during the early 20th century. It has been a private house since about 1928[7].

Parker's Lane

At the junction of Rectory Lane and Parker's Lane, No. 1 (*Howard Cottage*) and No. 3 form a pair of originally mirror-image brick cottages which were part of the Howard estate. There are remains of an original timber frame in *Howard Cottage*, suggesting that the present house was probably built around an early 17th century structure. Interesting features are a single central chimney stack, 'gothick' windows and trellis porches.

Woodfield Lane

No. 33 on this lane is a 17th century timber-framed cottage, with a fine outside end chimney stack and an outshot at the back; some flint can be seen in the lower walls. The central entrance faces a cupboard with a ventilated window, which may have been the position of the original staircase. A brick cottage (No. 35) with an inside end chimney has been built against it.

Agates Lane

Murreys Court (formerly New Purchase Farm)   This farm was one of the largest in Ashtead, and the farmhouse was probably built in the mid-17th century. There were kitchen quarters at the back, and two vaulted cellars. The house was extended in the early 18th century with a south bay. During the later part of Queen Victoria's reign it was brought up to date by Col A.C. Gleig, who added a second storey with dormer windows.

The elevation to Agates Lane was at one time symmetrical, but the original front door has gone and the entrance is now by a long covered passage from the re-positioned front door in the garden wall. The first floor windows on either side of the projecting part (which probably had a pediment) have been bricked up. Rubbed bricks surround the windows and are used at the quoins. There are later extensions to the house on the garden side, and the original

Fig. 70. The Old Rectory. Drawing by Gillian Wilson.

dog-leg stair with finely turned balusters became the back stair at this time. The reception parts of the house are panelled, with carved doors and interesting surrounds to the fireplaces, and there are two mottoes in Gothic lettering (one in French) around the dining room. The metal-lined shutters on the ground floor were put in by Col Gleig, who feared an invasion by the French. The bell on the road-side was to call workers from the fields.

Near the southern side of the house stands a large three-bay barn, on a brick plinth, with a staggered butt purlin roof, straight wind braces and lacking a ridge; it probably dates from the mid-17th century. Chisel-cut carpenters' assembly marks, in Roman numerals, can be seen on the timbers. The straight wind braces are unusual in this kind of roof, and are probably an early example of this; the barn is now tile hung. All the openings on the north side have been blocked up, and a stable has been added on the east end. Within living memory, it was used as a threshing barn, with the great doors open. The weather vane was made by Rowhurst Forge.

Ilex House Though records of the present house, with its three storeys and slate roof, date back only to the 17th century, it may well have replaced an earlier building. The entrance, with 'Classical' columns, is not central in the façade; the bay windows on either side were probably added later. There are sash windows with moulded frames to the openings projecting from the main wall. The house was once known as *Ruskerville Cottage*, then in 1881 it became *The Laurels* and sometime afterwards became a laundry; more recently, the name changed to *Ilex Lodge* and, in 1983, to *Ilex House*[8].

A brick-built stable with a tiled roof once stood to the north of the house and housed the local fire engine – and also, so it is said, a Derby winner!

Merry Hall, opposite *Murreys Court*, was probably built in the late 18th century, though some records refer back to the previous century. It is a dignified, almost symmetrical, brick house in Flemish Bond with two storeys, a cellar and attics. The roof is slated, and the moulded cornice has a concealed gutter on the west side. The chimneys for the front rooms lie on the outside of the end walls. Elegant stairs with plain banisters and a curving over-rail face the entry hall. The ground floor window on either side of the central projecting part has been blocked up. There is a 19th century addition to the north end, and more recent extensions at the back. The well-known writer Beverley Nichols lived here in the 1950's (see p. 201).

Pepys Cottage   (Nos. 60 and 62 Agates Lane), built between 1550 and 1600, is the oldest house in Ashtead after the *Wistaria Cottage/Forge Cottage* hall house. It is a good example of a two-storey, three-bay, timber-framed house with a narrow end bay for the framed hearth. It shows the typical features of a "smoke bay" house, and has a half-hipped roof, arching wind braces in the framing, and jowl posts. The forward wing was added later, with its hearth backing the brick hearth in the smoke bay. The building has been divided into two dwellings, and there are modern back extensions. There is no known connection with the Pepys family, but not long ago the cottage was the home of Mr. Cates, the cabby, well-known to many of the older inhabitants of Ashtead.

Ottways Lane

The Old Cottage   (No.11). set close to the Lane, is a late 17th century, timber-framed building of two storeys and attics, with a clasped purlin roof, straight wind braces and raking queen posts. There is an outside end chimney with an inglenook hearth. The framing suggests that it was originally a barn and was later converted into three small dwellings and finally into a single interesting house. In the mid-19th century, it was called *Ordnance Cottage*, because the men who were carrying out the Ordnance Survey work locally lived there[9]. But, from the last century until fairly recently, part of it was used as a bakery so that, not long ago, some Ashtead residents remembered going there when they were young to buy loaves and buns, which were also delivered to homes by donkey and cart.

Dormers, close to where Ottways Lane joins Harriotts Lane, is the former *Whitehouse Farm House*, which dates from the mid-19th century, although some parts may be older than this. The present building is an attractive, red brick house, with the service rooms at a lower level at the back. There is a brick porch, and dormer windows rise into a grey slate roof. The splendid central chimney stack has joined round flues from separate rooms, which unite in the roof. There is a large, partly renovated old barn in the garden at the back[10].

The Common
Two **Woodside Cottages,** formerly on the Common, have been

Fig. 71. Howard Cottage, Park Lane. Drawing by Betty Eldridge.

moved to the Weald and Downland Open Air Museum at Single-ton in Sussex. They were typical examples of the many boarded or rendered cottages built in the early 19th century.

Park Lane/Farm Lane/Epsom Road

Howard Cottage, where Park Lane joins Epsom Road (not to be confused with the cottage at the corner of Parker's Lane) was never part of the Howard estate. The house has been much altered and extended. The original was brick built, with a slated roof and cast iron latticed basement windows facing the main roof, and its main entrance on the north side. This provided living accomodation, a stone-flagged kitchen with dairy adjacent, and bedrooms over. In the 1880's, a new building was constructed at right angles, facing Park Lane. It was built in 'red rubbers' brick, and has wide sash windows and a timber porch with latticed side panels. Between this and the original house, there is a courtyard with a well and pump. The building has now been decorated in white and a Georgian style porch replaces the original. The house was later extended to the east, with a gable facing the main road, and two-storey bay window added between the original entrance and the new extension. The later extension is in keeping with the original house, with latticed casement windows in wood.

Hatchgate Cottages, Nos. 1 & 2 Farm Lane, are a pair of mirror-image double-pile brick dwellings with one roof over both, having a central brick partition, with entrances at either end. There used to be a delicate iron verandah along the west side, of which only the catches remain. The cottages probably date from the early 19th century.

Old Well House on Epsom Road was formerly known as *Hatchgate Cottage*. It is a symmetrical two-storey brick house with a central entrance and a facing stair inside. The rafters are nailed but there is no ridge. The well is in the front. An older cottage, formerly on the west end, has been replaced by a lean-to, and a brick wing has been added to the east end. The house is probably late 18th century, as there is an indenture of 1775.

The **Forest Lodge** site in Epsom Road, almost opposite the North Lodge of Ashtead Park, has had a varied history. In the early 19th century, the *Haunch of Venison* inn stood there, but during the 1860's Henry Parsons converted it into a house, where in 1871 he lived with a large household, including five servants. In the 1879 sale of Ashtead Park, *Forest Lodge* was bought for £3,700 on behalf of Lord Rosebery, although it was occupied at that time by Thomas C. March, who held important positions in the royal household, and who subsequently purchased the property. After his death, it was sold by his daughter, Arabella.

Augustus Meyers purchased the estate in 1901, and lived there for nearly fifty years. Soon after he acquired the property, he built the present *Forest Lodge*, set well back from the road behind the site of the original inn, which had stood near the present entrance. Some of the original land parcels of the estate, such as Haunch Shaw, a woodland of three acres, perpetuated the name of the former inn. The laying-out of the grounds, including the demolition of the earlier house, had been completed by 1911.

After the death of Augustus Meyers in 1949, *Forest Lodge* was purchased by Mrs. Netta Mountford Spence. The house was subdivided and the estate was broken up. In the late 1950's, despite opposition from Leatherhead Urban District Council, areas within the estate (now called Forest Way, Pepys Close and Devitt Close) were developed by New Ideal Homesteads with some fifty houses. During the 1960's, infilling in the form of individual detached houses took place between *Forest Lodge* and the main road; these included *Forest Lodge House*, an all-glass building of 1968, by Michael Manser.

Other Buildings

The *Leg of Mutton & Cauliflower* in The Street has been a hostelry for over 200 years. The present building dates from 1890, but at the rear there is some evidence of the earlier timber-framed structure. On the other side of The Street, the *Brewery Inn* dates in its present form from the 1930's, though at the back there are some remnants of the old 19th century building. The *Woodman* in Barnett Wood Lane was a small beer-house in the early 19th century, but its present building dates from 1939. For the early history of Ashtead's inns and public houses, see pp. 100–02

Peace Memorial Hall. This hall in Woodfield Lane was built in 1924 to mark the return to peace after the First World War. On the plaque inside the hall are the moving words; 'In thankfulness for peace and in gratitude for those who brought it'. It is an unpretentious single-storey building which is an important meeting place for many of Ashtead's social events[11].

Library. The Library in Woodfield Lane is one of the most recent public buildings in Ashtead, dating from 1968. It was designed by the County Architect, R.J. Ash, in buff brick with a crenellated roof line. There had been an interest in providing a County Library service for Ashtead as long ago as 1925, and three years later a small library was opened in Barnett Wood Lane School. After the war, the library moved in 1951 to the Constitutional Hall, where it stayed until the new library was built.

Ashtead Hospital and **Gilbert House**. The Ashtead Hospital, in the old chalk pit next to The Warren, was opened in September 1984. It is a fine, modern building, which caters for most medical and surgical specialities. Gilbert House, next to the Library in Woodfield Lane, has been a purpose-built medical centre since 1979. It was named after a highly respected doctor who practised in Ashtead for about 40 years.

Notes

1. I. Nairn & N. Pevsner, *Surrey* (1971), pp. 99–100.
2. G.J. Gollin, *Bygone Ashtead* (1987), pp. 31–9.
3. Alan A. Jackson (ed.) *Ashtead; A Village Transformed* (1977), p. 187.
4. G.J. Gollin (1987) *op.cit.*, pp. 66–9.
5. G.J. Gollin (1987) *op.cit.*, pp. 51–7.
6. Joan M. Harding, 'Applebough Cottage, Rectory Lane'. *Procs. LDLHS*, (1974) 3(8), pp. 246–7.
7. Alan A. Jackson (ed.) (1977) *op.cit.*, p. 189.
8. G.J. Gollin (1987) *op.cit.* pp. 115–6.
9. G.J. Gollin (1987) *op.cit.* p.120.
10. Alan A. Jackson (ed.) (1977) *op.cit.*, p. 149.
11. Peace Memorial Hall pamphlet (1984).

Index

compiled by J.C. Stuttard